Carolina Currents
Studies in South Carolina Culture

Carolina Currents
Studies in South Carolina Culture

Volume 3. Travel as Resistance

Edited by
Meredith A. Love and Christopher D. Johnson

Published by the University of South Carolina Press
Columbia, South Carolina 29208

uscpress.com

Printed in the United States of America

Library of Congress Cataloging-in-Publication Data can be found at http://catalog.loc.gov/.

ISBN: 978-1-64336-632-6 (paperback)
ISBN: 978-1-64336-662-3 (ebook)
DOI: https://doi.org/10.61162/9781643366623

The inclusion of this book in the Open Carolina collection is made possible by the generous funding of the University of South Carolina Libraries and Francis Marion University.

Contents

Volume 3, 2026

List of Illustrations

Driftwood Labyrinth, photograph by Tyler LaCross, taken on Driftwood Beach, Edisto Island, August 4, 2023. © Tyler LaCross.

Daybreak Prayer on Edisto Island
Melissa LaCross

I want to free myself entirely
like the Pacific breeze
that blew across country
a whole week straight
then circled and fell
before stilling itself
on this Carolina beach,

like the brown pelican that,
faced with wild gusts,
both soars into wind
and dives headlong,
oracle of survival.

In the resurrected heart,
which fears nothing,
the world has already died,
disappeared in rotation
then returned at dawn:
new sun, new dew
across wild oats,
even our watches
forget when to wake.

I want the dew.
I want to rise early,
lay among wise dunes,
see it form on my thigh.
I want to weep
when it evaporates.

I want the shore
with driftwood

trees, where a beached
whale found rest,
blue clay and sand
a charitable bed
to give itself back,
and I want
the white jaw bone
and baleen to come alive,
show me how to fish
in ravenous tides,
to plunge deep in darkness
and come up fed.

Melissa LaCross has a master of fine arts in creative writing from Vermont College of Fine Arts. She was born and raised in Florence, SC, and attended Francis Marion University. She has a master of arts in English from Clemson University. You can find her on Instagram or wandering trails with her husband, dog, and kids in tow.

Acknowledgments

Carolina Currents would not be possible without the generous support of Francis Marion University (FMU). Dr. Luther F. Carter, president of FMU, and Dr. Alissa Warters, university provost, have provided resources, guidance, and encouragement.

Editorial board members have urged colleagues to contribute to *Carolina Currents* and have graciously served as reviewers for the many essays we received. Several of our FMU colleagues have also served as reviewers: Caleb Doan, Dustin M. Meyer, J. Mark Blackwell, and John Rowan. I also thank J. Porter Lillis of the University of North Carolina, Pembroke.

Two student workers have assisted with production. Maggie Odom and Gracen Tyce have worked tirelessly on the bibliographies and notes. Their work has been tremendously helpful.

Our colleague Erica Johnson deserves special thanks. Erica has contributed to each volume of *Carolina Currents*. Two of her essays have been coauthored with students. She has also prepared book reviews, encouraged colleagues to contribute, and reviewed a number of submissions. Even when we've imposed unreasonable deadlines, Erica has always provided outstanding guidance and recommendations. Her commitment and generosity have made *Carolina Currents* better.

Christine Johnson has helped proofread the finished version.

The good people at the University of South Carolina Press have been, as always, wonderful partners. I acknowledge Michael McGandy, Aurora Bell, and Kerri L. Tolan, all of whom have been exceptionally helpful and patient. The University of South Carolina Libraries have provided vital funding to support the open access version of the volume.

Introduction

Christopher D. Johnson and Meredith A. Love

So hope for great sea-change
On the far side of revenge.
Believe that a further shore
Is reachable from here.

—Seamus Heaney, _The Cure of Troy_

Resistant Travel and Enduring Hope

During Jim Crow, railroad companies deliberately made the cars designated for Black passengers uncomfortable and dirty. They did so not to prevent African Americans from purchasing tickets but rather, as Roger C. Hartley notes, to encourage white passengers to perceive the "significance of their own Whiteness" and the "fact of their own superiority."[1] They did so, in other words, to make white travelers feel better about themselves. As Hartley explains, the railroad executives knew that Black passengers would continue to purchase tickets because they had no other means of travel. By forcing them into substandard cars, the companies could maintain Black revenue, even as they used Black suffering to appeal to white passengers' worst prejudices. The railroad companies' actions also, of course, spoke to African-American passengers, reminding them of their diminished social status and the power of authorities to impose dehumanizing conditions upon them. Hard seating and unswept floors carried powerful messages about status and subjugation.

Today's readers may be tempted to see the railroad companies' brutal actions as gestures from an age long past. Indeed, railroad cars are no longer segregated. Hotels, restaurants, and businesses can no longer refuse service based on race, and the Civil Rights Act of 1968 made sundown towns, where African Americans faced violence after working hours, illegal.[2] Our age, we might assume, has progressed toward justice and fairness, and in many ways it has. Yet the old impulses of discrimination and exclusion persist. Those in authority continue to harm the vulnerable, and cynical public voices continue to villainize those who are different to preserve their own influence and relevance.

Segregation, of course, was always about more than separating people. It was also about asserting racial hierarchies and erasing the experiences of marginalized populations. We see vestiges of these intentions in recent actions, such as the Defense Intelligence Agency's decision to purge references to Jackie Robinson, the Navajo Code Talkers, and the Tuskegee Airmen, and to the federal ban on activities related to Black History Month, Juneteenth, LGBTQ (Lesbian, Gay, Bisexual, Transgender, Queer/Questioning) Pride Month, and Holocaust Remembrance Day.[3] In each case, officials have worked to erase the identities and experiences of others and impose a restrictive, monolithic vision of American culture.

Within our state, actions such as the proposed anti-DEI (diversity, equity, and inclusion) legislation serve similar purposes.[4] By obscuring the horrific legacies of racism and silencing the voices of the oppressed, state leaders effectively divert attention away from enduring inequities. And those inequities are substantial. The poverty rate for Black South Carolinians (23.1%) remains more than double that of the state's white residents (9.3%).[5] Disparities in Black and white homeownership, a key dynamic for social mobility, increased between 1990 (15.2%) and 2020 (26.6%) and will likely increase further by 2040 (27.9%).[6] The preterm birth rate for Black mothers is 1.4 times higher than South Carolina's overall rate, and Black infant mortality is 1.8 times higher.[7] Recent studies have called attention to alarming diagnosis-to-treatment times for Black breast cancer patients.[8] Other investigations have documented the degree to which structural racism worsened maternal health inequalities for minority women during the COVID-19 pandemic.[9] A particularly disturbing 2025 report examines correlations between maternal social mobility and low birth weight. Downward social mobility, the study concludes, is more common for Black women than white women. Moreover, the "protective association" of upward mobility against low birth weight exists "only for the most highly educated Black women."[10] Collectively, these studies point out the severe realities that define experience for many South Carolinians. Sober minds recognize that no attack on DEI, no pledge to reward colorblind merit, and no scrubbing of curriculum will address the fundamental conditions that harm our fellow citizens.

Discrimination, however persistent, inevitably meets resistance. Those denied liberty and inclusion will invariably seek it. Even in the face of oppression they will, in the words of Richard Wright, continue "groping toward that invisible light" of freedom.[11] For many twentieth-century African Americans, resistance meant travel—the ability to break away from everyday concerns, visit family, see historical sites, and seek opportunity. But travel was fraught with uncertainty and danger. In response, a postal worker from Harlem named Victor Hugo Green began publishing *The Negro Motorist Green Book* in 1936. For thirty years, the many *Green Book* editions provided lists of hotels, tourist homes, restaurants, and other businesses that welcomed Black patrons. It encouraged African Americans to leave the places assigned to them and discover worlds beyond their own. It allowed Black musicians, entertainers, intellectuals, and civil rights leaders to meet and move about freely and safely. Debra Yeo, responding to Yorbura Richen's documentary film on the *Green Book,* notes that Green's publications created community by offering "a kind of parallel universe," a "secret road map" of empowerment.[12]

The first four essays in this volume, introduced in the following text, discuss *Green Book* businesses in South Carolina and provide useful research tips to those who want to learn more about the histories of their communities. The *Green Book* essays are followed by three essays that take the reader back to the days before emancipation. John Barrington provides a detailed portrait of an eighteenth-century biracial Baptist church in the rural community of Welsh Neck, now part of Marlboro County. Barrington demonstrates that the inclusion of enslaved people originated in both the idealism of the American Revolution and fears of British invasion and slave revolt. He introduces the reader to Reverend Elhanan Winchester, a once-strict Calvinist who eventually embraced Universalism and used his considerable rhetorical skills to integrate his congregation. Winchester was aided by Colonial Alexander McIntosh, who allowed those he enslaved to worship in Winchester's church. Integration in church did not, of course, cause enslavers to abandon the subjugation of their fellow worshipers, but it did, perhaps, encourage them to recognize the humanity and dignity of those they harmed.

Erica Johnson also investigates biracial faith communities in the Pee Dee. Focusing on Presbyterian churches in Aimwell, Hopewell, Indiantown, Salem, and Williamsburg, she presents a less idealistic depiction of integration. By the mid-nineteenth century, the egalitarian impulses of the American Revolution had long since faded, and the national divide on slavery had become inexorable. Christianity, with its celebrations of submission and promise of rewards beyond earthly life, became an instrument of control. It encouraged the enslaved to accept their station. At the same time, it mollified the consciences of enslavers who could rest easy knowing they had saved eternally those they harmed temporally. The fact that these actions took place within Presbyterian congregations suggests a bitter irony, given Presbyterianism's foundational suspicions of hierarchy and authority. Johnson substantiates her argument with the testimony of African Americans who grew up in those churches before and immediately after emancipation. Using the oral histories recorded during the 1930s, she brings firsthand perspectives to her discussion and shows the durable links that tie past and present. Decades after the Civil War and Reconstruction, the intersections of faith and oppression remained vivid for those who shared their stories.

Moving from ecclesiastical to judicial concerns, Stan Barnett recreates two trials from nineteenth-century Marion, in which enslaved people were charged and eventually convicted of murder. Like John Barrington and Erica Johnson, Barnett builds his argument on primary sources that have not received scholarly attention. Through the transcripts of court testimony, he shows how the enslaved interacted with the criminal justice system. Modern readers might be surprised to learn that enslaved people charged with murdering white enslavers would even receive trials. Barnett demonstrates not only that they did, but also that they benefited from some legal safeguards. At the same time, however, the courts viewed them as property. Were they executed, as both defendants were, the state might owe compensation to their enslavers. For enslaved Black people in nineteenth-century South Carolina, legal protections originated only in part from their humanity.

These three essays, all focused on the Pee Dee region, provide unexpected glimpses into the lives of the enslaved and meaningfully complicate our understandings of their experiences. Together, they expose many of the dynamics that made Victor Green's travel guides necessary and welcomed. Todd C. Couch's essay takes the reader into the present. Providing practical suggestions for improving the recruitment and retention of faculty, staff and students on rural campuses, Couch emphasizes the importance of connecting institutions of higher learning to the communities they serve. His observations are particularly applicable to those working and studying at our state's comprehensive teaching universities and technical colleges. In 2024, 206,566 students enrolled in South Carolina's public institutions. Of these, 132,129 (approximately sixty-four percent) enrolled in comprehensive teaching universities and technical colleges, which also enrolled higher percentages of women and minority students than the state's research universities.[13] Comprehensive and technical institutions play tremendously important roles in South Carolina. They prepare large numbers of students for careers and professions, they provide much-needed cultural experiences to underserved communities, and they invigorate rural economies. Couch shows how these institutions can attract and retain talented faculty and staff and how, by doing so, they can better serve students and surrounding areas.

The essay portion of the volume concludes with Andrew Geyer's interview with novelist Lynn Kostoff and Jo Angela Edwins's review essay of four recent volumes by South Carolina poets. For almost forty years, Kostoff has lived in South Carolina, working as both a university professor and writer. His novels, which follow many of the conventions of *noir*, take the reader on unexpected journeys and capture the richness and complexity of experience. Geyer's interview reveals the dedication and craft that allow for compelling fiction. Edwins, herself an accomplished poet, introduces the reader to authors who embody the rich diversity of our state. The collections reflect the poets' own resistant travels through loss and exclusion. Having transformed these experiences into art, they invite the reader to undergo similar journeys toward compassion and understanding. Although the poets confront many of life's harshest realities, they also offer hope that horrific events can become meaningful gifts of solace and insight.

In many ways, Edwins's review essay brings the volume back to Melissa LaCross's brilliant introductory poem, "Daybreak Prayer on Edisto Island." Reflecting on one of our state's most beautiful locations, LaCross looks deeply into the ocean, seeing not only its beauty but also the force of its "ravenous tides." Her hope is not to escape the ocean's power but to embrace it, "to plunge deep in darkness/and come up fed." She reminds us that journeys are often frightening and that nourishment comes from struggle. She also insists that beauty and profundity surround us. In these days, when so many certainties seem to be crumbling, we should remember the simple lessons that linger just below the surface of LaCross's poem and the essays in this volume: The urge to travel and discover abides, resistance against injustice is never futile, and even in the darkest depths there remains the promise of new light.

The *Green Book* in South Carolina

Warm temperatures, beautiful beaches, and "well-planned, good roads" were promised by Governor George Bell Timmerman Jr. in a South Carolina State Development Board tourism brochure published around 1955.[14] The swans and the magnolias, the anglers, and the Spanish moss featured on the brochure were an attempt to offset the negative assumptions that

Americans had about the South and the people who lived in it. Timmerman wanted to attract Northern tourist dollars, but he did not want to change the racial culture that would have made some Northern travelers uncomfortable. In fact, after winning the gubernatorial election in 1954, he did all that he could to ensure that South Carolina remained segregated. As reported in his *The New York Times* obituary, "he sought to thwart an order by the Interstate Commerce Commission for desegregation of long-distance travel in 1955, especially because it affected public waiting rooms. At the same time he opposed Federal court orders integrating public parks, bathing beaches and golf courses."[15] In other words, Timmerman welcomed only some to the state, insisting that, even in travel and leisurely pursuits, Black and white travelers should remain separate.

Black travelers during this period were acutely aware of the lack of hospitality and the possibility of violence that awaited them in South Carolina, and rather than look to brochures published by the state to guide their choices along the road, they turned instead to resources such as the *Green Book*. Inspired by travel guides for Jewish Americans, the *Green Book*, published by postal worker Victor Green, was one of the most popular guidebooks of the era.[16] It was published from 1936 to 1966 and had an estimated annual printing of twenty thousand copies, which were sold in Esso Gas stations, churches, and other locations.[17] It began as a sixteen-page guide to Black-friendly establishments in New York City; however, Green had a good many connections, and, by 1937, it was a national guide offering a state-by-state, city-by-city listing of restaurants, service stations, hotels, motels, and other businesses serving travelers. It eventually grew into a resource of more than one hundred pages.

The *Green Book* has enjoyed a great deal of public attention in recent years, primarily because of the release and acclaim of the 2018 award-winning film *Green Book*, directed by Peter Farrelly, which tells the story of the accomplished pianist Don Shirley who employs bouncer Tony "Lip" Vallelonga to drive him throughout the South on a concert tour in 1962. Shirley knows the potential dangers and pitfalls that await him on the road. The film depicts sundown towns and scenes where Shirley experiences discrimination and violence at the hands of whites. In one instance, Shirley and Lip are forced to stay in two different hotels when Shirley is prohibited from staying in the "white" hotel in Louisville. Shirley must stay at one listed in the *Green Book*—and it is bleak. The scene is dark; the parking lot where we see Shirley sitting outside (suggesting that there may not be air conditioning in the room) is run down and noisy. Shirley certainly appears out of place in this substandard establishment, a Black hotel that is clearly not as good as the white one. In many ways, this depiction is unfortunate. It assumes that *Green Book* businesses provided shabby accommodations and poor service. To be sure, many of the lodgings, known as tourist homes, were modest, often no more than spare rooms in a private residence, but there is little reason to imagine that they were uncomfortable or uninviting; nor should we assume that their surroundings were always dreary and poor. In a well-intentioned effort to show the depredations of segregation, the writers and director inadvertently erased or at least misrepresented important aspects of African-American life. The authors of the essays that follow seek to correct some of the assumptions created by movies such as *Green Book*. Exploring the lives of the men and women in South Carolina who operated *Green Book* businesses, they seek to show not only the struggles and injustices of Black experience in South Carolina but also its ingenuity and triumph.

The *Green Book* itself is only briefly mentioned in the film; however, it has certainly captured the public imagination. Interest in the origin of the publication and the sites listed within it has ballooned, with stories appearing in magazines, news outlets, podcasts, documentaries, and scholarly articles written by geographers, journalists, and historians. Additionally, several book-length publications have been released in just the past few years on the topic of the *Green Book*. In 2016, Alvin Hall completed a radio documentary on the *Green Book* that led to a twelve-day road trip. His 2019 podcast series, titled *Driving the Green Book,* then led to the publication of *Driving the Green Book: A Road Trip Through the Living History of Black Resistance.*[18] Candacy Taylor's 2020 book, *Overground Railroad: The Green Book and the Roots of Black Travel in America,* more than any other recent publication, delves deeply into the *Green Book.* Taylor includes hundreds of site photos and pages of *Green Book* content, covering topics such as music venues and the Black women who were often the owners of *Green Book* businesses. Gretchen Sorin's 2020 *Driving While Black: African American Travel and the Road to Civil Rights* and Mia Bay's 2021 *Traveling Black: A Story of Race and Resistance* chronicle challenges that Black travelers faced. Bay covers rail, car, and air travel, and Sorin focuses entirely on the indispensability of travel guides for Black travelers. Additionally, there have been numerous articles published in mainstream magazines and newspapers, as well as a 2010 children's book, *Ruth and the Green Book,* and a 2014 play titled *The Green Book: A Play.*[19]

On the state level, the South Carolina African American Heritage Commission, now known as the WeGOJA Foundation, has created an online travel guide—*The Green Book of South Carolina*—to direct travelers to more than three hundred sites important to African-American history in the state. In 2022, the foundation released *The Green Book of South Carolina: A Guide to African America Cultural Sites* as a hard-copy book.[20] Some *Green Book* sites are included in the guide, which seeks to expand our understanding of those sites and communities, and of the significance of sites that have been lost, and to help us plan excursions to visit those still standing.

In this third volume of *Carolina Currents*, we hope to introduce readers to the roles that *Green Book* sites played in different parts of the state over the years of its publication. All kinds of businesses—tourist homes, barber shops, taverns, funeral homes, hotels, restaurants, and services—from all over the state were represented over the course of the guide's history. Here, we aim to deepen our understanding about the people behind the businesses and addresses recorded under "South Carolina" in *The Negro Motorist Green Book* from 1936 to 1966. The brief, one-line listings actually tell us very little about these establishments—usually just a name and address. The research presented here animates those listings and tells us the stories of family-run businesses and how they created and sustained community, of towns whose vibrant Black business communities are left unrepresented by the *Green Book*, and of the work being done today to recover and preserve these stories and memories.

By the time the *Green Book* came onto the scene, American families were just starting to make enough money to afford automobiles. Families had some disposable income, and American workers enjoyed more leisure time on weekends and designated days off for vacation. Not surprisingly, as cars became more affordable and more common, and more roads began to open, there was also a proliferation in travel-related industries: Gas stations, hotels, and restaurants popped up all along these new interstates as families went on vacation. South Carolina has always attracted visitors seeking better winter weather, and some towns such as "Aiken, Camden, and Summerville had been frequented by wealthy northerners" since the 1880s "either as destinations or as stops enroute to Florida."[21] The state's commitment to tourism, however, did not gain real momentum until the 1920s. As cities began to focus on tourism as a money-making venture, they realized that there was little infrastructure to support large numbers of visitors. It was during this period that Charleston, in the midst of historic preservation efforts, opened two new hotels (Fort Sumter Hotel and the Francis Marion); Myrtle Beach's first major hotel, the Ocean Forest Hotel, was completed in 1930.

Black travelers were excluded from hotels such as Ocean Forest Hotel, and they were on alert, in constant worry about finding restrooms and service stations in addition to overnight accommodations. Oral histories conducted by researchers at the Beck Cultural Exchange Center in Knoxville, Tennessee, reveal that the Jim Crow laws in the South created a complex atmosphere for Black travelers: "For Black motorists, tourism was not simply the physical and technological work of driving, but it also required the emotional labor of managing the stress of driving within and against an atmosphere of White supremacy that always carried with it the uncertainty of how, when, and where one might encounter racial hostility while traveling."[22] This emotional weight was mitigated, in some part, by family and other networks that could provide addresses of relatives or friends who would welcome the travelers along the way. And although it could never guarantee absolute comfort or certainty, the *Green Book* allowed people some hope for hospitality on the road.

The first edition of the *Green Book* to include listings outside of New York, was published in 1938. It included twenty-five sites across South Carolina, in Aiken, Charleston, Columbia, Florence, Georgetown, and Spartanburg. Most of the listings were for hotels or women-run tourist homes. At the end of the issue, under South Carolina "Summer Resorts," there is a one-line entry naming Atlantic Beach on Ocean Drive. The following year, travelers would have found forty-five South Carolina listings, and the towns of Anderson, Darlington, Greenville, and "Mullens" [*sic*] were included, as were listings for barbers, drug stores, and other businesses. Overall, more than one hundred South Carolina establishments were listed in the nearly thirty annual editions that were published.

Throughout the years, the *Green Book* provided customers with numerous possibilities in the state's capital of Columbia. W. Maclane Hull introduces readers to one of the most prominent families in Columbia during the twentieth century—the Leevy family, whose service to the area stretches over seventy years. Leevy's Service Station was advertised in the *Green Book* from 1950 to 1955 and was part of a network of several businesses owned by Black families. Together, with the Leevy family, these establishments supported both the traveler coming through the state's capital and the permanent citizen of the city looking to establish and maintain community.

Another South Carolina city, Greenville, was home to more than a dozen *Green Book* sites, which also functioned as welcoming respites and important community hubs. Courtney L. Tollison and Rachel Gambrell take us deep into the stories of two of these businesses—212 John Street and Whittenberg's Service Station. As a tourist home owned by Lurleen and Isaac White, 212 John Street was near Textile Hall and often hosted performers who played there, including Duke Ellington. As part of the strong network of Black business owners and activists in Greenville, Abraham Jonah Whittenberg, owner of Whittenberg's Service Station, stands as an important contributor to the civil rights movement in the Upstate. In this essay, we learn about Whittenberg's many leadership positions within the movement and his personal drive to fight injustices on many different fronts.

Charleston, as another major city within South Carolina, was also home to around a dozen *Green Book* sites over the course of its publication. Although this may sound like a large number for a city during the mid-twentieth century, Barry Stiefel explains that these were not listed all at the same time and that there were very few options for those Black tourists who did visit the city. Stiefel's history of accommodations for Black travelers and his discussion of those sites that were included in the *Green Book* serves as a reminder that a city so rich in Black history often took pains to make Black visitors feel anything other than welcome.

Cherish Thomas, in the section's final piece, provides the reader with the mindset and tools necessary to explore *Green Book* sites in our communities. From the digital collections of the New York Public Library to other library databases to city directories, Thomas helps the reader get started on research that has the potential to reshape and illuminate local histories throughout the state.

Each of these contributions reminds us that there is history in South Carolina that has gone unmarked and that there are eminent South Carolinians who have gone uncelebrated. Of course, the *Green Book* is only one of the many artifacts that can point us to the undone work of researching and remembering. But within these issues, beyond those simple entries are stories of entrepreneurship and resourcefulness, of hospitality and community. The collection we have here is but an introduction to the stories that are still untold.

Christopher D. Johnson is professor of English and Trustees' Research Scholar at Francis Marion University. His most recent book is *Samuel Richardson, Comedic Narrative, and the Culture of Domestic Violence: Abused Pamela* (Cambridge Scholars Publishing, 2023). In addition to *Carolina Currents*, he is currently working on a book manuscript examining the rhetoric of early-modern biographies.

Meredith A. Love is professor of English and chair of English and philosophy at Francis Marion University, where she teaches courses in first-year composition, professional writing, gender studies, and rhetoric. For over six years, she has been researching the role of the *Green Book* as a tool of resistance. Currently, she is examining the visual rhetoric of the *Green Book* covers and how the images and artwork worked as persuasive tools to draw in readers. Her work has been published in *Rhetoric Review, College Composition and Communication,* and, most recently, the first volume of *Carolina Currents.*

NOTES

1. Hartley, *Monumental Harm,* 67.
2. See Loewen, "Sundown Towns and Counties: Racial Exclusion in the South."
3. See Dilanian et al., "Federal Agencies Bar Black History Month"; and "Defense Department Webpage on Jackie Robinson Goes Down."
4. Diversity, Equity, and Inclusion, H. 3927, 126th General Assembly (2025).
5. These data have been widely reported. See *Talk Poverty.*
6. "Forecasting State and National Trends in Household Formation and Ownership."
7. "2024 March of Dimes Report Card."
8. Babatunde et al., "Racial Disparities and Diagnosis-to-Treatment Time."
9. Hung et al., "Analysis of Residential Segregation and Racial and Ethnic Disparities."
10. Kappelman et al, "Black/White Disparities in Low Birth Weight."
11. Wright, *Black Boy,* 227.
12. Yeo, "The Real Book Behind *Green Book.*" See also Richen, dir., *The Green Book.*
13. Perez, *South Carolina Commission on Higher Education Statistical Abstract,* 3, 8, 10.
14. State Development Board Tourism.
15. Saxon, "George B. Timmerman, Jr., 82, Segregationist Leader in 50s," 30.
16. See Taylor, *Overground Railroad,* 19–20.
17. Townsend, "How the Green Book Helped African-American Tourists Navigate a Segregated Nation."
18. Hall and Weber, *Driving the Green Book.*
19. Ramsey et al. *Ruth and the Green Book*; Ramsey, *The Green Book: A Play.*
20. WeGOJA Foundation, and Parks, *The Green Book of South Carolina.*
21. Edgar, *South Carolina,* 493.
22. Edgar, *South Carolina,* 17.

WORKS CITED

"2024 March of Dimes Report Card for South Carolina." March of Dime Peristats, 2025. https://www.marchofdimes.org/peristats/reports/south-carolina/report-card.

Alderman, Derek, Kortney Williams, and Ethan Bottone. "Jim Crow Journey Stories: African American Driving as Emotional Labor." *Tourism Geographies* 24, nos. 1–2 (2019): 198–222.

Babatunde, Oluwole Adeyemi, Jan M. Eberth, Tisha M. Felder, et al. "Racial Disparities and Diagnosis-to-Treatment Time Among Patients Diagnosed with Breast Cancer in South Carolina." *Journal of Racial and Ethnic Health Disparities* 9 (2022): 124–34. https://doi.org/10.1007/s40615-020-00935-z.

Bay, Mia. *Traveling Black: A Story of Race and Resistance.* Harvard University Press, 2023.

Bollinger, Alex. "Marjorie Taylor Greene threatens to beat up Sarah McBride on day before Trans Day of Remembrance." *MSN*, November 20, 2024. https://www.msn.com/.

"Defense Department Webpage on Jackie Robinson Goes Down, Then Returns Amid DEI Purge." *Associated Press*, March 19, 2025. https://apnews.com/.

Dilanian, Ken, Alexandra Marquez, Claretta Bellamy, and Dan De Luce. "Federal agencies bar Black History Month and other 'special observances.'" *NBC News*, January 31, 2025. https://www.nbcnews.com/.

Edgar, Walter. *South Carolina: A History.* University of South Carolina Press, 1998.

Farrelly, Peter, dir. *Green Book.* 2018. Universal Pictures, 2018. 130 min.

"Forecasting State and National Trends in Household Formation and Ownership." Urban Institute, March 18, 2021. https://www.urban.org/.

The Green Book of South Carolina: A Travel Guide to S.C. African American Cultural Sites. 2025. https://greenbookofsc.com.

Hall, Alvin. *Driving the Green Book: A Road Trip Through the Living History of Black Resistance.* HarperOne, 2023.

Hall, Alvin, and Janée Woods Weber. *Driving the Green Book.* September 2020. https://alvinhall.com/radio/radio-podcast-driving-the-green-book.

Hartley, Roger C. *Monumental Harm: Reckoning with Jim Crow Era Confederate Monuments.* University of South Carolina Press, 2021.

Hung, Peiyin, Jihong Liu, Chelsea Norregaard, et al. "Analysis of Residential Segregation and Racial and Ethnic Disparities in Severe Maternal Morbidity Before and During the COVID-19 Pandemic." *JAMA Network Open* 5, no. 10 (2022): e2237711. doi:10.1001/jamanetworkopen.2022.37711.

Kappelman, Abigail L., Annie Ro, Lindsay Admon, Belinda L. Needham, and Nancy L. Fleischer. "Black/White Disparities in Low Birth Weight Across Maternal Trajectories of Social Mobility in South Carolina." *Social Science & Medicine* 366 (2025): 117675. https://doi.org/10.1016/j.socscimed.2025.117675.

Loewen, James William. "Sundown Towns and Counties: Racial Exclusion in the South." *Southern Cultures* 15, no. 1 (2009): 22–44.

Perez, Jeffrey L. *South Carolina Commission on Higher Education Statistical Abstract, 46th Edition 2024.* South Carolina Commission on Higher Education, 2024. https://che.sc.gov/sites/che/files/Documents/CHE%20Data%20and%20Reports/Statistical%20Abstracts/2024_Statistical_Abstract-WEB.pdf.

Ramsey, Calvin Alexander. *The Green Book: A Play.* Calvin Alexander Ramsey, 2014.

Ramsey, Calvin Alexander, Gwen Strauss, and Floyd Cooper (illustrator). *Ruth and the Green Book.* Carolrhoda Books, 2010.

Richen, Yoruba, dir. *The Green Book: Guide to Freedom.* Viacom, 2019.

Saxon, Wolfgang. "George B. Timmerman, Jr., 82, Segregationist Leader in 50s." *The New York Times.* December 3, 1994, Saturday, Late Edition-Final, 30.

Sorin, Gretchen. *Driving While Black: African American Travel and the Road to the Civil Rights.* Liveright Publishing, 2020.

State Development Board Tourism Promotional Brochure, ca. 1955, S 149013. South Carolina Department of Archives and History.

Talk Poverty, 2025. https://www.talkpoverty.org.

Taylor, Candacy. *Overground Railroad: The Green Book and the Roots of Black Travel in America.* Abrams Books, 2020.

Townsend, Jacinda. "How the Green Book Helped African-American Tourists Navigate a Segregated Nation." *Smithsonian Magazine,* December 18, 2024. https://www.smithsonianmag.com/.

WeGOJA Foundation and Joshua Parks (photographer). *The Green Book of South Carolina: A Travel Guide to African American Cultural Sites.* Hub City Press, 2022.

Wright, Richard. *Black Boy: A Record of Childhood and Youth.* Harper & Brothers, 1937.

Yeo, Debra. "The Real Book Behind *Green Book*: A Means to Keep Black Americans Safe But Also a Guide to Having Fun." *Toronto Star,* February 19, 2019. https://www.thestar.com/.

Leevy's Funeral Home

Generations of Greatness

W. Maclane Hull

Driving from downtown Columbia, eastward down Taylor Street toward Benedict College and Allen University, one will come across a striking building. Most likely, a pillar of slate at the corner, rising high above the rest of the building, will catch the eye. It is almost incongruous with the rest of the building's yellowish painted brick 1950s design. One might then notice an overhang jutting almost out into the street, embossed with the words "Leevy's Funeral Home." Established in 1932, with the current building constructed in 1951, Leevy's Funeral Home has been a center of the Midlands' African-American community. Indeed, it has not simply operated as a funeral home but has also functioned as a center for political organizing. The funeral home was listed in *The Negro Motorist Green Book* from 1950 through 1955 because of its importance to the African-American community.

This essay is not simply about the Leevy Funeral Home but also about the life of its founder, Isaac Samuel (I. S.) Leevy Jr. Leevy was a major figure in South Carolina's African-American community. He was a business and community leader, political activist, local civil rights movement icon, and a central figure in countless institutions within Columbia's African-American sphere. His story is essential to understanding Columbia's history. This essay also covers the history of the Leevy family and the funeral home after I. S. Leevy's passing in 1968. It gives special attention to his grandson, Isaac Samuel Leevy Johnson who, inspired by his childhood working in the funeral home, entered politics, becoming one of the three first Black South Carolina legislators since the Reconstruction era, serving throughout most of the 1970s. He was a founding partner of Johnson, Toal & Battiste, a law office that he continues to run today. Furthermore, he took over the funeral home in 1995, which he now runs with his sons, Reverend Christopher Leevy Johnson and George Johnson.

Born in the small Kershaw County community of Antioch, Isaac Samuel (I. S.) Leevy Jr. (May 3, 1876–December 9, 1968) was the son of Isaac Samuel Leevy Sr. and Laura Hunter Leevy. He was one of ten children and grew up poor. His father was born into slavery. His mother was born free before Emancipation.[1] Growing up, Leevy attended Mather Academy in the county seat of Camden, taking odd jobs to pay tuition. During and after his time at Mather, Leevy was involved with the local church, opened a pressing shop, and served as a public school teacher before enrolling in the Hampton Institute in Virginia to learn to tailor. He graduated from Hampton in 1906, having achieved an academic degree from night school classes along with an industrial degree in tailoring. During this time, he kept in contact with Mary Kirkland from Kershaw County, who was then attending the South Carolina Agricultural and Mechanical Institute. After graduating from their academic programs, the couple married in June 1909. They had four children: Ruby Geneva, Isaac Kirkland, Carroll Moten, and Marian Naomi.[2] Mary became instrumental in his business and political life, always at his side and serving as his eyes when he started to lose his sight in the 1940s. She was always "active in the community and continued to devote her time to making the funeral home a continuing success."[3]

Leevy first arrived in Columbia in 1907 on a visit to Allen University's commencement. There he met Reverend Richard Carroll, a prominent South Carolinian best known for his annual conventions on race relations, which underscored the importance of economic development in Black communities. Reverend Carroll was a conservative in the same vein as Booker T. Washington, which endeared him to the white community in South Carolina, especially the editors of the white-owned *State* newspaper.[4] Carroll invited Leevy back to Columbia and took him on as a protégé. Leevy traveled with Carroll to speaking engagements and civic race meetings. Their relationship gave Leevy meaningful engagement with issues related to civil rights and the pursuit of racial equality. It also brought other, more tangible benefits, as many of Carroll's friends subsequently patronized Leevy's tailoring shop.[5]

Immediately after moving to Columbia, Leevy began establishing his name through a series of business and social accomplishments. He co-organized the Negro State Fair Association of South Carolina with Reverend Carroll and Dr. A. C. Collins in 1908. Although segregated, Black state fairs had existed since Reconstruction. Carroll, Collins, and Leevy's was the first fully funded annual event. This new Colored State Fair took place on the same fairgrounds as the then-whites-only State Fair one week after that event. The Colored State Fair—later, the Palmetto State Fair—included animal exhibits, marching band shows, and an annual football match between the two local HBCUs: Allen University and Benedict College. It ran every year (except 1919, on account of the flu pandemic) until 1969, when the fairs

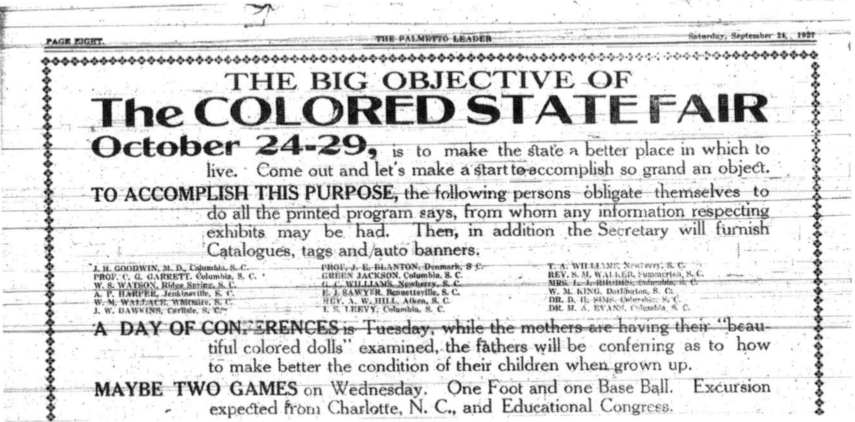

Figure 1.1. An advertisement for the Colored State Fair from 1927, listing I. S. Leevy as a main coordinator of the event. *The Palmetto Leader*, September 24, 1927, p. 8. Historical Newspapers of South Carolina, University of South Carolina Libraries, Columbia, SC.

were integrated.[6] One article from 1909 described the Colored State Fair as "the best exhibition of thrift and progress among the Negroes ever shown in South Carolina" and an example of community uplift.[7]

In 1921, Leevy also helped found the Victory Savings Bank—one of just four Black-owned banks in the nation through at least 1955–of which he was, at times, the vice president, president, and director.[8] Leevy closed his tailor store and opened a department store in 1917, which also housed a barber shop, beauty salon, tailoring shop, and dressmaking shop. That store closed ten years later because of economic downturn, and he opened a furniture store, which closed in 1929.[9]

In addition to his business interests, Leevy became a powerful advocate for education. He pushed local school officials to improve the facilities and resources offered to Black students in the city's segregated and unequal schools. By World War I, there was a dearth of high schools accessible to African Americans throughout South Carolina. In a state where barely half the white teenagers attended school, even fewer Black teenagers did, and Black schools received roughly ten percent of the state funding allocated to white schools.[10] The only school available to Richland County's Black children was Howard School, a two-story wood-frame building established in 1869 by the Freedmen's Bureau. Soon after he arrived, Leevy petitioned the city to open a second African-American school. The city eventually agreed and built the Booker T. Washington School in 1916. It initially only served

Grades one through ten, adding Grade eleven in 1924 and Grade twelve in 1947. Booker T. Washington was the only Black high school in Columbia from its opening until 1948 and was the first Black school accredited by the South Carolina Department of Education.[11] By the 1920s, a growing Black population in Columbia and white flight from the Waverly neighborhood created a need for a third African-American school. Leevy fought the city to allow Black students to attend the abandoned white Waverly school.[12] In 1936, Leevy helped establish another school with Charlotte Jackson in the Kendall Town suburb of Columbia. It was initially named the Jackson-Leevy Graded School, but Ms. Jackson withdrew her name, leaving it as the Leevy Graded School. A few years later the school was moved and renamed Carver Elementary School.[13]

In 1928, Leevy opened an Esso gas station at 1831 Taylor Street, which became a "nexus for civic activity and a haven for black travelers."[14] It included a gas pump and full-time mechanic. Leevy noted that he opened the station because "nowhere in Columbia . . . were Negroes engaged in the filling station business."[15] Four years later, he opened Leevy's Funeral Home, housing it within the gas station's building. He had previously operated a funeral home in the Ridgewood section of Richland County with partners Reverend H. M. Holloway of Brookland Baptist Church and P. M. Bowling.[16] However, Leevy decided that the partnership was not working and that the funeral home would be more successful downtown. He dissolved the partnership and reopened the business, run entirely by himself, at the Taylor Street location. This served as his base of political, religious, and social operations for the remainder of his life. Leevy's Funeral Home also included ambulance service, which was essential for Black communities at a time when hospitals often did not have them. Soon after he had established the funeral home, Leevy fought and succeeded to establish a Black chaplain and mortician at the State Hospital.[17] In all of these activities, I. S. Leevy worked to fill the holes that Columbia had in its Black community.

Leevy's choice of a funeral home was hardly accidental. The most prominent figures in Black communities in the Jim Crow era were often either church leaders or funeral directors, as these were among the few white-collar careers available to African Americans.[18] Indeed, funeral directing and undertaking was often the most accessible professional career available to African Americans post-Reconstruction, as preaching, teaching, and medicine had higher bars for qualification. Moreover, according to E. Franklin Frazier, undertaking was the only career that contained members of both the Black bourgeois and the professional classes.[19] Funeral directors operated completely independent of white patronage, the only Black professional or businessperson aside from the preacher to be so racially self-sufficient.[20] When he opened his home on Taylor Street in 1932, Leevy joined several other Black entrepreneurs who had entered the mortuary business during the interwar years, including four others in Columbia: Champion & Pearson, Johnson-Bradley, Manigault & Williams, and Pinckney's.[21]

In addition to their relative independence, Black funeral directors were highly regarded by their communities. Their relationship with the dead and grieving made them "an agent of one of the most personal rites associated with the church," requiring them to be the moral pillars of their communities.[22] People often looked up to funeral directors because they knew them at a personal level. The importance of community, public grieving, and funerary practices within Black communities created close relationships among African-American residents and funeral directors.[23] According to the Reverend Christopher Leevy Johnson, funeral directors had a higher standing in Black communities than white ones because of the shared economic, social, and cultural histories specific to African-American communities. He noted that other ethnic funeral homes functioned in similar roles, such as those in Jewish communities, but only Black funeral homes had such a racially restricted client base.[24] This close relationship with their communities, cultivated through the extraordinarily personal nature of their work, equipped many directors to speak out on behalf of their communities and assume positions of broader public leadership. As Johnson noted, "even before the civil rights movement, Negro funeral directors were instrumental in spearheading voter registration drives, voter education projects, job placement, philanthropic activity and community service."[25] Leevy's grandson, I. S. Leevy Johnson, was fascinated by this role of funeral directors and similarly noted how death became "a magnet that drew the black community together."[26]

Throughout the Jim Crow era, African-American funeral directors were among the most politically active members of their communities. Suzanne Smith notes how Black funeral directors had a unique position to straddle the private and public spheres. They "used their public role as community leaders in a variety of ways, most notable to combat racial discrimination," and this was prevalent throughout the nation from the end of Reconstruction.[27] Alcee Labat, the director of Labat & Ray in New Orleans, helped lead efforts against segregation amid the *Plessy v. Ferguson* trial. Charles C. Diggs Sr. also used his success and influence in the funeral business to run for office in Detroit in the 1920s and 1930s. More generally, funeral directors used hearses to drive people to polls, provided ambulances to rural areas, and—as in the case of Leevy's—promoted voting rights efforts.[28] The fact that they did not rely on white patronage allowed funeral directors such as I. S. Leevy to become prominent activists with less fear of economic reprisal. Broadly, Black businesses in segregated southern cities promoted communal pride and helped keep local African Americans united in the face of racial oppression.[29] Funeral directors maintained an even more prominent stature in Black communities, again because of their more exclusive clientele and the extremely intimate nature of their work. These dynamics allowed many like Leevy to become local "race men," or prominent men who "dedicate[d] their life to directly contributing to the betterment of Black people."[30]

In 1951, Leevy chose one of his sons, Isaac Kirkland "Kirk" Leevy, to construct a new gas station and funeral home. It replaced the building that had previously served as his gas station at the same location since 1930. After designing the building, Kirk hired several friends for the electrical, flooring, and brickwork. They began construction in August and completed the project by the end of 1952.[31]

From its completion, the building was striking. Most of the building is a two-story, flat-roof, stone structure, reflecting midcentury modern design. However, the southeast corner of the building features a slate, stacked-stone façade that extends several feet above the rest of the building. The second floor of this corner of the building contained a chapel, the stained-glass window of which can still be seen on the southern elevation. An overhang emblazoned with the business's name covers the main entrance. Although Leevy closed the service station soon after the new building's opening, the Leevy family retained one of the original gas pumps, which still stands in a recessed corner under this overhang. The pump represents both the origins of the funeral home and the reason for its inclusion in the *Green Book*. From 1950 through 1955, *The Negro Motorist Green Book* designated 1831 Taylor Street as a safe haven for Black travelers, listing it as one of Columbia's service stations.

Leevy's Funeral Home and service station was one of many *Green Book* sites in Columbia, one part of a vast, intimate network. Leevy's business stood on the outskirts of the historic Waverly district, where Black residents opened businesses and even their homes to locals and Black travelers. Columbia's first suburb, the Waverly district, was first developed in the 1860s and 1870s, and by the turn of the twentieth century had become the center of Columbia's Black population. Roughly bounded by Taylor Street, Gervais Street, Harden Street, and Millwood Avenue, it was home to the city's twin HBCUs, Allen University and Benedict College; the Good

Figure 1.2. Modern exterior of Leevy's Funeral Home, 1831 Taylor Street, Columbia, SC. Photograph by W. Maclane Hull, October 31, 2019.

Figure 1.3. One of the original gas pumps, still held by the entrance to Leevy's Funeral Home. Photograph by W. Maclane Hull, October 31, 2019.

COLUMBIA (con't.)

RESTAURANTS
Green Leaf—1117 Wash. St.
Savoy—Old Winnsboro Rd.
Cozy Inn—1509 Harden St.
Mom's—1005 Washington St.
Brown's—1014 Lady St.
Blue Palace—1001 Washington St.
Waverly—2515 Gervais St.

BEAUTY PARLORS
Amy's—1125½ Washington St.
Obbie's—1119½ Washington St.

BARBER SHOPS
Holman's—2138 Gervais St.

BEAUTY SCHOOLS
Poro—2481 Millwood Ave.
Madare Bradley—2228 Hampton St.

TAVERNS
Moon Glow—1005 Washington St.

SERVICE STATIONS
A. W. Simkins—1331 Park St.
Caldwell's—Oak & Taylor Sts.
Waverly—2202 Taylor St.
Leevy's—1831 Taylor St.

DRUG STORES
Count's—1105 Washington St.

TAXI CABS
Blue Ribbon—1024 Washington St.

Figure 1.4. Listing for Leevy's Service Station in the 1953 *Negro Motorist Green Book* (page 62). Schomburg Center for Research in Black Culture, Manuscripts, Archives and Rare Books Division, The New York Public Library.

Samaritan-Waverly Hospital; an extensive civil rights organizing network; and most of Columbia's Black professionals. These professionals opened groceries, health clinics and dentist offices, retail shops, restaurants, and pharmacies within Waverly, turning it into a relatively self-sufficient neighborhood open to the city's African-American population.[32] The *Green Book* eventually listed many of these businesses, including restaurants such as Magnolia, Treye's and Waverly, and service stations such as Waverly's Service and Thomas's Drug Store.[33]

Among Waverly's many *Green Book* sites were tourist homes, essentially the personal homes of African-American professionals in the city opened to travelers, especially civil rights organizers. Tourist homes were among the most popular places that "offered multiple options for African Americans looking to minimize the indignities of racism."[34] Because they were private homes, the owners could better conceal them from racist reprisal. Dr. W. D. Chappelle Jr. owned a tourist home at 1301 Pine Street. Chappelle was a physician who operated the People's Infirmary, one of the only sources of health care for Columbia's African-American people, and his father, an African Methodist Episcopal bishop, had served as Allen University's president from 1897 through 1899.[35] The Chappelle tourist home, operated by Dr. Chappelle's wife, was listed in the *Green Book* from 1938 through 1940, 1947 through 1957, and 1959 through 1967. Simmie Hiller Smith operated another tourist home on 929 Pine Street, which was listed in the *Green Book* from 1947 until 1967. Smith, a dressmaker, hosted everyone from Allen University students to musicians such as Duke Ellington. In her basement, she taught locals and travelers alike how to sew. Smith died in 1955, and her daughter, Delores Hiller Frazier, continued operating the guest home along with her husband, Benjamin, one of the first men to desegregate Columbia's fire department.[36]

Beauty parlors and barber shops were also integral parts of the *Green Book* network and Black communities. These businesses provided "alternative public space[s] where patrons could meet, freely converse, and receive quality, convenient service without fear of the harassment and degradation that often awaited them in the white-controlled spaces of mid-century Columbia."[37] Much like funeral homes, barber shops and salons were among the few avenues of entrepreneurship for Black men and women in the Jim Crow era. Holman's Barber Shop—listed from 1939 to 1941 and from 1948 to 1955—was one of these. Lewis Holman began barbering while a student at Allen in the late 1910s, opening his first Waverly barber shop in 1928. He operated in various locations over the following decades before establishing a permanent spot at 2128 Gervais Street in 1945. Here, Black men played games, socialized, and discussed political issues, growing an interconnected civil rights community.[38] The same was true for women's beauty salons. Ruth Collins Perry operated a beauty shop in Waverly at 1221 Pine Street, listed in the *Green Book* from 1939 through 1941. Beauty parlors like Perry's provided safe spaces for "cultural and aesthetic expression in a society where beauty norms were defined by white standards."[39] They also provided areas where Black women could socialize freely and politically organize. Black women were often the bedrock of civil rights organizing activity and much of their planning possibly took place in beauty parlors.[40]

Green Book sites also flourished outside Waverly. Beauty parlors such as Amy's and Obbie's and restaurants such as Green Leaf, the Blue Palace, and Mom's were all located on Washington Street in the city's downtown area.[41] Modjeska Monteith Simkins's Motel Simbeth was one of the most well-known *Green Book* sites outside Waverly. Located roughly eight miles north on modern-day Two Notch Road, the Motel Simbeth appeared in the *Green Book* from 1956 until 1961 with a special "recommended" star. Throughout the years, it hosted countless travelers, including famous musicians, such as James Brown, who stayed at the motel whenever they performed in Columbia. The Motel Simbeth also served local Columbians searching for a safe space. Simkins's niece, Henrie Monteith Treadwell; Robert Anderson; and James Solomon made history in 1963, when a judge ordered them admitted to the University of South Carolina, ending the school's nearly one hundred years of post-Reconstruction segregation. While attending the University of South Carolina, Anderson and Treadwell stayed at the Motel Simbeth just to have some peace. The motel was later demolished, but Simkins continued to operate her home on Marion Street in Columbia as an "office, meeting place, and for lodging of civil rights associates."[42]

I. S. Leevy understood the responsibility he was undertaking as a funeral home director and continued to build his public reputation. Once he took over, he began to raise the profile of his funeral home, running advertisements in *The State, Palmetto Leader, Lighthouse and Informer,* and several other South Carolina newspapers. The advertisements promoted Leevy's dedication to providing affordable and accessible service to even the most impoverished African-American people of the Midlands, stating "No Deserving Poor Refused." Leevy's grandson remembers: "I learned at an early age that my granddaddy was dedicated to improving the quality of life for everyone. He had a commitment to helping others. . . . And that was instilled in me from an early age."[43]

In time, Leevy's Funeral Home played an even greater role when it served as a central base for Columbia's civil rights movement. Although Leevy himself never won elected office, he became one of midcentury Columbia's leading African-American political figures. A fierce critic of the one-party system that had strangled Southern politics since the end of Reconstruction, Leevy believed in a competitive two-party South Carolina that would allow equal involvement of Black and white people, even in an era when the African-American vote was almost exclusively Republican.[44] Leevy attacked the conservative, "Lily White" faction of the Republican Party.[45] In 1944, after the Supreme Court's denunciation of the Democrats' white primaries in *Smith v.*

Allwright, many Black South Carolinians, such as John H. McCray—editor of the *Lighthouse and Informer,* a local Black newspaper—formed the Progressive Democratic Party, hoping to win interracial support for Franklin D. Roosevelt. The national Democratic Party under Roosevelt wanted to make inroads with the African-American communities, and McCray's efforts sought to shift the Democrats' power in the South away from segregationists, such as Strom Thurmond, and toward a more progressive, racially inclusive party. With the support of the National Association for the Advancement of Colored People (NAACP), the Progressive Democrats managed to register over fifty thousand African Americans to vote by 1946.[46] Leevy, however, continued to work for the Republican Party, hoping to attract the "many Negroes who still fondly cling to the hope that the party of Douglas and Lincoln will come into power again and champion complete freedom for them, a second Emancipation Proclamation."[47]

Under the Republican Party, Leevy ran in numerous local elections and worked to further establish the party among South Carolina's Black communities. In 1940, "Tieless" Joe Tolbert appointed Leevy chairman of Richland County's Republican Party to spread the Republican Party to South Carolina, which barely existed in the state.[48] Tolbert, a white man, had a somewhat sordid reputation among the African-American community due to his use of racist slurs in public speeches and his general lack of interest in growing the party by attracting Black voters. Still, he and the national party appreciated Leevy's outspoken criticism of Democrats and his reputation as a respected businessperson.[49] Leevy believed in the Republican Party because of its role in Reconstruction, but he was never hesitant to criticize the party. For example, he called out the national party during the Eisenhower years for working with Dixiecrats and ignoring the South Carolina party.[50]

Leevy ran for office multiple times, including for South Carolina's Second District congressional seat in 1954. However, he faced intense opposition by the Progressive Democrats and McCray, mainly due to his association with Tolbert. Other members of the Progressive Democrats such as O. E. McKaine wished to work with Leevy and create an all-Black coalition but were overruled. Despite the opposition from McCray and lack of electoral victories, Leevy remained loyal to Tolbert and the Republican Party until 1964. It was Barry Goldwater's nomination for president that finally caused Leevy to defect–Goldwater's opposition to the 1964 Civil Rights Act was the final straw.[51]

I. S. Leevy used both the original service station and the 1951 funeral home as the base of his operations to fight for voting and political rights.

Independence from white patronage provided a valuable shield for voting rights activities. As civil rights activists escalated their registration and education efforts during the 1950s and 1960s, white reprisals likewise increased. Bob Moses, for example, was brutally assaulted outside courthouses in Mississippi for his efforts in the 1960s. Medgar Evers, James Chaney, Andrew Goodman, and Michael Schwerner were murdered for working to register African-American people to vote. More locally, employers fired workers and teachers, including Charleston's Septima Clarke, for refusing to give up their NAACP membership. George Elmore, owner of a Columbia five-and-dime and secretary for Richland County's Progressive Democratic Party, faced death threats, burning crosses, and white refusals to restock his store after he successfully challenged the state's Democratic Party's barring of Black voters.[52] In Calhoun Falls, Reverend Archie Ware was beaten with clubs and left for dead after casting a vote in the 1946 primary.[53] All African-American people in the South had to tread carefully in white society for their own protection, and Black communities were especially wary about voter registration.

Leevy, however, remained undaunted. He founded the Lincoln Emancipation Club in the mid-1940s, using the funeral home for covert voter registration. The club pushed "all state and local religious, fraternal and various other secular organizations to strive for 100 percent registration of their respective membership by May 1956," but was advertised as "a non-partisan and non-racial organization, dedicated to the establishment of at least a two-party system" to prevent unwanted retaliation.[54] Club members held annual Emancipation Day Celebrations, which served as registration drives, until 1960. After he opened the funeral home, Leevy convinced a member of the voter registration office to lend voter registration machines to the funeral home. Leevy then invited Columbians to learn about the voter registration process. Members of the Leevy family, especially I. S.'s grandson, I. S. Leevy Johnson, taught citizens how to use the machines. The goal was to prepare African-American voters to pass even the most rigorous tests white registrars could put before them.[55] Leevy also traveled to churches throughout the Midlands, imploring clergy and congregation alike to register and vote. When ministers complained of the mixing of politics and religion, Leevy responded, "Until we develop some civic and political leaders outside the church. We've got to involve church people in civic affairs [*sic*]."[56]

Leevy had close relationships with many other local civil rights leaders and national organizations. He continued to work with the Columbia chapter of the NAACP, which he had helped found in 1917.[57] After Martin Luther King, Jr. founded the Southern Christian Leadership Conference (SCLC) in 1957, Leevy joined as an executive board member and representative of Columbia, positions he retained through the early 1960s.[58] These connections, along with his local stature, allowed him to host national figures. For example, in 1959, SCLC held their fall meeting in Columbia. During the meeting's off-time, King, Ralph Abernathy, and other SCLC leaders congregated in the funeral home's chapel, the only location big enough to hold them all. During the meeting, Leevy, the SCLC, and the Columbia community discussed voter registration methods.[59] Leevy was especially close to the legendary civil rights figure Modjeska Monteith Simkins, who described him as "my beloved compatriot with whom I maintained a glowing friendship for many years."[60]

By the time the new funeral home was constructed, Leevy's sight had deteriorated badly, and he soon became completely blind. His wife, Mary, his son Kirk, and his grandchildren, including I. S. Leevy Johnson, helped run the business and took him to political events throughout the region. Mary Kirkland Leevy, his wife of fifty-six years, died June 17, 1965. Leevy passed away three years later, on December 9, 1968, at age ninety-one. His death received front-page coverage from *The State*, and memorials in various newspapers listed his many political and business achievements, painting him as a man who affected genuine change in Columbia.[61]

Isaac Samuel Leevy ran the funeral home until his death and its ownership remained in family hands. Dr. Carroll Moten Leevy, his son, oversaw the estate and appointed Leevy Johnson and Claude McCollom as co-managers. Carroll Leevy had graduated from Columbia's Booker T. Washington High School and Tennessee's Fisk University when he applied for medical school in 1942. The Medical College of South Carolina in Charleston barred him from attending, despite I. S. Leevy's petitioning the state's General Assembly. Instead, he attended the University of Michigan Medical School. He specialized in medical research, working with Roosevelt's National Youth Administration's National Advisory Committee and the US Army Specialized Training Program, earning his MD in 1944. He moved to New Jersey for his residency, where he remained for the rest of his life. Kirk Leevy, however, frequently overturned decisions made by Johnson and McCollom and convinced his brother Carroll to give I. S. Leevy Johnson an ultimatum: stay with Leevy's or practice law.[62] For someone raised in the funeral home, and who expected to spend the rest of his life there, it was a difficult but ultimately consequential decision.

Isaac Samuel Leevy Johnson was born May 16, 1942, to Ruby Leevy Johnson—I. S. Leevy's daughter—and O. J. Johnson. His parents separated when he was young, and Ruby and her children moved into the funeral home. I. S. Leevy Johnson quickly became his grandfather's main assistant. His family raised him with the expectation that he would take over one day; Leevy taught him about business, politics, community, and funerary practice. Johnson described his youth as "a combination of family and business, since we lived in the Funeral Home. The business aspect of our lives heavily influenced the family aspect."[63] He was able to meet Martin Luther King, Jr., during the SCLC's Columbia meeting and guided his then-blind grandfather at the 1956 Republican National Convention in San Francisco. Johnson recalls being inspired by Leevy's care for marginalized people. "He was my role model," Johnson recalled, "and I grew up wanting to be just like him.... He always fought for the underdog."[64]

After graduating from C. A. Johnson High School in 1960, Johnson enrolled in mortuary school. I. S. Leevy was fixated on the idea that students should live on campus, and the only mortuary program in the United States that provided dormitory space was the University of Minnesota. The two years at Minnesota were difficult for Johnson, being one of the few Black students on campus and being away from his family for the first time. Following the completion of his degree, he returned to South Carolina and enrolled at the local HBCU Benedict College while fulfilling a state-required two-year apprenticeship. He achieved a business degree at Benedict and enrolled at the University of South Carolina Law School in 1965. He hoped that training in law would allow him to better assist the funeral home and advocate for the communities it served. Johnson was able to pursue his law degree without having to split time with the funeral home, yet he faced immense pressure. He was only the second Black student to attend the law school; the first student had enrolled the previous year but did not finish. In 1968, Johnson became the first African American to finish the program. That same year, he married Doris Wright and lost his grandfather.[65]

When faced with Kirk Leevy's ultimatum, Johnson decided to continue his law practice. He opened the I. S. Leevy Johnson Law Firm and quickly developed a solid local reputation. In 1969, a group of prominent Black South Carolinians gathered at the Masonic Temple on Gervais Street to elect one of their own to the state's General Assembly. Since the passing of the Voting Rights Act of 1965, "the number of registered [African-American] voters mushroomed" to two hundred twenty thousand in 1970 but had yet to see major electoral victories.[66] Indeed, the state's government had remained all white for the entire twentieth century. This group, which included Lincoln C. Jenkins, Modjeska Monteith Simkins, Reverend C. J. Whitaker and others, sought to change this unfortunate history. With support from the Democratic Party's white faction, the group nominated Columbia lawyer James Felder, Charleston funeral director Herbert Fielding, Charleston political organizer James Clyburn, and I. S. Leevy Johnson to run for the South Carolina House of Representatives. Since the then-white supremacist Democratic Party had taken control of the state after the end of Reconstruction, one of the many ways they attempted to keep African-American people out of political office was decrying them as incompetent and unqualified for politics. Even after the passage of the Civil and Voting Rights Acts, South Carolina's Black leadership focused on each candidate's qualifications. Johnson was not only an accomplished lawyer; he also carried the prestige of the family name: "The name recognition helped: I was I. S. Leevy's grandson."[67]

In 1970, I. S. Leevy Johnson realized his grandfather's dreams. Johnson's namesake had fought for Black voting rights for decades. He had tried to enter office to change things from the inside but never won an election. On November 3, 1970, Johnson, along with Felder and Fielding, was among the first African Americans in the century to be voted into the South Carolina General Assembly.[68] Looking back at those years, he recalled, "I just wish that [my grandfather] and my grandmother had been alive to see things they have allowed me to achieve," crediting all the political and community work they accomplished during their lives as the reason he could achieve so much.[69] Johnson lost reelection in 1972 during a nationwide Nixon-Republican wave fueled by white backlash against the school redistricting measures that had integrated Richland County schools.[70] He won his seat back in 1974, serving until his political retirement in 1980. In office, he helped found the South Carolina Black Caucus, served as vice-chairman of the Judiciary Committee, and introduced bills to make school textbooks free and expand the state's Supreme Court.[71]

While Johnson was in office, Kirk Leevy continued to run the funeral home. In 1977, he approached Carroll about purchasing the business from the trust, but he died in 1978 before the sale could take place. His children, Gregory and Gloria Leevy, continued his dream, purchasing the funeral home in 1978 with a loan from First Palmetto Bank. Gregory, who returned home after touring as an actor, served as executive director, obtaining his funeral director's license while Ben Piper and Robert Bostick oversaw the daily functions. Gregory was frequently absent, directing and performing at the local Trustus Theatre while Gloria was busy with her own law practice, leaving Piper, Bostick, and the staff to run the funeral home.[72] Piper and Bostick would both leave in the early 1980s. Bostick partnered with Willie

Tompkins, also a former Leevy's employee, to open the Bostick-Tompkins Funeral Home three blocks away from Leevy's. Bostick and Tompkins had been the public faces of Leevy's, and the community began shifting its patronage to the people they knew. Leevy's Funeral Home's finances began to suffer, but Gregory and Gloria resisted selling, even to an interested I. S. Leevy Johnson. However, in 1994, Gregory and Gloria defaulted on payments and filed for Chapter 11 bankruptcy. In 1995, the presiding judge for their case, William Thurmond Bishop, began selling the funeral home's assets. As the sole bidder, Leevy Johnson became the owner of Leevy's Funeral Home in June 1995. Gregory continued to act and direct while Gloria continued her law practice, both later moving to Greenville, SC.[73]

Before he purchased his grandfather's funeral home, Leevy Johnson continued his successful legal career. In 1975, he expanded his law firm, partnering with one-time law school classmate and then law professor, William T. Toal, and a recent Emory Law School graduate, Luther J. Battiste. The new Johnson, Toal & Battiste P. A. was the first integrated law firm in South Carolina. Toal was white, and the firm hired paralegals and clerks of all races. Johnson, Toal & Battiste focused on fighting for poor and marginalized people and developed a reputation for being, in the words of former South Carolina Chief Justice Ernest Finney, "articulate, prepared and on the cutting edge on the issues which are of vital concern to the African-American community."[74] After a heart attack and finding distaste with political campaigning, Johnson resigned from elected office in 1980 and focused on his law firm. In 1983, the South Carolina Bar elected him as its secretary, and in 1985, he was unanimously elected president, the first Black lawyer to lead the Bar.[75] Johnson worked to improve the image of lawyers in the state and give hope to Black communities. He embraced his blackness "because it offers hope to black people who may have questions about the sincerity and determination of the judicial system today."[76] His reputation as a lawyer grew nationally throughout the rest of the century. Even superstar attorney Johnnie Cochran allegedly described himself as "the I. S. Leevy Johnson of Los Angeles."[77]

Johnson was also prominent in education, much like his grandfather. Governor Dick Riley appointed him chair of the Trustee Board of South Carolina State College (SCSC) in 1980, a position he held for ten years. He then spent an additional five years on the board as a regular member. SCSC saw unprecedented growth under his leadership, achieving university status in 1990.[78] Johnson resigned from the board in 1995, in part because of the institution's financial scandals. His main reason, however, was that he had finally purchased Leevy's Funeral Home after three decades of waiting.

After becoming the sole owner of the funeral home in June 1995, Johnson appointed Ben Piper as manager and worked to gain back the community's trust. His statewide reputation certainly helped. He remodeled the home, "bought a new fleet of cars, landscaped Lincoln cemetery, and purchased uniforms for the staff."[79] Johnson revived his grandfather's tradition of helping all those in need, donating services to those who passed in tragedies. Even when offered Matthew Perry's vacant district judge seat, Johnson turned it down to focus on the funeral home.

I. S. Leevy Johnson continues to run the funeral home, along with his law practice. Leevy's Funeral Home purchased a neighboring car maintenance shop in 1999, converting it into a chapel. In 2005, the space between the Funeral Home and new chapel was covered and converted into parking for the Funeral Home's fleet of vehicles.[80] It remains a family practice. Johnson's son, Reverend Dr. Christopher Leevy Johnson, is president and managing director; and another son, George Johnson, is general counsel for the Funeral Home and managing shareholder for Johnson, Toal, and Battiste. I. S. Leevy Johnson's wife, Doris Wright Johnson, has worked as the funeral home's public relations director in addition to her career as an educator at Booker T. Washington High and Benedict College.[81]

Johnson has received various high honors for his careers in politics, law, and funerary practice. In 1999, he received South Carolina's highest civilian achievement, the Order of the Palmetto, recognizing his achievements, and in 2003, Interstate 277 was named after him.[82] I. S. Leevy Johnson would perhaps consider his greatest, or at least most personal, achievement to be inducting his grandfather, I. S. Leevy, into the South Carolina Business Hall of Fame in 1996. In his speech, Johnson credited his grandfather with all his success and eulogized him, saying, "Let no one here say that this is the last tribute of respect that he'll pay him, but let every moment of every day be spent in honoring all that Mr. Leevy stood for."[83]

W. Maclane Hull recently earned a PhD in history at the University of South Carolina. He completed his master of arts in public history in 2021. His research focuses on the rise and intersections of mass incarceration and hip-hop culture in the United States. He successfully nominated Leevy's Funeral Home to the National Register of Historic Places in 2021.

NOTES

1. Johnson, *Undertakings*, 158. Reverend Christopher Leevy Johnson is the son of Isaac Leevy Johnson and great-grandson of I. S. Leevy. Johnson's dissertation covers not only Leevy's Funeral Home but two other Black-owned funeral homes in the nation and the role of Black funeral directors in African-American communities.
2. Leevy, "A Cornerstone of Columbia's History," 16; Leevy-Kirkland Wedding Invitation; Johnson, *Undertakings*, 158–59. Marian Leevy passed at only age eighteen. See I. S. Leevy Johnson, interview by James Shadd.
3. "S. C. History: Leevy—Black Pioneer," 4.
4. Leevy, "A Cornerstone of Columbia's History," 16; Harlan, "The Secret Life of Booker T. Washington," 401–2; Donaldson, "Carroll, Richard."
5. Johnson, *Undertakings*, 162.
6. Stroup, *Meet Me At the Rocket*, 39–48; Underwood, "The Colorful South Carolina State"; Brinson, "The Colored State Fair."
7. "Colored State Fair to Meet at Batesburg."
8. "Lincoln Day Celebration," 1; "Personal Biography of Isaac Samuel Leevy," 1.
9. "Personal Biography of Isaac Samuel Leevy," 1; "S.C. History: Leevy—Black Pioneer"; "I. S. Leevy, Columbia Business Man, Gets Service Award"; Leevy, "A Cornerstone of Columbia's History"; Johnson, *Undertakings*, 167.
10. Bullock, *A History of Negro Education*, 180; Bartels, *History of South Carolina Schools*, 15.
11. Leevy, "A Cornerstone of Columbia's History"; Johnson, *Undertakings*, 163–64; Found, "Booker T. Washington High School Auditorium," Section 8.
12. "New Industrial School Planned By Negros," 1; Johnson, *Undertakings*, 164.
13. Leevy, "A Cornerstone of Columbia's History"; "S.C. History: Leevy—Black Pioneer"; Johnson, *Undertakings*, 166.
14. Johnson, *Undertakings*, 168.
15. "I. S. Leevy, Columbia Business Man."
16. Leevy, "A Cornerstone of Columbia's History," 17; I. S. Leevy Johnson, interview by W. Maclane Hull.
17. Leevy, "A Cornerstone of Columbia's History," 17; "Personal Biography of Isaac Samuel Leevy"; Johnson, *Undertakings*, 171.
18. Johnson, *Undertakings*, 5.
19. Frazier, *Black Bourgeoisie*, 48.
20. Johnson, *Undertakings*, 7.
21. *Hill's Columbia . . . Directory*, 938. I. S. Leevy Johnson has also stated that it was one of Leevy's sons, Kirkland Leevy, who first suggested entering the funeral home business. See I. S. Leevy Johnson, interview by James Shadd.
22. Johnson, *Undertakings*, 8; I. S. Leevy Johnson, interview by James Shadd.
23. Smith, "To Serve the Living," 249–62; Rev. Christopher Leevy Johnson, interview by W. Maclane Hull.
24. Johnson, *Undertakings*, 8–9. See also, Holloway, *Passed On*, 15–57.
25. Johnson, *Undertakings*, 11.
26. O'Shea, "A Real Go-Getter Heads S.C. Bar," 1.
27. Smith, "To Serve the Living," 251.

28. Smith, "To Serve the Living," 249–62; Johnson, *Undertakings*, 173–76.

29. Ingham, "Building Businesses, Creating Communities," 641.

30. Assata Shakur, quoted in "Race Men." For more on "race men and women" and race representatives, see Carby, *Race Men*; and Mack, *Representing the Race*, 12–37.

31. "Leevy's Will Build $23,000 Funeral Home," 11; I. S. Leevy Johnson, interview by Hull. A 1956 Sanborn map states that the building was completed in 1952, but other sources claim the new funeral home was open as early as 1951. See *Sanborn Fire Insurance Map*, 47.

32. Parramore and Brown, Section 8; "Waverly Protection Area: Historic Preservation Guidelines."

33. For a full list of all extant and demolished Columbia *Green Book* sites, see "Columbia's Green Book Sites."

34. Crawford, "Cornwell, Harriet M., Tourist Home," Section 8.

35. Chappelle Jr.'s grandson is Dave Chappelle, an internationally famous comedian.

36. The Smith House was one of the few extant *Green Book* tourist houses in Columbia. In April 2023, however, it was destroyed by fire. It is unclear whether the fire resulted from deterioration or arson. See "929 Pine Street"; and Hughes, "This SC home where Duke Ellington once stayed has a storied history."

37. "Holman's Barber Shop."

38. "Holman's Barber Shop."

39. "Ruth's Beauty Parlor."

40. Taylor, *Overground Railroad*, 236.

41. All of these sites have been demolished, likely because of urban redevelopment in Columbia's downtown. See "Columbia's Green Book Sites."

42. Waldrop, "'Walking through History'"; Allen, "Searching for Motel Simbeth"; and "South Carolina: Modjeska Monteith Simkins House."

43. Johnson, *Undertakings*, 184; I. S. Leevy Johnson, interview by Hull.

44. Workman, "Leevy, Modjeska Simkins and Other Negro Republicans."

45. McKaine, "The Palmetto State."

46. Brinson, *Stories of Struggle*, 6–7; Richards, "Progressive Democratic Party"; Burton, "Civil Rights Movement."

47. "S. C. History: Leevy—Black Pioneer."

48. Nickles, "Attorney of the Week."

49. Johnson, *Undertakings*, 174.

50. I. S. Leevy to Vel J. Washington.

51. McCray, "John McCray to Arthur Clement"; "Leevy's Hymntime"; Johnson, *Undertakings*," 181.

52. For a small selection of voter registration and white reactionary violence in the civil rights era, see McMillen "Black Enfranchisement in Mississippi"; Branch, *Parting the Waters*; Cagin and Dray, *We Are Not Afraid*; Dittmer, *Local People*; Payne, *I've Got the Light of Freedom*; and Santoro, "The Civil Rights Movement and the Right to Vote."

53. *Elmore v. Rice et al.*, 10.

54. "W. E. Solomon Addresses Richland Lincoln Emancipation Club"; "Emancipation Day Talk to Be Made by Bishop"; "Lincoln Day Celebration in Columbia Saturday"; "Impressive Attendance at Lincoln Day Celebration," 1.

55. I. S. Leevy Johnson, interview Hull.
56. Eulogy for Isaac Samuel Leevy.
57. Clancy, "Leevy Marks Anniversary of NAACP."
58. Leevy drew deep inspiration from Dr. King, seeing in him someone who believed in and fought for the same ideals Leevy had his whole life: an end to segregation and an expansion of voting and civil rights, combined with a religious devotion Leevy had always preached. See "Annual Meeting of the Southern Christian Leadership Conference Pamphlet."
59. "Mass Letter from I. S. Leevy, Matthew D. McCollom, and Milton E. Cox"; Leevy, "Invitation to SCLC meeting"; I. S. Leevy Johnson, interview by Hull.
60. Leevy, "A Cornerstone of Columbia's History." For her part, Modjeska Simkins owned and operated her own *Green Book* site, the Motel Simbeth. Along with providing housing for Black travelers, Simbeth served as a base of operations for various Columbia civil rights actions. For example, in 1955, Simeon Booker of *Jet* and Reverend Albert C. Redd stayed at the motel to investigate a South Carolina White Citizens Council boycott of Black businesses, one that sought to "starve" NAACP-sympathetic African Americans. See "South Carolina's Plot to Starve Negroes"; Carlisle, "#TBT: Who is Modjeska Monteith Simkins?"; and Allen, "Searching for Motel Simbeth."
61. "City Mortician I. S. Leevy Dies After Short Illness," 1, 6; "I. S. Leevy Obituary"; "I. S. Leevy, Carolinian"; "Leading Mortician Dies in Columbia"; Montgomery, "On The Record."
62. Carroll Leevy's research on liver disease has subsequently earned him international acclaim. See Johnson, *Undertakings*, 189; and Richards, "Leevy, Carroll Moton."
63. I. S. Leevy Johnson, interview by Hull.
64. Quoted in Johnson, *Undertakings*, 187.
65. Johnson, *Undertakings*, 187–88; I. S. Leevy Johnson interview by Hull.
66. Edgar, *South Carolina: A History*, 541.
67. Quoted in Johnson, *Undertakings*, 191.
68. James Clyburn's campaign failed, but he went on to serve as Governor John West's advisor and on the state's human affairs commission. He stepped down from this position in 1992 to successfully run for South Carolina's Sixth District seat in the US House of Representatives. See Krell, "Negroes Win House Seats"; O'Shea, "A Real Go-Getter Heads S.C. Bar"; and Burris, "Blacks Finally Elected in 1970," B1.
69. I. S. Leevy Johnson, interview by Hull.
70. O'Shea, "Richland Elects GOP Slate," 1; Bishop Redfern II, open letter; Johnson, *Undertakings*, 193.
71. Mauldin, "Bill Would Allow Free Textbooks for Poor," 12; "Johnson: Expand Supreme Court," 51.
72. "Gregory Kirkland Leevy."
73. Lofton, "Funeral Home Changes Hands in Family," B1; "Gregory Kirkland Leevy"; Johnson, *Undertakings*," 205–09.
74. Thomas, "25 Years of Striving for a Goal," G1.

75. Among his other awards for his law career were the Matthew J. Perry Medallion from the Columbia Lawyers' Association in 2000, the Spirit of Excellence Award from the American Bar Association in 2014, and honorary doctorates from Benedict College, Allen University, and Morris College. See Isaac Washington, "On Paying Dues"; Milkie, "Johnson Making Own History Today With Swearing In," *Times and Democrat*, 1; O'Shea, "A Real Go-Getter Heads S.C. Bar," 1; Johnson, *Undertakings*, 195, 198–203; "Isaac Samuel 'I. S.' Leevy Johnson"; and "I. S. Leevy Johnson."

76. O'Shea, "A Real Go-Getter Heads S.C. Bar," 1.

77. Johnson, *Undertakings*, 214.

78. Johnson, *Undertakings*, 195–97.

79. Johnson, *Undertakings*, 211.

80. Richland County Tax Assessor Reports, https://property.spatialest.com/sc/richland/#/property/R11403-09-10; I. S. Leevy Johnson, interview (2019).

81. "Staff"; "Attorneys."

82. Rees, "277, Farrow Rd. named for I. S. Leevy Johnson."

83. Monk, "S.C. Business Hall of Fame Inducts Three," 214.

WORKS CITED

"929 Pine Street." *Historic Columbia*, accessed September 10, 2025. https://www.historiccolumbia.org/online-tours/lower-waverly/929-pine-street.

Allen, Katharine. "Searching for Motel Simbeth." *Historic Columbia*, accessed September 10, 2025. https://www.historiccolumbia.org/blog/searching-motel-simbeth.

"Annual Meeting of the Southern Christian Leadership Conference Pamphlet." 1961. Box 33, South Carolina Council on Human Relations Records. South Caroliniana Library, University of South Carolina.

"Attorneys." Johnson, Toal & Battiste, PA., accessed September 10, 2025. https://www.jtblawfirm.com/attorneys.

Bartels, Virginia B. *The History of South Carolina Schools*. Center for Educator Recruitment, Retention, and Advancement, 2004.

Branch, Taylor. *Parting the Waters: America in the King Years, 1954–63*. Simon & Schuster, 1989.

Brinson, Claudia Smith. "The Colored State Fair: The Segregated Fair, 1890–1971." *Stories of Struggle*, accessed September 10, 2025. https://storiesofstruggle.com/the-colored-state-fair.

Brinson, Claudia Smith. *Stories of Struggle: The Clash Over Civil Rights in South Carolina*. University of South Carolina Press, 2020.

Bullock, Henry Allen. *A History of Negro Education in the South: From 1619 to the Present*. Harvard University Press, 1967.

Burris, Roddie. "Blacks Finally Elected in 1970." *The State*, February 17, 2002, 4.

Burton, Orville Vernon. "Civil Rights Movement." *South Carolina Encyclopedia*, July 20, 2022. https://www.scencyclopedia.org/sce/entries/civil-rights-movement/.

Cagin, Seth, and Philip Dray. *We Are Not Afraid: The Story of Goodman, Schwerner, and Chaney, and the Civil Rights Campaign for Mississippi.* Macmillan, 1988.

Carby, Hazel V. *Race Men.* Harvard University Press, 2000.

Carlisle, Lois Carlisle. "#TBT: Who is Modjeska Monteith Simkins?" *Historic Columbia,* accessed September 10, 2025. https://www.historiccolumbia.org/blog/tbt-who-modjeska-monteith-simkins.

"City Mortician I.S. Leevy Dies After Short Illness." *The State,* December 10, 1968.

Clancy, Paul. "Leevy Marks Anniversary of NAACP." South Carolina Council on Human Relations, n.d. Isaac Samuel Leevy papers, 1905–1973. South Caroliniana Library, University of South Carolina.

"Colored State Fair to Meet at Batesburg, S.C." *The People's Recorder,* September 11, 1909.

"Columbia's Green Book Sites." *Historic Columbia,* accessed September 10, 2025. https://www.historiccolumbia.org/GreenBook.

Crawford, Lindsay. "Cornwell, Harriet M., Tourist Home." National Register of Historic Places Nomination Form. US Department of the Interior, National Park Service, 2007, Section 8.

Dittmer, John. *Local People: The Struggle for Civil Rights in Mississippi.* University of Illinois Press, 1995.

Donaldson, Bobby J. "Carroll, Richard." *South Carolina Encyclopedia,* accessed September 10, 2025. https://www.scencyclopedia.org/sce/entries/carroll-richard/.

Edgar, Walter. *South Carolina: A History.* University of South Carolina Press, 1999.

Elmore v. Rice et al. 72 F. Supp. 516 (E.D.S.C. 1947).

"Emancipation Day Talk to Be Made by Bishop." *The State,* December 29, 1946.

Eulogy for Isaac Samuel Leevy by Rev. M. D. McCollom, December 12, 1968. Box 4. African American History in South Carolina Vertical Files collection. South Caroliniana Library, University of South Carolina.

Frazier, E. Franklin. *Black Bourgeoisie.* The Free Press, 1957.

Found, Jill. "Booker T. Washington High School Auditorium." National Register of Historic Places Nomination Form. US Department of the Interior, National Park Service, 2018, Section 8.

"Gregory Kirkland Leevy: April 24, 1953–January 6, 2009." Thomas McAfee Funeral Homes, accessed September 10, 2025. https://thomasmcafee.com/obituary/gregory-kirkland-leevy.

Harlen, Louis R. "The Secret Life of Booker T. Washington." *The Journal of Southern History* 37, no. 3 (1971): 393–416.

Hill's Columbia (South Carolina) City Directory: 1931. Hill Directory Co., Inc., 1931.

Holloway, Karta. *Passed On: African American Mourning Stories.* Duke University Press, 2002.

"Holman's Barber Shop." National Park Service, 2022. https://www.nps.gov/.

Hughes, Morgan. "This SC home Where Duke Ellington Once Stayed Has a Storied History. A Fire Just Destroyed It," *The State,* April 12, 2023. https://www.thestate.com/.

"I. S. Leevy Johnson." Johnson, Toal & Battiste, PA, accessed September 10, 2025. https://www.jtblawfirm.com/attorneys.

"I. S. Leevy, Carolinian." *The Columbia Record*, December 14, 1968. Isaac Samuel Leevy papers, 1905–1973. South Caroliniana Library, University of South Carolina.

"I. S. Leevy, Columbia Business Man, Gets Service Award for Ten Years Service." *Palmetto Leader*, n.d. Isaac Samuel Leevy papers, 1905–1973. South Caroliniana Library, University of South Carolina.

"I. S. Leevy Obituary." 1968. Isaac Samuel Leevy papers, 1905–1973. South Caroliniana Library, University of South Carolina.

I. S. Leevy to Vel J. Washington. Personal letter, October 30, 1954. Box 2, Folder 30. John Henry McCray Papers 1929–1989. South Caroliniana Library, University of South Carolina.

"Impressive Attendance at Lincoln Day Celebration: Hinton Calls for 40,000 Negro Voters County Organization Plan Initiated." *The Palmetto Leader*, February 19, 1955. Box 4. African American History in South Carolina Vertical Files collection. South Caroliniana Library, University of South Carolina.

Ingham, John N. "Building Businesses, Creating Communities: Residential Segregation and the Growth of African American Business in Southern Cities, 1880–1915." *The Business History Review* 77, no. 4 (2003): 639–65.

"Isaac Samuel 'I. S.' Leevy Johnson." n.d. Box 3, African American History in South Carolina Vertical Files collection. South Caroliniana Library, University of South Carolina.

"Johnson: Expand Supreme Court." *The State*, January 11, 1980.

Johnson, Christopher Leevy. *Undertakings: The Politics of African American Funeral Directing*. PhD diss., University of South Carolina, 2004.

Johnson, I. S. Leevy. "Oral History with I. S. Leevy Johnson." Interview by James Shadd III. The Walker Local and Family History Center Digital Collections. Richland Library, May 1, 2023. https://localhistory.richlandlibrary.com/digital/collection/p16817coll19/id/76/rec/1.

Johnson, I. S. Leevy. Interview by W. Maclane Hull, October 24, 2019.

Krell, Kent. "Negroes Win House Seats." *The State*, November 4, 1970.

"Leading Mortician Dies in Columbia." *The Afro-American*, December 21, 1968. Isaac Samuel Leevy papers, 1905–1973. South Caroliniana Library, University of South Carolina, Columbia.

"Leevy's Hymntime." October 11, 1964. Topical Papers, Speeches, 1964–1971 and n.d. Modjeska Simkins Papers. South Caroliniana Library, University of South Carolina.

Leevy, I. S. "A Cornerstone of Columbia's History." *Progressive Magazine*, February 1995, 17. Box 4. African American History in South Carolina Vertical Files collection. South Caroliniana Library, University of South Carolina.

Leevy, I. S. "Invitation to SCLC meeting." Topical Papers, Southern Christian Leadership Conference, 1961–1982. Modjeska Simkins Papers. South Caroliniana Library, University of South Carolina, 1961.

Leevy, Rev. Christopher Johnson. Interview by W. Maclane Hull, October 31, 2019.

"Leevy's Will Build $23,000 Funeral Home." *The State*, August 1, 1951.

Leevy-Kirkland Wedding Invitation. Isaac Samuel Leevy papers, 1905–1973. South Caroliniana Library, University of South Carolina.

"Lincoln Day Celebration in Columbia Saturday." *The Palmetto Leader*, February 12, 1955.

Lofton, Dewanna. "Funeral Home Changes Hands in Family." *The State*, July 2, 1995.

Mack, Kenneth W. *Representing the Race: The Creation of the Civil Rights Lawyer.* Harvard University Press, 2012.

"Mass Letter from I. S. Leevy, Matthew D. McCollom, and Milton E. Cox." July 29, 1959. Box 4. African American History in South Carolina Vertical Files collection. South Caroliniana Library, University of South Carolina.

Mauldin, Douglas. "Bill Would Allow Free Textbooks for Poor." *The State*, April 15, 1976.

McCray, John H. "John McCray to Arthur Clement Regarding the Problems of Rev. Beard Running on the Tolbert-Leevy Ticket." August 11, 1946. Folder 13, Box 3. John Henry McCray papers. South Caroliniana Library, University of South Carolina.

McKaine, O. E. "The Palmetto State." *Norfolk Journal and Guide*, September 15, 1945. Box 4. African American History in South Carolina Vertical Files Collection. South Caroliniana Library, University of South Carolina.

McMillen, Neil R. "Black Enfranchisement in Mississippi: Federal Enforcement and Black Protest in the 1960s." *Journal of Southern History* 43, no. 3 (1977): 351–72.

Milkie, Joyce W. "Johnson Making Own History Today With Swearing In." *Times and Democrat*, June 20, 1985.

Monk, Fred. "S. C. Business Hall of Fame Inducts Three." *The State*, May 24, 1996.

Montgomery, John A. "On The Record: Outstanding South Carolina Negro." *The Columbia Record*, January 3, 1969. Isaac Samuel Leevy papers, 1905–1973. South Caroliniana Library, University of South Carolina.

"New Industrial School Planned By Negros Here." *The Palmetto Leader*, February 7, 1925.

Nickles, Beverly. "Attorney of the Week: I. S. Leevy Johnson." *The Star Reporter*, May 17, 1990.

O'Shea, Margaret N. "A Real Go-Getter Heads S.C. Bar." *The State*, June 23, 1985.

O'Shea, Margaret N. "Richland Elects GOP Slate." *The State*, November 8, 1972.

Parramore, Mary R., and Frank Brown III. "Waverly Historic District." National Register of Historic Places Nomination Form. US Department of the Interior, National Park Service, 1989, Section 8.

Payne, Charles. *I've Got the Light of Freedom: The Organizing Tradition and the Mississippi Freedom Struggle, With a New Preface.* University of California Press, 2007.

"Personal Biography of Isaac Samuel Leevy." n.d. Box 33. South Carolina Council on Human Relations Records. South Caroliniana Library, University of South Carolina, Columbia.

Redfern, Bishop II. Open Letter. 1972, Box 4. African American History in South Carolina Vertical Files Collection. South Caroliniana Library, University of South Carolina, Columbia.

Rees, Chris. "277 Farrow Rd. Named for I. S. Leevy Johnson." *WISNews*, June 23, 2003. https://www.wistv.com/story/1331912/277-farrow-rd-named-for -isleevy-johnson/.

Richards, Miles S. "Leevy, Carroll Moton." South Carolina Encyclopedia, Institute for Southern Studies, 2022. https://www.scencyclopedia.org/sce/entries/ leevy-carroll-moton/.

Richards, Miles S. "Progressive Democratic Party." South Carolina Encyclopedia, Institute for Southern Studies, 2022. https://www.scencyclopedia.org/.

"Ruth's Beauty Parlor." National Park Service, August 9, 2021. https://www.nps .gov/places/ruth-s-beauty-parlor.htm.

"S.C. History: Leevy—Black Pioneer: Isaac Leevy—A Family Tradition." *Black On News*, November 1973, 4. https://digital.tcl.sc.edu/digital/collection/isleevy/ id/15/rec/1.

Sanborn Fire Insurance Map from Columbia, Richland County, South Carolina. Sanborn Map Company, 1956. https://www.loc.gov/item/sanborn08131_010/.

Santoro, Wayne A. "The Civil Rights Movement and the Right to Vote: Black Protest, Segregationist Violence and the Audience." *Social Forces* 86, no. 4 (2008): 1391–1414.

Shakur, Assata. Quoted in "Race Man." *The Ohio State University Libraries: Research Guides: Africana Studies,* accessed September 10, 2025. https://guides.osu.edu/ africana/raceman.

"South Carolina: Modjeska Monteith Simkins House." National Park Service, June 28, 2021. https://www.nps.gov/places/south-carolina-modjeska-monteith -simkins-house.htm.

"South Carolina's Plot to Starve Negroes." *Jet*, October 20, 1955, 8–13.

Smith, Suzanne. "To Serve the Living: The Public and Civic Identity of African American Funeral Directors." In *Public Culture: Diversity, Democracy, and Community in the United States*, edited by Marguerite S. Shaffer. University of Pennsylvania Press, 2008.

"Staff." Leevy's Funeral Home, accessed September 10, 2025. https://leevy.com/ staff/.

Stroup, Rodger E. *Meet Me at the Rocket: A History of the South Carolina State Fair.* University of South Carolina Press, 2019.

Thomas, Maurice. "25 Years of Striving for a Goal." *The State*, December 17, 2000.

Underwood, Tut. "The Colorful South Carolina State Fair was Once Black and White." South Carolina Public Radio, October 19, 2022. https://www .southcarolinapublicradio.org/.

Waldrop, Melinda. "'Walking Through History': Reflecting on an Era's Significance." *Columbia Regional Business Report*, February 4, 2019.

Washington, Isaac. "On Paying Dues." *The Palmetto Post*, July 4–10, 1985.

"Waverly Protection Area: Historic Preservation Guidelines." City of Columbia Planning & Development, December 6, 2016. https://planninganddevelopment .columbiasc.gov/districts/#waverly.

"W. E. Solomon Addresses Richland Lincoln Emancipation Club." *The Palmetto Leader*, April 30, 1955.

Workman, W. D., Jr. "Leevy, Modjeska Simkins and Other Negro Republications in State Are Supporting Gerald." Unlisted newspaper, c. 1950. Newspaper clippings, 1946–1949. Modjeska Simkins Papers. South Caroliniana Library, University of South Carolina, Columbia.

Greenville in the *Green Book*

Whittenberg's Service Station and 212 John Street

Courtney L. Tollison and Rachel Gambrell

Between 1939 and 1966, *The Negro Motorist Green Book* included fourteen unique sites for Greenville County. Two of those sites echo larger themes that characterize the Jim Crow era. First, the history of 212 John Street reveals the extent to which segregation ordinances applied to all African-American people, regardless of wealth, status, or fame. The *Green Book* listed the home from 1946 to 1954, although it likely functioned as a tourist home before and after this period.[1] Second, Whittenberg's Service Station was a full-service garage located at 600 Anderson Street that appeared in the *Green Book* in 1948 and 1950–1955.[2] Whittenberg's Service Station reflects the experiences of civil rights activists who courageously persisted in the struggle, despite the imperiling impact it had on themselves and their families.

212 John Street

Before opera star Marian Anderson desegregated the Dyckman Hotel in Minneapolis, and performers Harry Belafonte, Lena Horne, and Nat King Cole successfully challenged Las Vegas's segregated hotel policies, African-American performers were bound by law to stay in segregated hotels, private homes, or tourist homes.[3] Over the course of its thirty-year run, the *Green Book* listed two tourist homes for Greenville County, one operated by Miss M. J. Grimes and another by Mrs. W. H. Smith.

From at least 1930, Lurleen Smith and her husband, William Henry "Kid" Smith, lived in Greenville's Southernside neighborhood at 212 John Street with their daughter, Helen.[4] Kid Smith was the proprietor of a billiards and pool hall, known as the Railroad Men's Athletic Club, and a professional gambler.[5] When he died in 1935, Lurleen and her daughter stayed in the home and began taking in African-American boarders and providing overnight accommodations to visitors. In the early 1940s, Lurleen married Isaac White, who moved into her large home at 212 John Street.[6] Isaac White worked at various times at the Poinsett Hotel, as manager of the Broad Street Café and as a school principal. He was also an events promoter who handled the logistics for performers visiting the area, including their overnight accommodations.[7]

From the 1930s to the 1960s, Greenville hosted high-profile Black performers, including Marian Anderson, Louis Armstrong, Roy Brown, Ruth Brown, Cab Calloway, Duke Ellington, Ella Fitzgerald, Willis "Gator" Jackson, Ivory Joe Hunter, "Little" Esther Phillips, Della Reese, and Sarah Vaughn.[8] According to interviews with local residents, including Lurleen White's granddaughter, Lurleen and Isaac White hosted many of these visiting musicians in their two-story clapboard home, which was built around 1910.[9] It was located approximately half a mile from Textile Hall, where these musicians usually performed.

In the early and mid-twentieth century, Black performers enchanted white audiences, but as soon as the show was over, Jim Crow ordinances prevailed. This was not strictly a southern policy. Rat Pack performer Sammy Davis Jr. once recalled that, in Las Vegas, known as the "Mississippi of the West" among African-American people in the 1950s, his skin had "no color" onstage. The moment he walked offstage, however, he and other Black musicians were "colored again. . . . The other acts could gamble or sit in the lounge and have a drink, but we had to leave through the kitchen with the garbage."[10]

Some of the Black acts in Greenville, including Ella Fitzgerald, were advertised as "white-only" performances, although most were open to Blacks and whites.[11] Isaac White, however, often worked with visiting artists to arrange another performance exclusively for African Americans. These after-party performances occurred at his home, where the performers stayed overnight. Advertisements for these postperformance parties never listed the featured musician's name. In Duke Ellington's case, a member of his band served as the headliner on the handbill, with admission costing approximately one-third of the cost to attend the Ellington's performance at Textile Hall. These intimate performances in "Mrs. W. H. Smith's Tourist Home" circumvented Jim Crow laws and represent a discreet display of African-American agency.[12]

As the promoter for many of these high-profile African-American performers, Isaac White often relied on local African-American businesses, including *Green Book* site Gibb's Pharmacy, to publicize his events and sell tickets. In Greenville, African-American businesses were part of a small, connected, cohesive network. Whittenberg's Service Station similarly served as a site to purchase tickets to philanthropic and other events that benefited the African-American community, such as a 1965 speaking engagement by

Roy Wilkins, the executive secretary of the National Association for the Advancement of Colored People (NAACP).[13]

Whittenberg's Service Station

In 1948, Whittenberg's Service Station owner Abraham Jonah Whittenberg was a thirty-year-old Black man in a city that had recently been in the national spotlight. Rebecca West of the *New Yorker* and other national journalists had covered Greenville's 1947 trial of two dozen white men accused of lynching Willie Earle, an African-American man five years younger than Whittenburg.[14] Many viewed the simple fact that there was a trial as sign of racial progress. However, the acquittal of twenty-eight men by an all-white, all-male jury indisputably affirmed the local racial imbalance of power. The verdict enraged Whittenberg and eventually inspired him to become active in the movement for racial justice. Decades later, Whittenberg highlighted the impact of the lynching: "If it had not happened, I probably would not have been so eager to work for the betterment of blacks. It was the fertilizer for growth."[15]

His political activism began in the 1940s and continued throughout much of his life. He served as chairman of the Greenville City Election Commission, vice chairman of voter registration for the Greenville County Democratic Party, president of the Greenville branch of the NAACP, a member of the Chamber of Commerce's biracial committee, and a delegate to the 1972 Democratic Party National Convention.

In October 1959, during Whittenberg's time as the local NAACP president, he helped host Jackie Robinson, who was credited with breaking the color barrier in major league baseball. As Robinson was leaving, he was threatened with arrest after sitting in a "whites only" section at the Greenville airport. Embarrassed and angry, Whittenberg and other protestors planned and executed a march on the airport on January 1, 1960. Images of hundreds of African Americans marching to overturn Jim Crow policies drew national attention. One month later, four college students from North Carolina Agricultural and Technical University sat in at a Woolworth's in Greensboro, a moment that historians long considered the beginning of the activist phase of the civil rights movement in the South. The march on the airport spurred protest activity at the library, downtown lunch counters, and local churches that eventually resulted in overturning local Jim Crow ordinances.

After having inspired such progress toward desegregation, Whittenberg turned his efforts toward his eleven-year-old daughter, Elaine. After

Brown v. The Board of Education in Topeka, Kansas, Whittenberg became frustrated with the lack of action toward school desegregation in Greenville County. With support from his wife, Eva, who worked as a maid at the Christie Pediatric Group, he sent letters to superintendent Dr. M. T. Anderson requesting that Elaine be transferred from Gower School to Anderson Street School, a "whites-only" school. In an interview with *The Greenville News*, Whittenberg stated, "Any parent, if they love their child, wants the very best for their child.... We are assuming that the school board will accept the transfer.... If she is refused, we intend to take whatever legal steps are necessary."[16]

Superintendent Anderson denied Whittenberg's request, along with those of five other families who had also requested transfers to white schools. Staying true to his word, Whittenberg and his attorneys filed a lawsuit against the School District of Greenville in 1963. After a hard-fought case, Whittenberg won the lawsuit. Token desegregation began in Greenville schools in April 1964 when Elaine and five other African-American students became the first to attend "whites-only" schools.[17]

A. J. Whittenberg's activism did not come without consequences. Soon after Elaine broke the racial barrier, he was forced to close his service station. Whittenberg's activism "was disastrous for his business," his daughter recalled soon after her father's death. Although the loss of the family business undoubtedly brought great stress to the Whittenberg family, it likely paled in comparison with the stress caused by the threats they received. In an oral history from April 2002, Elaine described the horrors that her family faced: "My father had many threats. And we had threatening letters. Our phone was mainly unlisted, but his business phone was inundated with threats and even people threatening him openly." She explained how her father once received a letter in the mail that included a picture of Elaine with a noose around her neck.[18]

In 2010, a new elementary school opened in Greenville, named in honor of A. J. Whittenberg.[19] Greenvillians are now much more aware of A. J. and Elaine Whittenberg's courage and the price they paid for their perseverance.

Conclusion

Sixty years after the *Green Book* ceased publication, estimates suggest that less than twenty percent of the sites listed are extant. For South Carolina, as of 2021, approximately thirty percent of the *Green Book* listings remain.[20] Most of the fourteen sites listed in the *Green Book* for Greenville area are gone. Whittenberg's Service Station no longer exists, although A. J. and

Elaine Whittenberg's legacy endures at the school named in his memory. 212 Asbury Avenue (the former 212 John Street) stands as one of the few extant *Green Book* sites in Greenville County.[21] It is an important site of not only African-American agency but also the perpetuation of African-American culture, as evidenced by the increase in local media attention and community support for its preservation in the 2020s.[22] As noted by others in this issue, researching *Green Book* sites remains important work, as each site— including the location, proprietors, and customers—provides its own stories and rich evidence of the resistance and ingenuity of African Americans in our communities' history.

Courtney L. Tollison is the Distinguished University Public Historian and Scholar at Furman University, where she has taught since 2004. She is the author of *Furman University, World War II and Upcountry South Carolina: "We Just Did Everything We Could"; "Our Country First, The Greenville": A New South City During the Progressive Era and World War I;* and *Furman University, 1826–2026: An Illustrated History.*

Rachel Gambrell is a third-year history major at Furman University from Greenville, South Carolina. Her research focuses on American history, specifically twentieth-century social justice movements and the underrepresented figures involved in their successes. Rachel's current work as an intern for the preservation of 212 Asbury Avenue, a former *Green Book* tourist home, has inspired her contributions to this essay.

NOTES

1. According to Greenville, SC City Directories, the address of 212 John Street changed to 212 Asbury Avenue sometime between 1945 and 1949. In the *Green Book* listings, however, it remained 212 John Street.
2. Green, *The Negro Motorist Green Book,* 1948.
3. See Belafonte, *My Song,* 158–59; Gavin, *Stormy Weather,* 243.
4. According to the US Census, 1930, William Henry Smith and Lurleen Hallums married on January 19, 1916. See also Greenville County, South Carolina, US, Marriage License Index, and Bainbridge, "A Railroad Runs Through History of Greenville's Southernside Community." Official records are inconsistent in the spelling of Lurleen's name.
5. US Census, 1920. See also "212 Asbury, South Carolina Historic Properties Survey," and "South Carolina Death Records, and U.S.," and "City Directories, 1822–1995."
6. Bainbridge, "A Railroad Runs Through History of Greenville's Southernside Community"; "Greenville, SC City Directory (1943)"; and "U.S., City Directories, 1822–1995."

7. Jeter, "Still Standing"; "Greenville, SC City Directory (1945)."
8. See advertisement appearing in *The Greenville News* on March 21, 1947; September 11, 1949; April 10, 1950; June 3, 1951; April 13, 1952; and March 10, 1953.
9. "212 Asbury, South Carolina Historic Properties Survey."
10. Salem, *The Late Great Johnny Ace*, 122–23; Green, "The Mississippi of the West," 57.
11. *The Greenville News*, November 10, 1945.
12. Despite the fact that Lurleen Smith married Isaac White and is listed in census records and city directories from the early 1940s on as Lurleen White, the *Green Book* continued to use Mrs. W. H. Smith as the contact for her tourist home between 1946 and 1954.
13. "NAACP Plans Member Drive," *The Greenville News*, December 9, 1965, 24.
14. West, "Opera in Greenville."
15. Hoover, "The Lynching of Willie Earle; O'Neill, "Memory, History, and the Desegregation of Greenville," 288; Whittenberg, interview by William Gravely, 13 December 1982; Whittenberg, interview by William Gravely, 28 November 1989.
16. Steadman, "Transfer to Anderson School."
17. Boyce, "…More Good People in the World"; O'Neill, "Memory, History, and the Desegregation," 293–94.
18. Boyce, "…More Good People in the World." According to the 1963 Greenville, SC City Directory, the Whittenbergs lived at 903 Dunbar Street.
19. Located at 420 Westfield Street, the A. J. Whittenberg School of Engineering, enrolls four hundred seventy-nine students in Grades K–5. The school has received more than twenty awards and honors, including recognition as a National Blue Ribbon School in 2020. See "2024–25 Profile."
20. "Green Book Properties Listed in the National Register." This article quotes Jennifer Reut, an architectural historian with the National Trust for Historic Preservation.
21. Letter from Ramon Jackson to Unknown Recipient, undated, in author's possession. Jackson was the South Carolina African American Heritage Coordinator for the South Carolina Department of Archives and History.
22. See Jeter, "Still Standing."

WORKS CITED

"212 Asbury, South Carolina Historic Properties Survey." South Carolina Department of Archives and History, accessed September 10, 2025. http://schpr.sc.gov/index.php/Detail/properties/31401.

"2024–25 Profile: A. J. Whittenberg School of Engineering." Greenville County Schools, October 15, 2024. https://www.greenville.k12.sc.us/Schools/profile.asp?schoolid=ajw.

Bainbridge, Judy. "A Railroad Runs Through History of Greenville's Southernside Community." *The Greenville News*, March 5, 2019. https://www.greenvilleonline.com/story/life/2019/03/05/bainbridge-railroad-runs-through-history-greenvilles-southernside/3053493002/.

Belafonte, Harry, with Michael Shnayerson. *My Song: A Memoir of Art, Race, and Defiance.* Canongate Books, 2012.

Boyce, Elaine Wittenberg. ". . . More Good People in the World." By Justin Baldwin. *Champions of Civil and Human Rights in South Carolina.* A Digital Exhibition by the Department of Oral History at the University of South Carolina, April 23, 2002. https://digital.library.sc.edu/exhibits/champions/volume-3-2/part-2/elaine-wittenberg-boyce-more-good-people-in-the-world/.

"Death County or Certificate Range: Greenville," accessed September 10, 2025. https://ancestry.com.

Gavin, James. *Stormy Weather: The Life of Lena Horne.* Atria Books, 2009.

Green, Michael S. "The Mississippi of the West?" *Nevada Law Journal* 57 (Fall 2004): 57–70.

Green, Victor H. *The Negro Motorist Green Book.* Victor H. Green & Co., 1948. Schomburg Center for Research in Black Culture, Manuscripts, Archives and Rare Books Division, The New York Public Library. https://digitalcollections.nypl.org.

"Green Book Properties Listed in the National Register of Historic Places." National Park Service, 2022. https://www.nps.gov/.

"Greenville County, South Carolina, U.S. Marriage License Index, 1910–2010," accessed September 10, 2025. https: ancestry.com.

"Greenville, SC City Directory (1935)," accessed September 10, 2025. https://ancestry.com.

"Greenville, SC City Directory (1943)," accessed September 10, 2025. https://ancestry.com.

"Greenville, SC City Directory (1945)," accessed September 10, 2025. https://ancestry.com.

"Greenville, SC City Directory (1963)," accessed September 10, 2025. https://ancestry.com.

The Greenville News, accessed September 10, 2025. https://www.newspapers.com.

Hoover, Dan. "The Lynching of Willie Earle, SC's Last, Foreshadowed Changing Time." *The Greenville News,* April 9, 2018.

Jeter, John. "Still Standing: Southernside Neighborhood Looks Back on Troubled History, Ahead to Unity Park." *Greenville Journal,* February 21, 2020. https://greenvillejournal.com/.

"NAACP Plans Member Drive." *The Greenville News,* December 9, 1954, 24. https://www.newspapers.com.

O'Neill, Stephen. "Memory, History, and the Desegregation of Greenville." In *Toward the Meeting of the Waters,* edited by Vernon Burton and Winfred B. Moore. University of South Carolina Press, 2008.

Salem, James M. *The Late Great Johnny Ace and the Transition from R &B to Rock 'n; Roll.* University of Illinois Press, 2001.

South Carolina Death Records; Year Range: *1925–1949*; Death County or Certificate Range: *Greenville.* South Carolina Department of Archives and History; Columbia, South Carolina. Ancestry.com, accessed September 10, 2025. https://ancestry.com.

Steadman, Ethel A. "Transfer to Anderson School Here Is Asked By Negro Girl."
    The Greenville News, August 9, 1963, accessed September 10, 2025. https://www
    .newspapers.com.
"US Census, 1920," accessed September 10, 2025. https://ancestry.com.
"US Census, 1930," accessed September 10, 2025.https://ancestry.com.
"US City Directories, 1822–1995," accessed September 10, 2025. https://ancestry
    .com.
West, Rebecca. "Opera in Greenville." *New Yorker*, June 6, 1947. https://www
    .newyorker.com/magazine/1947/06/14/opera-in-greenville.
Whittenberg, A. J. Interview by William Gravely, 13 December 1982. William
    Gravely Oral History Collection on the Lynching of Willie Earle. South Caro-
    liniana Library, University of South Carolina.
Whittenberg, A. J. Interview by William Gravely, November 28, 1989. William
    Gravely Oral History Collection on the Lynching of Willie Earle. South Caro-
    liniana Library, University of South Carolina.

African-American Tourism and Travel to the Holy City

The Short List of Green Book *Sites in Charleston, South Carolina*

Barry L. Stiefel

Starting in the 1920s, Charleston, SC, developed a budding tourism economy based on its historic sites, a by-product of the Charleston Renaissance (1918–1941), a period that lasted between the First and Second World Wars when the city experienced a flourishing in the visual arts, literature, and historic preservation that celebrated Charleston's culture and past. Although interrupted by World War II, touristic boosterism continued soon after, but with a very European American–centric perspective of the city's history that excluded the African-American perspective on the past. For example, the Old Slave Mart Museum had an incredibly offensive exhibit on antebellum slavery, depicting it as a positive experience. Even though the Mart had been a place for buying and selling people, when the museum opened in 1938, the exhibit's founder Miriam Wilson, showed her beliefs that slavery was not brutal and was mainly a way to civilize Black people.[1] Other sites were simply not accommodating, such as the Charleston Museum, which began in 1917, (re)allowing African-American school children accompanied by a teacher to attend when they had a reservation. However, African-American adults who were not part of a school group were denied admission.[2] Using the *Negro Motorist Green Book* (hereinafter called the *Green Book* because of variations in titles that evolved over the years) as a lens for viewing the African-American experience, this article will investigate the interface of white supremacy with Charleston's twentieth-century touristic image and what we can learn from the handful of Charleston-area amenities listed in this directory. With this historical context, preservationists and public historians can better identify and preserve sites related to the *Green Book* in Charleston.

Because of examples such as the Slave Mart Museum and Charleston Museum, the city's touristic experience was not attractive to African-American people from elsewhere, and so few came. Charleston was South Carolina's largest city during this period, yet the 1946 edition of the *Green*

Book lists only five "tourist homes."[3] A tourist home was similar in concept to a bed and breakfast, where African-American travelers could find lodging and one meal a day. These five locations were the only listed amenities in the *Green Book* for 1946, indicating that not many out-of-town African-American visitors could be accommodated at any time. This is in comparison with other South Carolina towns with lower populations, such as Columbia (with forty-one listings), Greenville (nine listings), Mullins (ten listings), and Spartanburg (fourteen listings), which had a greater number of listed amenities in 1946 and in other years.

Circa 1930, on the eve of the first publication of the *Green Book*, just under fifty percent of Charleston's population was African American, but these residents would have only needed this directory when traveling to other places.[4] The lack of Charleston-area amenities listed in the *Green Book* is not a reflection of African American–owned and friendly businesses in the city. Although the *Green Book* listed a few other Charleston businesses in other years, such as the James Hotel and Brooks Grill, the total number of business listings was always small. For example, Harleston's Tavern was Charleston's only restaurant mentioned in the *Green Book* for 1946, but thirty additional restaurants for people of color are listed in Charleston's 1946 city directory.[5] Thus, there were many places where African-American people could go out to eat in Charleston; however, it appears that customers at restaurants for Black people were primarily local and not travelers from elsewhere.

As late as 1977, after the *Green Book* had ceased production, local African-American businessman Arthur Clement Jr. observed "in Charleston there are no Negro tour guides, no brochures, no pamphlet handouts put out by the Chamber of Commerce nor any other local tourist group" even though the "Negro tourist in America last year spent some $400 million in plane fares visiting places around America. When you add hotel, motel, and entertainment expenses, the total outlay reaches astronomical proportions."[6] So, although there were African-American tourists and travelers, they did not come to Charleston in large numbers, despite the city's large African-American population.

Since the nineteenth century, people of African descent have taken an interest in being a part of Charleston's tourism industry. As early as the 1810s, free Black man Jehu Jones Sr. established the Jones Hotel, which he and his family ran as a successful business for decades. Jones also established a second resort hotel on nearby Sullivan's Island as well as another in New York. The Jones Hotel served wealthy European American and European travelers, and the service at the Jones Hotel was so well reputed that the enslaving elite often had their enslaved cooks apprentice at the hotel.[7] Thomas Hamilton of Scotland, who visited the Jones Hotel in the early 1830s, claimed:

> [e]very Englishman who visits Charleston will, if he be wise, direct his baggage to be conveyed to Jones's hotel. It is a small house, but everything is well managed, and the apartments are good. Our party at dinner did not exceed ten, and there was no bolting or scrambling. Jones is a black man. . . . The pleasure of getting into such a house,—of revisiting the glimpses of clean tablecloths and silver forks,—of exchanging salt pork and greasy corn cakes [fare of travel], for a table furnished with luxuries of all sorts,— was very great. For a day or two, I experienced a certain impulse to voracity, by no means philosophical; and sooth to say after the privations of a journey from New Orleans, the luxury of Jones's iced claret might have converted even Diogenes into a *gourmet* [emphasis original].[8]

Free Black woman Eliza Lee established the Mansion House Hotel during the antebellum period to compete with the Jones Hotel, which had an equally commendable reputation. She and her husband eventually took over the Jones Hotel in 1852. Despite Black ownership of the Jones Hotel and the Mansion House, Black patrons were likely not guests at these establishments because of the period's racist expectations. There were also too few free Black people with wealth to sustain a segregated hotel for their demographic.[9] Indeed, Prince Carl Bernhard, of Saxe-Weimar-Eisenach, observed during his visit to the Jones Hotel in 1825,

> I took up my abode at the Jones's Hotel, a well supported and finely situated house, whose host was a mullato [*sic*]. In consequence of [the Denmark] conspiracy among the slaves a few years previous [in 1822], supposed to have been instigated by colored people . . . very severe laws were passed, and no free colored person having once crossed over the boundary of the State was allowed to return. . . . I was informed that if I had brought a free black servant with me, he would have been put in custody till I left the State, or I must deposit a considerable security for him.[10]

Prince Bernhard's testimony highlights the high level of risk for a free Black person to travel any great distance in the early United States. Prince Bernhard also observed that Mrs. Jones, Jehu's wife (first name not provided) and a free Black woman, was marooned in New York City for years because of this situation. She had traveled to New York City to visit family shortly before the

Denmark Vesey conspiracy and now "dared not attempt to return home," out of fear of what harm could come to her, including re-enslavement.[11] Jones' son, Jehu Jones Jr., had an interest in museums and mentions in passing visiting the Charleston Museum, contrasting it with his experience in Philadelphia when he was denied access to a museum because of racism.[12] In another instance during the antebellum, period, although possibly not at the precise moment of Jones Jr.'s visit to the Charleston Museum, there was an exhibit that entailed a stuffed zebra with "a Negro Boy riding on his back."[13] Examples such as this encouraged the objectification of people from Africa. A century later, the Charleston Museum had rice-husking demonstrations conducted by local African Americans dressed in traditional slave-era attire.[14] Black people put on display within old Charleston by the white majority further complicated tourism for African-American travelers by making them feel uncomfortable. This was, of course, in addition to the trials and tribulations that existed for African Americans traveling to and from Charleston. From this, we can surmise anecdotally that some financially successful free Black people in the United States in the nineteenth century were interested in tourism and traveled domestically, but to do so was also very risky to their personal welfare.

As can be seen from the Jones Hotel eyewitness accounts, European Americans and Europeans were frequent customers. However, for African-American people, even those with wealth, travel to continental Europe was difficult before 1865 because the State Department would not issue passports for them, even when they were free. Passports were not needed for entry to the British Empire, including Canada, which was significant for those seeking freedom on the Underground Railroad.[15] However, while traveling domestically, finding places to stay, places to eat, and leisure activities was often challenging not only because of race-based discrimination. An example of this is documented in 1869, when, "Robert Stevens, negro of Charleston, South Carolina [sued] against the Richmond and Fredericksburg Railroad, for putting his wife [May] in a second-class car by force after selling her a first-class ticket . . . the Judge [John C. Underwood], in his charge to the Jury, which was half black, said distinction on account of color was a relic of barbarism. . . . The jury brought a verdict of $1,600 [about $38,800, today] damages for the plaintiffs."[16] This case underscores the systemic racism African Americans faced, even when they had legally purchased the same services as white individuals. After Reconstruction and the *Plessy v. Ferguson* (163 U.S. 537, 1896) case, it would be decades before the juries in much of the United States comprised fifty percent African Americans. If Judge John C.

Underwood (1809–1873) had not been an abolitionist, the court ruling that upheld "separate but equal" treatment could not have been dated much earlier and called "*Robert Stevens v. Richmond, Fredericksburg, and the Potomac Railroad*," because of this travel by railroad incident that originated from Charleston. The *Plessy v. Ferguson* ruling upheld as legal not only Jim Crow segregation but also, as I discuss later, the objectification of people from Africa.[17]

Victor H. Green published the *Green Book* between 1936 and 1966 (although it was suspended from 1942 to 1945 because of World War II) in the Harlem neighborhood of New York City. Green wanted to provide useful information for African Americans who were considering travel throughout the United States, where racially segregated businesses posed a great potential for "running into difficulties, embarrassments."[18] On the eve of the *Green Book*'s debut, besides being discriminated against, African Americans in New South-Charleston were being objectified in ways that were offensive and that glorified the Old South aura of the city's ambiance. For example, in *Uptown/Downtown in Old Charleston: Sketches and Stories,* Louis D. Rubin Jr., who was in his youth at this time, reflected on how "Black people Downtown were 'colorful' and 'primitive' and wore bandannas and spoke Gullah, and they went about the streets hawking fish and shrimp and produce, and everyone knew their picturesque vending cries. The women wore uniforms to work and had names like Viola and Evalina. Downtown was steeped in history. . . . [the] older Downtown homes had outbuildings behind them that had once been slave quarters. Downtown there was culture and art, and painters and etchers made illustrations."[19] Thus, it can be seen through Rubin's youthful, white privileged eyes how African-American people played decorative roles in Charleston's cultural landscape in a similar manner as the romanticized old buildings and Spanish-moss–covered trees that were being depicted in Charleston Renaissance art. Examples of the illustrations made by the painters and etchers that Rubin references can be seen in the contemporaneous *Charleston Welcomes You: America's Most Historic City* travel brochure produced by the Chamber of Commerce in 1938. On the brochure's cover is an old, balding, African-American man, holding his hat respectfully in hand while standing to the side of an open, black wrought-iron gate, welcoming the reader to the city.[20] Through the gate is a picturesque, manicured flower garden in the foreground with several of Charleston's old and iconic buildings in the middle and background, including the steeples of the white elite churches, St. Michael's and St. Philips, that lend to the municipality's nickname, "the Holy City." Within the brochure are additional pages depicting romanticized—and sanitized—photographs of Charleston historic buildings, old trees, and occasional African-American bodies as part of the attraction, portrayed in the acquiescent roles that Rubin articulated. Events such as Charleston's Azalea Festival further reinforced African-American iconic roles in tourism, which attracted northern white vacationers.[21] As Stephanie Yuhl has observed in her opus, *A Golden Haze of Memory: The Making of Historic Charleston*, "[b]y clinging to their memories and little else, Charleston's white elites successfully situated their politicized notions of the past, present, and future at the center of city life,"[22] and this dominated the African-American experience in Charleston in ways that were often adverse.

Accounts from early twentieth-century African-American visitors include varying opinions on Charleston's touristic situation. Leila Pendleton, an African-American community activist and educator in Washington, DC, believed that places such as Fort Sumter and Charleston harbor were witnesses to nineteenth-century African-American struggles for freedom, which were important events that led to emancipation and to Robert Smalls's courageous escape on a Confederate supply ship.[23] Confederate War monuments, such as John C. Calhoun's, are reminders that white supremacy should not be forgotten. When Booker T. Washington and his entourage visited Charleston as part of the South Carolina State Negro Business League tour in 1909, they admired the city's historic architecture and cultural traditions.[24] However, other early twentieth-century African-American visitors to Charleston were of a different opinion. W. E. B. DuBois commented that he was disgusted by the vestiges of slavery and Jim Crow oppression that he observed during his visit in 1917, and others shared DuBois's sentiments for decades to come and across racial lines.[25] As late as the 1970s, a *New York Times* travel reporter reflected, "how does a black man see that same history? . . . How does a tour of Charleston's slave Market strike his soul? . . . Does he see the same ghosts I [i.e., a white man] do, or far more sinister ones?"[26] In comparison, when looking more broadly at African American–produced travel literature from the nineteenth and early twentieth century that was published for public consumption, the prevalence of destinations written about are in Europe, the Mediterranean, Mexico, and Central America. Although some ventured to African countries, such as to Liberia, as part of the American Colonization Society's efforts, most African-American tourists in North America did not feel that their travels were worth writing about—or, at least, there was little to report in a positive light.[27]

The African-American population in Charleston during the late nineteenth and early twentieth centuries was far from trivial, hovering above fifty percent of the city's total population. African-American people constituted from thirty-four to seventy-two percent of any given ward. Charleston's neighborhoods were the least segregated compared with other southern cities, such as New Orleans, Richmond, Memphis, and Savannah. This resulted in there not being a concentrated African-American residential district nor a commercial main street. Therefore, African-American businesses in Charleston were scattered across the city and dependent on white patrons. However, the city's economy and boosterism never diversified to incorporate African-American tourists from elsewhere as part of the municipality's revenue generation agenda.[28]

Charleston was among several southern American cities in the early twentieth century that sought to diversify their economies through heritage tourism. Others included New Orleans, St. Augustine, Natchez, and Williamsburg, although only New Orleans (also a large city) had substantial infrastructure listed in the *Green Book* to accommodate African-American travelers (more than fifty-eight businesses listed in 1946). These data contradict an earlier assumption on an inverse relationship between the number of listings for a given community and the racial demographics of the community in question because both Columbia, SC, and New Orleans appear to be more alike in their *Green Book* listing depth.[29] However, in reflection on other Southern historic cities that boostered heritage as part of their respective economic stimulus agenda during this period, another correlation emerges. Within the 1946 *Green Book*, St. Augustine had two establishments (both tourist homes), and Natchez and Williamsburg were not even listed.[30] Although they were smaller, St. Augustine, Natchez, and Williamsburg should have had far more listings by the logic of this former reasoning. Although African Americans worked at Colonial Williamsburg and St. Augustine's resorts and were involved with the Natchez Pilgrimage festival, African-American tourists were not allowed to stay at any hotel in or near the respective historic districts.[31] Historic Charleston was not centrally administrated like Williamsburg with the Rockefellers and the Flagers in St. Augustine, yet the situation for Black people had many similarities.

From 1865 to 1917, as well as from 1932 to 1952, Charleston lacked a hotel that would accommodate Black travelers. At least one of the tourist homes hosted out-of-town Black guests long before the creation of the *Green Book*, illustrating how the *Green Book*'s function was organizing already existing information. There may have been other tourist homes before the 1930s that have since been forgotten. For example, in 1888, Frederick Douglass stayed at 99 Coming Street (listed as A. Serrant's tourist home in the *Green Book*) when he visited Charleston as part of a lecture tour across several southern states.[32] His stay in Charleston inspired the local Black community and challenged his own views on American racial politics. In his later speech, "I Denounce the So-Called Emancipation as a Stupendous Fraud," delivered on April 16, 1888, in Washington, DC, Douglass criticized the post–Emancipation Proclamation treatment of Black Americans. He argued from his personal observations while staying in South Carolina and Georgia that the proclamation, although legally freeing slaves, did not grant them true freedom or equality. Instead, it left them vulnerable to systemic racism, violence, and disenfranchisement.[33] The Coming Street location where Douglass stayed was near the center of Black culture in Charleston during the late nineteenth century, including the Mount Zion African Methodist Episcopal Church and the Avery Normal Institute, which played crucial roles in the Black community's spiritual, social, and intellectual life. Douglass's stay at 99 Coming Street is historically significant, because it highlights the ongoing struggle for racial equality and the challenges faced by Blacks in post-Reconstruction.

The situation of racial discrimination of Black visitors is exemplified by how the city government and Chamber of Commerce discouraged the accommodation of African-American tourism too, similar to Williamsburg, Natchez, and St. Augustine. Most African-American visitors to Charleston during these decades came to visit friends or family, or for business, not for recreation.[34] Thus, the early twentieth-century Black visitors to Charleston for whom we have accounts, such as Washington, did not stay in a hotel but with family, friends or associates, or at a tourist home like the ones later listed in the *Green Book*. The attraction closest to Charleston for Black tourists during this time was the racially segregated Atlantic Beach, located one hundred ten miles northeast of the city near Myrtle Beach.[35] There was also a small campground near Walterboro, approximately fifty miles west of Charleston, that accommodated Black travelers.[36] Atlantic Beach and the Walterboro-area campground also show a Black preference for places that were an escape from present discrimination and historical reminders of it.

Other distinguished Black travelers, such as Washington and members of the South Carolina State Negro Business League, reserved an entire railcar to avoid public displays of Jim Crow humiliation that would force them to yield their seats to other white passengers. In Charleston, it was customary for the Black elite to acquire the largest houses that they could afford to both show off their wealth and host distinguished guests, which came with additional social prestige. Large Black-owned homes would also host parties, weddings, meetings, and other gatherings that whites otherwise hosted at hotels because there were no other venues.[37] This situation also reinforced a sense of community belonging among Black Charlestonians.

Traveling to and around a destination, whether by train or automobile, presented unique challenges for Black citizens in the Jim Crow era. Candacy A. Taylor documents the experience of her stepfather, Ronald Burford, who, as a child, witnessed his father encounter a county sheriff checkpoint in Tennessee during the 1950s. During the incident, Burford's father had to falsely tell the sheriff that his automobile belonged to his white employer and that the women and child were domestics he was chauffeuring for work, and not his car or his family, to keep the car from being stolen (or worse) by the sheriff out of jealousy. Well into the 1960s, African-American motorists often took with them ice coolers with food, spare cans of fuel, portable toilets, and bedding to use on their road trips because of the racism encountered during travel.[38] Another incidence of this in South Carolina from before the advent of the *Green Book* is found in the "Greenville County Sheriff Sales Books for Automobiles Seized While Transporting Contraband Liquors, 1925–1927." In June 1925, Sheriff Samuel D. Willis confiscated a Cadillac Touring Car from a "Negro from Charlotte," which was subsequently auctioned off to William Felix Mauldin for one hundred twenty-five dollars.[39] No other discussion is made about the identity of the "Negro from Charlotte" or what they were carrying, in comparison with the other entries within the Sales Book, where full names are given in addition to frequent mentions of the quantities of alcohol involved. Could this have been the process for a jealous sheriff to clear title on an automobile stolen from an African-American owner? During the 1920s, a new Cadillac Touring Car sold for more than three thousand dollars, a price normally out of reach for Mauldin, who was formerly employed at a textile mill. One hundred twenty-five dollars would also be an enviable, quick pay bump for a racist, underpaid sheriff in Greenville County. When he purchased the Cadillac for one hundred twenty-five dollars, Mauldin had a new career as a driver for his own car service.[40] Thus, African-American motorists had to be careful about travel to and from their destinations in addition to the discriminatory challenges encountered where they went.

During World War I, the Hametic Hotel established and accepted Black customers before going out of business in 1932, four years before the publication of the first *Green Book*. The Great Depression adversely affected African Americans, so few could afford to stay at the Hametic Hotel (or reserve an entire railcar to avoid humiliating Jim Crow segregation). The Hametic Hotel was in the former Faber House (built in 1839), located at 635 East Bay Street, conveniently a block away from Charleston Union Station (burned in 1947).[41] This significant hotel had twenty-five bedrooms, a reception hall, dining room, parlor, and kitchen.[42]

Between 1936 and 1966, the *Green Book* listed a total of ten locations in Charleston, with an additional non-location-specific entry for First Class taxi service. As mentioned before, five of these listings appeared in the 1946 case study year, which was about the average number listed in any given *Green Book* edition. When mapped across the Charleston peninsula, two very distinct correlations become readily apparent, especially when visualizing the Hametic Hotel as an associated site that went out of business on the eve of the *Green Book*'s debut:

1. Charleston's *Green Book*'s listings are located far from the touristic historic district as it existed between 1931 and 1966; and
2. Charleston's *Green Book*'s listings are predominantly located in a corridor spanning the width of the city's midpeninsula, with the older listings skewed toward Charleston Union Station in the east and the more recent listings located near the Ashley River Bridge (for US Highway 17) in the west, reflecting the national and local shift in travel mode from rail to automobile.

These findings reflect Derek Alderman's, Ethan Bottone's, and Joshua Inwood's significant observations regarding the places listed in the *Green Book*, highlighting their role as African-American counterpublic spaces. These locations were not just safe havens for African-American travelers during the era of segregation but also vibrant, dynamic places that reflected the evolving needs and aspirations of the African-American community. The data from different editions of the *Green Book* reveal how these spaces changed over time, adapting to new social, economic, and political realities. This dynamism is evident in the shifting listings and the emergence of new businesses and services, illustrating the resilience and resourcefulness of the African-American community in creating and maintaining these vital spaces.[43]

Figure 3.1. Present-day photograph of the Faber House, 635 East Bay Street, Charleston, SC. The Faber House served as the Hametic Hotel until 1932. Photograph by Barry L. Stiefel, 2024.

Closer inspection of the survey reveals that the Hametic and James Hotels served as bookends to this corridor, with the Hametic Hotel greeting African Americans who came by rail and the James Hotel accommodating those traveling by automobile. Tourist homes are very common throughout the *Green Book*. They were frequently women-operated businesses that enabled host families to have an additional income, such as those operated by Elizabeth Alston, Annie Mayes, Huldah L. Harleston, and Annabell Serrant. Some of the restaurants were also joint spousal and extended family

Figure 3.2. Present-day photograph of Mrs. Mayes's tourist home, 82½ Spring Street, Charleston, SC. The building, now a private residence, served as Mrs. Mayes's tourist home from the 1930s until the 1960s. Photograph by Barry L. Stiefel, 2024.

operations, like Queen's Restaurant and Scott's Restaurant. Several of the people who operated *Green Book* businesses worked at other Charleston hospitality- or food-related establishments, further exhibiting a transference or application of skill, knowledge, and economic necessity of more than one income.

On the eastern side of the peninsula is also the Cooper River Bridge, specifically listed in the 1941 edition of the *Green Book*, seeming to indicate that African-American motorists could travel on it. Unlike the Ashley River Bridge, which was free to cross, the Cooper River Bridge charged a toll until 1946.[44] The Avery Normal Institute (125 Bull Street), a school for Black students, was listed once in the *Green Book* for 1947.[45] Although historian John N. Ingham observes that Charleston did not have an exclusive African-American commercial area, there does appear to be a specific corridor that served African-American visitors through those listed in the *Green Book*, implying that African-American businesses in other parts of the city focused on either local clientele of both races and/or white tourists.

African-American business included the informal economy of the street hawkers observed by Rubin, who plied their trade within the touristic historic district while playing the objectified roles that white civil authorities and tourists expected of them. As late as 1954, only one question on the city's sixty-question tour guide licensing program was devoted to African-Americans in Charleston and that was the identification of the Avery Normal Institute for Black students.[46]

In *Overground Railroad*, Taylor states that based on her personal experience visiting approximately five thousand *Green Book* sites, fewer than twenty-five percent remain.[47] Within Charleston, seven of ten remain, which is an exceptionally high survival rate considering Taylor's statistics, although none of the original businesses are still in operation. Before publication of this article, little has been investigated by scholars on the *Green Book* sites of Charleston comprehensively. Although some of the buildings fall within Charleston's historic district today, this is due to relatively recent expansions of the district. None of the former *Green Book* listed buildings are specifically recognized for this past either. In 1985, the South Carolina Department of Archives and History historic property survey inventoried 15 Nassau Street but did not identify it as historically exceptional.[48] In response to the 2018 motion picture, *Green Book*, Hanna Raskin wrote an article for the *Post and Courier* titled "Before 'Green Book' Was a Movie, Charleston Restaurants Were in the Guidebook."[49] Nic Butler at the Charleston County Public Library also wrote a website article titled "The Green Book for Charleston, 1938–1966"[50] in February 2019; however, the film features none of Charleston's sites. Raskin and Butler did important first explorations of Charleston's *Green Book* sites that serve as the foundation for this article. Butler also addresses businesses such as the City Taxi Company and the Waverly tourist home, which are incorrectly listed in the *Green Book* as being in Charleston, so they are not included in this study. Those businesses that did function in Charleston are the following, and they are organized in order of *Green Book* appearance.

In the map reproduced here, the Hametic Hotel is depicted with a six-pointed star and "o," and the surviving *Green Book* sites are identified with five-pointed stars and numbered according to the brief descriptions that follow. Lost *Green Book* sites are identified by an "X" and their corresponding number. The approximate borders of Charleston's Old and Historic District, as it existed between 1931 and 1966, are also identified on the map with a thick line boundary. The Sanborn Fire Insurance Map is from the Library of Congress. All other additions and edits to the map are by the author.

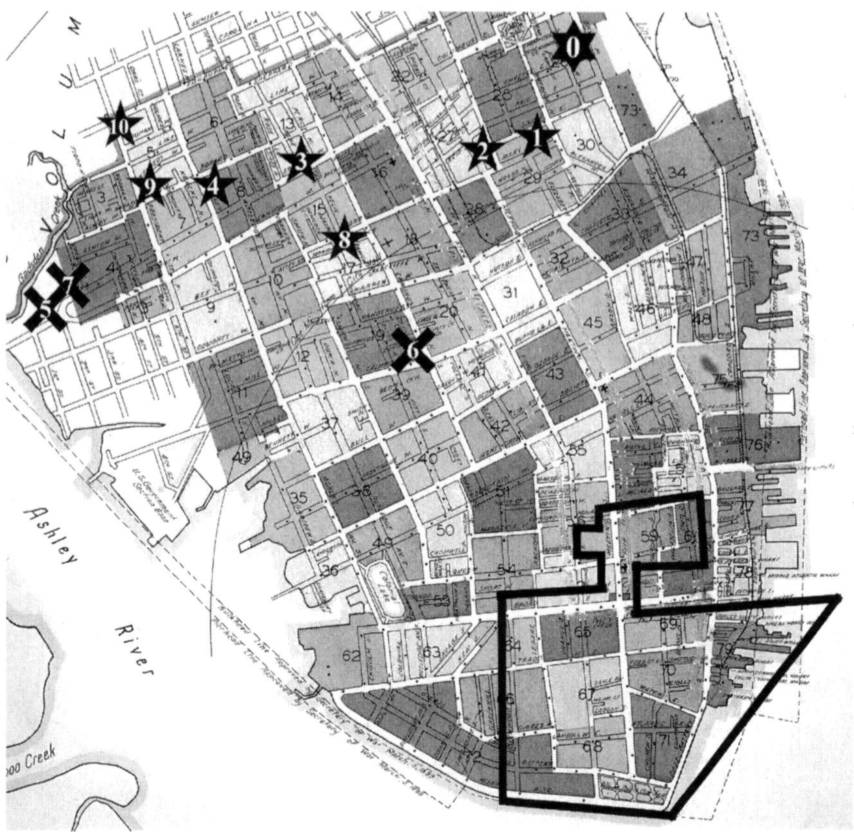

Figure 3.3. The Sanborn Fire Insurance Map from Charleston County, SC, 1944, showing locations of Charleston *Green Book* businesses. This was used for mapping the Hametic Hotel and the city's ten *Green Book* listings in relation to the urban-built environment and transportation infrastructure. Library of Congress, Geography and Map Division, Sanborn Maps Collection.

0. Hametic Hotel, 635 East Bay Street, which operated from ca. 1917 to 1932, closed shortly before the *Green Book* debuted, and is provided as a geographic reference in relation to the railroad and other *Green Book*–listed locations.[51]
1. Mrs. Alston, 43 South Street (tourist home), was among the first cohort of businesses in Charleston listed in the *Green Book*, spanning from 1938 to 1946. This establishment was run by Elizabeth Alston with her husband, Isaac Alston.[52]
2. Mrs. Gadsden, 15 Nassau Street (tourist home), was among the first cohort of businesses in Charleston listed in the *Green Book*, spanning from 1938 to 1967. The property's name is attributed to the original owner, Mrs. Gadsden.[53]

3. Annie Mayes, 82½ Spring Street (tourist home), was among the first cohort of businesses in Charleston listed in the *Green Book*, spanning from 1938 to 1967. Mayes, who is also identified as a laundress, hosted intermittent travelers.[54]

4. Huldah L. Harleston's, 250 Ashley Avenue (tourist home and tavern), was among the first cohort of businesses in Charleston listed in the *Green Book*, spanning from 1938 to 1950. Harleston, who was widowed with children, sold prepared foods from the house and hosted intermittent travelers.[55]

5. Green Grill, 186 Spring Street, was in the *Green Book* from 1939 to 1941. Susan Green, a professional cook, likely sold prepared foods from the house. The building was demolished during the 1960s as part of the urban renewal "Crosstown Expressway" development, now called the Septima P. Clark Parkway, after the civil rights activist.[56]

6. A. Serrant, 99 Coming Street (tourist home), was in the *Green Book* from 1941 to 1952. Annabell Serrant, who passed in 1943, was married to Gabriel Serrant, a Haitian immigrant and waiter at the Fountain Inn.[57] This property was acquired by the College of Charleston in 1976 and demolished sometime after, where now stands the School of Math & Science Building.

7. James Hotel, 238 Spring Street, built in 1951, was in the *Green Book* from 1952 to 1967. It was the only "colored" hotel listed in the Charleston city directory along with an attached restaurant. The hotel was operated by Edward and James Washington near the Ashley River Bridge. Distinguished hotel guests included Hank Aaron, Count Basie, James Brown, Fats Domino, and Duke Ellington.[58] The building was demolished in the 1960s as part of the urban renewal "Crosstown Expressway" development.

8. Brooks Restaurant, 58 Morris Street, was in the *Green Book* from 1959 to 1961. It started as a small café that opened in 1934 and expanded into a larger restaurant in 1950. The business relocated in 1967 and closed in 1979. The Brooks Café and Restaurant was a family-operated business, including Henry, Albert, and Benjamin Brooks. A Brooks Motel was also opened after 1963, but the Brooks had ceased advertising in the *Green Book* two years earlier. The Brooks Restaurant also hosted political meetings, including those involved with the civil rights movement.[59]

9. Queen's Restaurant, 55 Kennedy Street, was in the *Green Book* from 1959 to 1961, operated by Queen and George Breach.[60]

10. Scott's Restaurant, 237 Fishburne Street, was in the *Green Book* from 1959 to 1961, operated by Beatrice and William Mack. William also worked at Bullwinkel's, a local bakery.[61]

Figure 3.4. Present-day photograph of L. Harleston's tourist home and tavern, 250 Ashley Street, Charleston, SC. The building was included in the *Green Book* from 1938 until 1950. Photograph by Barry L. Stiefel, 2024.

The occurrence of the *Green Book* happened amid Jim Crow segregation. As previously mentioned, before the *Green Book* the Hametic Hotel welcomed Black customers from 1917 to 1932. After the *Green Book* ceased in 1966, segregated accommodations for African-American travelers were still needed. For example, the J&P Motel and Café (also called the Esau Jenkins Shop and Hotel) was established, testifying to the continuing endemic racism in Charleston and the need for accommodations for African Americans after the Civil Rights Act of 1964.[62] As Clement observed, the continued neglect of white Charlestonian interest in African-American tourists was highly present in 1977. Not until the mid-1980s were the first official

Figure 3.5. Present-day photograph of 55 Kennedy Street, a private residence that served as Queen's Restaurant in the 1950s and 1960s. Photograph by Barry L. Stiefel, 2024.

African-American history tours, a guidebook, and the Moja Arts Festival that celebrates African-American and Caribbean cultures organized in Charleston. Also, it was in the 1990s that Charleston tourism specifically advertised to an African-American audience.[63] These efforts resulted in the identification and preservation of African-American-associated historic sites in the Charleston area, most significantly the Gullah Geechee Cultural Heritage Corridor, established in 2006. These are great improvements, but they fall far short of addressing past wrongs.

On February 11, 1945, the historian E. Horace Fitchett of the historically Black Claflin College presented an address to the Charleston Interracial Committee, calling for (among many other things) the "equal accommodations for Negroes as provided under the law, be actually provided on all public transportation facilities, and that discriminatory practices now common in travel be abolished."[64] Visiting from Orangeburg, SC, Fitchett undoubtedly stayed at one of the tourist houses mentioned in the 1941 and 1946 editions of the *Green Book* (they are the same) or with other friends/family he knew. Two decades passed before the Civil Rights Act required Fitchett's comment to come into law, which was the premise for the end of the publication of the *Green Book* in 1966. However, many more years of begrudged integration had to pass before the hearts and minds of the public made a substantial enough shift for some change within the city and the country.

Jennifer B. Hawes, a reporter for the *Post and Courier*, describes the African-American past in Charleston at the moment of the city's 350th anniversary in 2020 as a "Forsaken history." She observes that many "key places in Charleston's racial past [are] long neglected."[65] Hawes covers multiple places, including sites that need to be revisited for their historic significance, such as Colonel William Rhett's wharf (where the first imported Africans were sold at auction in 1696) and William Payne's auction house (where hundreds of enslaved people were also auctioned), but also those that have been forgotten, such as the African Church, the Work House next to the City Jail, John Mood's silversmith shop (where slave badges were made), and the James Hotel. Indeed, the James Hotel is the only property from the twentieth century that was discussed by Hawes as a very significant site from Charleston's African-American past, although—and unfortunately—it is no longer extant (the site is currently a parking lot for a fast-food establishment after the "Crosstown Expressway" development). The James Hotel was a site of African-American agency, whereas many of the other sites discussed by Hawes were places of oppression.

Although the James Hotel, along with two other *Green Book* sites, are gone, there are seven other formerly listed locations that survive, which is a much higher percentage than in many other cities. This study has found that none of the seven surviving sites have any indication that they were once listed in the *Green Book* (no placard, official historical designation, etc.). The Hametic Hotel, which predates the *Green Book,* is on the National Register of Historic Places, and its association as a hotel that serves African-American customers is part of its official history, but it is called the Faber House after its original nineteenth-century, single-family, white occupant. Although this building was a recipient of the Preservation Society's Carolopolois Award in 1972 for exemplary restoration work, this site lacks an interpretative marker about the historical significance of this place, whether as the Hametic Hotel or the Faber family's home. Currently, these seven Green Book sites exhibit a high level of integrity and form a coherent heritage corridor across the midsection of Charleston's peninsula, serving as a landmark counternarrative to the establishment and administration of the city's original Old and Historic District as it existed between 1931 and 1966. More could be developed on the interpretation and public history of the seven *Green Book* historic buildings to improve public awareness and how it responded to the racism that plagued the Old and Historic District during these decades.

Future steps taken must involve the participation of African Americans—inclusive of those from elsewhere who traveled to Charleston as well as those who lived in Charleston—especially considering that the authors Hawes, Raskin, and Butler, who have published on some of these historic places, are not African American. African-American voices are needed to define why Charleston's *Green Book* historic buildings matter. This is where the community and preservation organizations working in Charleston and elsewhere in South Carolina could create partnerships with government and community leaders to mark and interpret these historic sites that can serve as a continuing guide in our evolving understanding of the intersection of race, travel, and power in the United States.

Barry L. Stiefel is a professor at the College of Charleston's historic preservation and community planning program, which is part of the Department of Art and Architectural History. He is interested in how local preservation efforts affect regional, national, and multinational policies in cultural resource management and natural heritage conservation. He has completed numerous publications, including ones that address sustainability in heritage preservation; cultural–ethnic architectural history; historic transportation mobility; human-centered historic preservation; community building through historic places; diversity, equity, and inclusion in historic preservation; and preservation education.

NOTES

1. Coats, "In Charleston, Black history is being told through a new lens."
2. Anderson, *A Bluestocking in Charleston*, 63.
3. One tourist home, 250 Ashley Avenue, was also identified as Harleston's Tavern.
4. Agbor-Taylor, "South Carolina's Black Majority."
5. List of Black-owned businesses from 1946 compiled by Charleston County Public Library, unpublished vertical file, South Carolina Room.
6. Clement, "The Negro as a Visitor," *Charleston Evening Post*, A1.
7. Moss, *The Lost Southern Chefs*, 16–17; and Paracka, *The Athens of West Africa*, 36.
8. Hamilton, *Men and Manners in America*, 278.
9. Powers, *Black Charlestonians*, 43–44; and Peck, "Four Years Under Fire," 358–66.
10. Bernhard, *Travels Through North America*, 5.
11. Bernhard, *Travels Through North America*, 5.
12. Stiefel, "'Our Museum—Another Handsome Contribution,'" 103–14.
13. Mix, "Charleston Museum of Natural and Artificial Curiosities," 4.
14. Kytle and Roberts, *Denmark Vesey's Garden*, 194.

15. Stordeur, *Colored Travelers*, 105.

16. "News by Telegraph," 3.

17. Sandoval-Strausz, *Hotel*, 292.

18. Green, *The Negro Motorist Green Book*, 1.

19. Rubin, *Uptown—Downtown in Old Charleston*, 1–2.

20. Chamber of Commerce, *Charleston Welcomes You*.

21. Jackson and Wilson, eds. "Tourism, Cultural," 227–29.

22. Yuhl, *A Golden Haze of Memory*, 19.

23. Pendleton, *A Narrative of the Negro*, 158–59.

24. Jackson, "Booker T. Washington in South Carolina," 192–220.

25. Kytle and Roberts, *Denmark Vesey's Garden*, 178–79.

26. Kytle and Roberts, *Denmark Vesey's Garden*, 301.

27. Smith, "African American Travel Literature," 197–213.

28. Ingham, "Building Business, Creating Communities," 639–65.

29. Butler, "The Green Book for Charleston, 1938–1966."

30. Green, *The Negro Motorist Green Book*, 36, 78–79.

31. See Knight, *"Disreputable Houses of Some Very Reputable Negroes"*; Brundage, *The Southern Past*, especially 294–98, 309; and Colby, *Wicked St. Augustine*.

32. Butler, "Frederick Douglass in 1888 Charleston."

33. Douglass, "I Denounce the So-Called Emancipation as a Stupendous Fraud."

34. Kytle and Roberts, *Denmark Vesey's Garden*, 305.

35. See Suttles, *Atlantic Beach*.

36. Workman, "2 Held After 7 Robberies at Walterboro," 1.

37. Jackson, "Booker T. Washington in South Carolina, March 1909," 192–220.

38. Taylor, *Overground Railroad*, 1–5.

39. Greenville County (SC) Sheriff, "Sales Books for Automobiles Seized While Transporting Contraband Liquors."

40. "Mauldin, W. F.," US Census, 1920.

41. Juncker, "Africa in South Carolina,"144–52.

42. Eiland and Fesak, "National Register of Historic Places Inventory."

43. Alderman, Bottone, and Inwood, "Teaching and Enlivening the Green Book."

44. See Annan and Gabriel, *The Great Cooper River Bridge*.

45. Butler, "The Green Book for Charleston, 1938–1966," D6.

46. Kytle and Roberts, *Denmark Vesey's Garden*, 294.

47. Taylor, *Overground Railroad*, 1–5.

48. Geiger Brown Renfrow Architects.

49. Raskin, "Before movie, Charleston restaurants were in 'Green Book,'" D6.

50. Butler, "The Green Book for Charleston, 1938–1966."

51. Eiland and Fesak, "National Register of Historic Places Inventory—Nomination Form: Faber House."

52. Butler, "The Green Book for Charleston, 1938–1966."

53. Butler, "The Green Book for Charleston, 1938–1966."

54. Butler, "The Green Book for Charleston, 1938–1966."

55. Butler, "The Green Book for Charleston, 1938–1966."

56. Raskin, "Before movie, Charleston restaurants were in 'Green Book,'" D6.

57. Butler, "The Green Book for Charleston, 1938–1966," D6.

58. Smyth, "Segregation in Charleston in the 1950s: A Decade of Transition," 99–123.

59. Surface, *Lost Restaurants of Charleston*, 73–74.

60. Raskin, "Before movie, Charleston restaurants were in 'Green Book,'" D6.

61. Raskin, "Before movie, Charleston restaurants were in 'Green Book,'" D6.

62. Eiland and Fesak, "National Register of Historic Places Inventory–Nomination Form: Faber House."

63. Ashworth and Tunbridge, *The Tourist-Historic City*, 259.

64. Fitchett, "New Horizons in Interracial Cooperation and Understanding in the South."

65. Hawes, "Forsaken History."

WORKS CITED

Agbor-Taylor, Phylisha. "South Carolina's Black Majority (1708–1920)." *Black Past,* January 24, 2022. https://www.blackpast.org/.

Alderman, Derek H., Ethan Bottone, and Joshua Inwood. "Teaching and Enlivening the Green Book." Tourism Reset, June 17, 2019. https://www.tourismreset.com/.

Anderson, Allen L. *A Bluestocking in Charleston: The Life and Career of Laura Bragg.* University of South Carolina Press, 2001.

Annan, Jason, and Pamela Gabriel. *The Great Cooper River Bridge.* University of South Carolina Press, 2002.

Ashworth, Gregory J., and J. E. Tunbridge. *The Tourist-Historic City: Retrospect and Prospect of Managing the Heritage City.* Routledge 2001.

Bernhard, Carl. *Travels Through North America During the Years 1825–1826, Vol. 1.* Carey, Lea & Carey, 1828.

Brundage, W. Fitzhugh. *The Southern Past: A Clash of Race and Memory.* Harvard University Press, 2009.

Butler, Nic. "Frederick Douglass in 1888 Charleston." Charleston County Public Library, January 31, 2025. https://www.ccpl.org/charleston-time-machine/frederick-douglass-1888-charleston.

Butler, Nic. "The Green Book for Charleston, 1938–1966." *Charleston Time Machine,* podcast audio, February 22, 2019. https://www.ccpl.org/charleston-time-machine/green-book-charleston-1938-1966.

Charleston Chamber of Commerce. *Charleston Welcomes You: America's Most Historic City.* J. J. Furlong & Sons, 1938.

Coats, Jalen. "In Charleston, Black history is being told through a new lens." *National Geographic,* June 24, 2021. https://www.nationalgeographic.com/.

Colby, Ann. *Wicked St. Augustine.* History Press, 2020.

Douglass, Frederick. "I Denounce the So-Called Emancipation as a Stupendous Fraud." *History Is A Weapon,* accessed September 8, 2025. https://www.historyisaweapon.com/defcon1/douglassfraud.html.

Eiland, Alexis, and Mary Fesak, "National Register of Historic Places Inventory—Nomination Form: Faber House." National Park Service, 2019.

Fitchett, E. Horace. "New Horizons in Interracial Cooperation and Understanding in the South." Paper presented at the Charleston Interracial Committee, Mount

Zion AME Church, Charleston, SC, February 11, 1945. Unpublished document, Charleston County Library, South Carolina Room, Vertical File.

Geiger Brown Renfrow Architects. 15 Nassau Street. South Carolina Department of Archives and History Historic Property Survey, 1985. Unpublished document, Charleston County Library, South Carolina Room, Vertical File.

Green, Victor H. *The Negro Motorist Green Book*. Victor H. Green & Co., 1949.

Greenville County Sheriff's Office. Sales Books for Automobiles Seized While Transporting Contraband Liquors, 1925–1927 (Series L 23196, Record Group 000023). South Carolina Department of Archives and History.

Hamilton, Thomas. *Men and Manners in America*, vol. 2. W. Blackwood & T. Cadell, 1834.

Hawes, Jennifer B. "Forsaken History: In Her 350th Year, Key Places in Charleston's Racial Past Long Neglected." *Post and Courier*, November 13, 2020. https://www.postandcourier.com/.

Ingham, John N. "Building Business, Creating Communities: Residential Segregation and the Growth of African American Business in Southern Cities." *The Business History Review* 77, no. 4 (Winter 2003): 639–65.

Jackson, David H. Jr. "Booker T. Washington in South Carolina, March 1909." *The South Carolina Historical Magazine* 112, no. 3 (July 2012): 192–220.

Jackson, Harvey H., and Charles R. Wilson, eds. "Tourism, Cultural." In *The New Encyclopedia of Southern Culture*, Vol. 16, *Sports and Recreation*, edited by Harvey H. Jackson. University of North Carolina Press, 2011.

Juncker, Clara. "Africa in South Carolina: Mamie Garvin Field's *Lemon Swamp and Other Places*." In *Black Imagination and the Middle Passage*, edited by Diedrich Maria, Henry Louis Gates Jr., and Carl Pedersen. Oxford University Press, 1999.

Knight, Nora A. "Disreputable Houses of Some Very Reputable Negroes": Paternalism and Segregation of Colonial Williamsburg Paternalism and Segregation of Colonial Williamsburg." Unpublished bachelor's thesis, Bard College, 2016.

Kytle, Ethan J., and Blain Roberts. *Denmark Vesey's Garden: Slavery and Memory in the Cradle of the Confederacy*. New Press, 2019.

Mix, John. "Charleston Museum of Natural and Artificial Curiosities." *City Gazette and Daily Advertiser*, December 26, 1816, 4.

Moss, Robert F. *The Lost Southern Chefs: A History of Commercial Dining in the Nineteenth-Century South*. University of Georgia Press, 2022.

"News by Telegraph." *New Orleans Tribune*, 19 February 1869, 3.

Pendleton, Leila. *A Narrative of the Negro*. Press of R. L. Pendleton, 1912.

Paracka, Daniel J. *The Athens of West Africa: A History of International Education at Fourah Bay College Freetown Sierra Leone*. Routledge, 2003.

Peck, William F. "Four Years Under Fire." *Harper's New Monthly*, August 1865, 358–66.

Powers, Bernard E. *Black Charlestonians: A Social History 1822–1885*. University of Arkansas Press, 1994.

Raskin, Hanna. "Before 'Green Book' was a Movie, Charleston Restaurants Were in the Guidebook." *Post and Courier*, January 23, 2019, D6.

Rubin, Louis D., Jr., *Uptown–Downtown in Old Charleston: Sketches and Stories*. University of South Carolina Press, 2010.

Sandoval-Strausz, A. K. *Hotel: An American History.* Yale University Press, 2007.

Smith, Virgina W. "African American Travel Literature." In *The Cambridge Companion to American Travel Writing,* edited by Alfred Bendixen and Judith Hamera. Cambridge University Press, 2009.

Smyth, William D. "Segregation in Charleston in the 1950s: A Decade of Transition." *The South Carolina Historical Magazine* 92, no. 2, (1991): 99–123.

Stiefel, Barry L. "'Our Museum—Another Handsome Contribution': A Comparative Case Study of the Charleston Museum's Design and Visitation During its First Formative 150 Years." *Collections: A Journal for Museum and Archives Professionals* 1, no. 2 (2015): 103–14.

Stordeur, Pryor E. *Colored Travelers: Mobility and the Fight for Citizenship Before the Civil War.* University of North Carolina Press, 2016.

Surface, Jessica. *Lost Restaurants of Charleston.* The History Press, 2019.

Suttles, Sherry A. *Atlantic Beach.* Arcadia Press, 2009.

Taylor, Candacy A. *Overground Railroad: The Green Book of Black Travel in America.* Abrams Press, 2020.

US Census, *Family Search,* 1920, accessed September 10, 2025. https://familysearch .com.

Workman, W. D., Jr. "2 Held After 7 Robberies at Walterboro." *News and Courier,* January 9, 1939, 1.

Yuhl, Stephanie E. *A Golden Haze of Memory: The Making of Historic Charleston.* University of North Carolina Press, 2005.

Tracking the *Negro Motorist Green Book*

A Practical Guide for the Amateur Historian

Cherish Thomas

East Cheves and Jarrott.

"*No.*"

East Cheves and McFarland.

"*No.*"

East Cheves and Johns.

"*No.*"

I whispered quietly to myself, as I flipped through a collection of archival photographs, all of which were taken in the 1950s at the intersections of various streets in the predominantly Black neighborhood of East Florence.

East Cheves and Griffin.

"*No.*"

I was hoping to find an image of Ace's Grill, which was located on the corner of East Cheves and Kemp Street. It was the first Florence restaurant to be listed in the *Negro Motorist Green Book* in 1949.

East Cheves and Ballard.

"*No.*"

East Cheves and Ives.

"*No.*"

East Cheves and Ravenel...

East Cheves and Fairview...

East Cheves and Kemp!

At last, there in a photograph and barely within frame was what may very well be the last existing image of Ace's Grill.

I first became aware of Ace's Grill and other Florence *Green Book* businesses several months prior. Like many others, I had seen the movie *Green Book* and became curious about businesses from my region listed in that important travel guide.[1] I decided to visit the Florence County Library and take a look for myself. As I skimmed through a copy of the 1953 edition of *The Negro Motorist Green Book,* I discovered, much to my surprise, that several businesses in Florence were represented: Richmond Rest, 108 S. Griffin Street; Ebony Guest House, 712 North Wilson Street; Ace's Grill, 114 East

Cheeve[2] Street; Wright's, 110 South Griffin Street.[3] This discovery initially surprised me, as I had not expected a national travel guide for African Americans to represent Florence. However, I came to learn that Florence marks the halfway point between New York City and Miami, Florida, thus making it a convenient stopping point for weary travelers and that the *Green Book* featured eight local Florence businesses throughout its thirty-year publication. At the time, however, I simply wondered, *Why Florence . . . ? What became of these businesses?* I was eager to learn more, but after consulting with staff at both the Florence County Library and the Florence County Museum, I realized that public knowledge of these *Green Book* businesses seemed to begin and end within the pages of the travel guide.

Figure 4.1. Ace's Grill, 114 Cheves Street, Florence, ca. 1955. Florence County Museum.

The pursuit of truth is never without challenge. After consulting with these local institutions, I submitted my question to the unfailing wisdom of man's greatest achievement of the twentieth century: Google. It's one thing when human knowledge fails you, but despair knows no further depth as when Google fails you too! Therefore, I decided to take it upon myself to look beyond the digital and into the real world.

This essay is for those who wish to dig deeper and conduct their own *Green Book* research, as I did. Sharing tips and strategies from my own experience in researching local *Green Book* businesses, I hope to empower others to discover forgotten histories within their own communities. Although not an exhaustive account of my successes and failures, the essay provides practical tips for those getting started with *Green Book* research. My hope is to provide a guide from which others can grow, modify, and expand their knowledge in ways that are rewarding and useful within their own community.

New York City postal worker Victor H. Green published the *Green Book* from 1936 to 1966.[4] Although the guide was modified over the course of its publication, each edition featured business listings arranged by state and/or country and city. The listings provided the name and address (sometimes only the street name) of the business being advertised. Before 1956, the *Green Book* also classified each listing into categories such as restaurants, tourist homes, service stations, barber shops, and hotels. Each new edition of the *Green Book* was updated to reflect changes as businesses closed, moved locations, or changed names. Other times, business owners may have chosen not to continue advertising in the *Green Book*. As such, I have found that when investigating *Green Book* businesses, researchers should first identify the number of businesses listed within the chosen city, the types of businesses listed, and the years in which each business was listed.

To complete this work, researchers will find The Schomburg Center for Research in Black Culture website indispensable. The Center is part of the New York City Public Library and includes digitized collections of poems, personal papers of historic figures, photographs, maps, and twenty-three digitized editions of the *Green Book*.[5] To navigate, you simply click on the individual issue and flip through the pages as you would the pages of a physical book. From cover to cover, you can examine each page of each edition, organized by state and, sometimes, by county.

For researchers in South Carolina, the *Historic Columbia* website provides another valuable resource.[6] The creators have curated a list of sites in the capital city. The National Historic Trust for Historic Preservation and the South Carolina Department of State Archives and History offer helpful information on sites that have been marked and researched by historians.[7]

Once you have identified sites within your area, a second helpful step is to place those businesses within the past and present landscape of your chosen city. It is often difficult to imagine the evolution of a city's landscape when you are several decades removed from the source material. Very probably, the city looks different now than it did during the decades in which the *Green Book* was in print and its businesses in operation. When visiting the address of a local *Green Book* listing, you may discover that a parking garage now stands where you were expecting to find a barber shop. Similarly, if your GPS struggles to locate Griffin Street, it may be because Griffin Street no longer exists, as many older neighborhoods have been demolished and replaced by new businesses or roadways.

Real-world "field trips" to *Green Book* sites can be tremendously rewarding and valuable, but they often require a map published around the same time when the businesses were listed. Local libraries, archives, museums, and historical societies are all likely to have such maps within their collections, some of which may be accessible online. Comparing these older maps with current ones, you may find that a street name or building number has been changed or that the original addresses of the businesses no longer exist. For example, today there is no 100th block of South Griffin Street in East Florence. It was once located off East Cheves Street and was home to Richmond Rest until the late 1950s. It was also the site for Wright's for a few years. These streets were located in the heart of East Florence's residential neighborhood that has since become subsumed by the McLeod Regional Medical Center.

In addition to physically locating businesses on past and present city maps, Google Maps can also help to better orient your research. You may find that a business is still in operation or that a building is extant. Use caution, however, as Google Maps is a tool designed primarily to identify and locate present-day businesses, not those of the early to mid-twentieth century. Nevertheless, once you have determined the present-day location of a business, the Street View and 360-degree feature of Google Maps can depict the state and exterior condition of the building and the land on which it was built. Often when navigating Street View, a building that no longer exists may appear, or a significant architectural change to a building may become apparent, such as the addition of a new wing of a house or the refurbishment of a storefront facade.

Google Street View may also be valuable for obtaining images of businesses that are no longer extant and in documenting their buildings' architectural evolution. This was the case with Richmond Rest, a *Green Book* tourist home in Florence, whose first and second locations had been demolished before I began my research. By utilizing Google Street View in 2019, I was able to obtain images of the second location from 2012. Not only did these images provide insight into the physical characteristics of the tourist home, but also the "Image Capture" stamp informed me that the house was demolished sometime during or after 2012. It was this stamp that established a set of parameters into which I was able to channel the rest of my research.

Another helpful tool is a geographic information system (GIS) map, which is a type of map used to visualize and analyze landscape data. Municipalities commonly utilize GIS maps for city and county planning, zoning, and tax purposes. South Carolina's Information Highway provides online access to current county GIS maps.[8] The simplest means of searching a GIS map is by address, as you would with Google Maps. For *Green Book* researchers, GIS maps provide a bird's-eye view of businesses and often list useful information such as tax map numbers, names of current property owners, and acreage. The maps also provide links to recent digital city and county property cards, tax assessor records, deeds, and plats. The offices of local tax assessors and clerks of court preserve hard copies of these records as well as older records. Before paying a visit to either, be sure to know the current address, the tax map number, and the names of the current owners of the property that you are researching. This information will allow you to research changes to the property and in ownership over decades. Organizational and indexing methods for deed and plat books vary from one municipality to the next, so be sure to consult with the staff on the proper procedures for searching the records. Records are generally available for public research free of charge, but offices may require an appointment. Typically, researchers can also print copies of records for a small fee.

City directories, often available for free at a local library or for a fee on Ancestry.com, have proven to be the most significant resources for my research. Cross-referencing *Green Book* listings with local city directories is the simplest method of verifying existing information and obtaining new data, such as years of business operation and changes in location, names of proprietors, and insights on tourist homes.

1. Years in operation and changes in location. Consulting a local city directory
   can help establish a window of operation for each business through which

you can focus your research efforts. Begin by looking up each business in the directory for the year in which it first appeared in the *Green Book,* or the closest available year. From here, work forward and backward through the available directories. In doing so, you can confirm the first year in which a selected business began operations, as well as the year it closed. Changes in location also become apparent.

2. Names of proprietors. Identifying the names of *Green Book* proprietors is essential in telling the full story of their businesses and the culture they fostered. Some *Green Book* listings include the full names of the proprietors; others do not. Certain listings only include a partial name, such as "C. C. Godbold" or "Wright's," and other listings only include the name of the business such as "Spring Valley Motel" or "Ebony Guest House." Cross-referencing the listed address in the city directories will often reveal the full names of the proprietors included in parentheses or brackets within the business listing.

   You will also sometimes find that the listed proprietor was employed in other work outside the *Green Book* business. For example, James Miller, the proprietor of the Spring Valley Motel, was also the principal of Holmes Elementary, Florence's only elementary school for Black students. Miller's wife, Marian, was the librarian for Florence's only Black high school, Wilson High School. Likewise, Paul Wright, owner of "Wright's," was involved in multiple other business ventures that were never included in the *Green Book.* Establishing a "first-name basis" with *Green Book* proprietors also allows you to cross-reference their names in other resources such as census records, newspaper articles, and municipality records.

3. Insights on tourist homes. Occasionally, directory listings include the names of tourist home residents as members of the proprietor's (homeowner's) household. Although this information alone is useful, the inclusion of the resident's name in the listing can provide insight into the physical structure of the tourist home and its operation. For example, the listing of a resident's name in the directory implies that the resident had a separate mailing address from the homeowner. For example, residents of the John McDonald tourist home were listed in the city directories as residing in the "rear" of the house. This information suggests that paying residents lived in their own private section of the house, separate from the McDonald family, perhaps like a duplex apartment. This arrangement contrasts that of other tourist homes in which residents rented a room within the house and shared communal living spaces with the proprietor and their family.

Once you know the basic facts of each *Green Book* business, you can expand your research by investigating other primary sources. Databases and archives of primary resources such as newspaper articles, deeds, plats, postcards, letters, business cards, business records, photographs, and oral histories can help illustrate the broader social, political, economic, and cultural contexts in which the *Green Book* businesses operated. The University of South Carolina Libraries and the South Carolina State Library have compiled a tremendous archive of historical newspapers, which is full-text searchable.[9] Your local or state library, museum, historical society, or university are also excellent places to seek out primary sources. And remember, libraries can often provide free access to materials that may otherwise be blocked by expensive paywalls. You can find more information about these types of sources in the "Resources for Research" listing at the end of this article.

When researching, whether online or in person, try to be as specific as possible in your queries and requests. When visiting the library, rather than asking general questions about Mable's Motel, inform the staff of what you already know: "I'm looking for information on Mable's Motel. It's listed in the *Green Book* as being located on Highway 52 in Darlington, SC. It was owned by Mrs. Mable Robinson and was in operation from the 1940s to the 1980s." This detailed phrasing gives the library staff much more information to work with and can lead to a wealth of information. Perhaps there is a vertical file that contains news clippings of major events that occurred at Mable's Motel or a photograph collection of businesses that once occupied Highway 52, or a report of a historic survey conducted on Black businesses in the city of Darlington in 1970.

The exception to the "be as specific as possible" rule comes into play when searching digital databases. Being *too* specific in your search often renders too few results, yet being *too* general can render an abundance of broad, irrelevant results. A good rule of thumb when searching digital databases is to search both exact names and phrases as well as any known variants of those same names and phrases. For example, when searching for names of people, such as "Mable," "Lillie," and "Catherine," search also for alternative spellings such as "Mabel," "Lily," and "Katherine."

This technique is especially important when searching census records, which are only as accurate as the enumerator's auditory understanding of the name spoken, as well as the enumerator's spelling and the legibility of their penmanship. Moreover, if a street has been renamed since the time the *Green Book* business was in operation, or if the street is commonly referred to

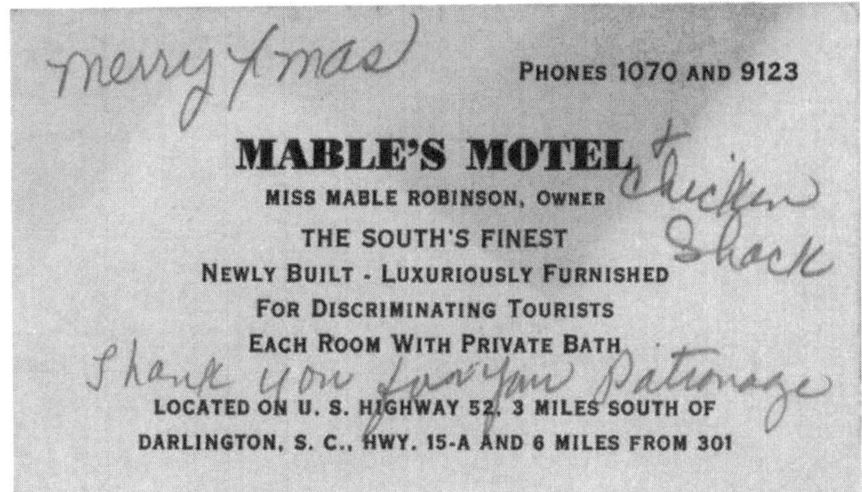

Figure 4.2. Business card for Mable's Motel and Chicken Shack, Highway 52, Darlington, SC, with handwritten holiday greeting, ca. 1950. John Henry McCray Papers, South Caroliniana Library, University of South Carolina, Columbia, SC.

by more than one name (e.g., "Cheeves" vs. "Cheves"), be sure to search for both. Remember, digital databases are only as intelligent as their algorithms! These subtle research strategies can unlock troves of relevant information that may otherwise remain undiscovered.

It is possible to conduct historical research and craft narratives apart from the communities in which your *Green Book* proprietors lived and worked, but having "boots on the ground" within the community and working to establish relationships with local residents will help establish an inclusive historical narrative. As the researcher, you should always take the initiative and reach out to individuals and community organizations with ties to your subject matter, be they relatives, friends, neighbors, religious institutions, or civic clubs. In short, you must get out and talk to people.

However, it can be challenging to identify a living participant or witness. If a living witness does, indeed, exist, there are scenarios in which engagement may be impossible or ill advised, ranging from a lack of travel funds to sensitivity of the subject matter. Nevertheless, when attempting to initiate contact, keep in mind that it is human nature to be wary of the intentions of strangers and those outside our own trusted communities. This wariness can become a roadblock for researchers seeking information from a community that is not their own. The following is a list of questions you should be prepared to answer when seeking to establish a relationship with a local community and while engaging with the community throughout the research process:

1. Who are you? What is your name? Where are you from? Are you representing yourself or a school/company/institution?—Be genuine and sincere. Do not presume that the influence of your personal reputation or the prestige of your institution is sufficient justification to gain insider knowledge and access. Always presume community members to be the primary authority on the subject. Address them with deference and humility, and be quick to listen rather than speak. Never act as if you are entitled to the information and resources that are within their possession.
2. What do you want to know or do? Whom or what are you researching? Why? What do you need from the community? Do you only seek information, or do you need access to tangible resources and spaces?—Be as specific as possible about what you wish to obtain from the community upfront.
3. What are your intentions? What do you intend to do with the information and materials once you have them? What is the end goal or finished product? Are you writing a book? Publishing an article? Giving a lecture? How involved do you or your institution expect the community to be in the research and in the formation and enjoyment of the finished product? How involved will you or your institution permit the community to be? What are the benefits for the community?
4. Money and publicity. Who is funding the research and the finished product? Will you or your institution be earning profits or garnering publicity throughout the research process or from the finished product? If so, will any profits be returned to the community? In what forms? Will the community be appropriately credited for their contributions to the finished project? Does the community desire to be credited for their contributions? How would they like to be credited?

Being open and transparent about yourself, your institution, and the purpose of your research helps establish and maintain trust. Often, unexpected circumstances will impede, delay, or halt your research altogether. This is not unusual. However, if this happens, be sure to maintain regular contact with the community and follow through with any claims or promises that you have made. Being in possession of information or resources does not grant you the authority to have your way with it, nor does it give you permission to abandon the community by cutting off communication or leaving promises unfilled. These are harmful, exploitive actions that will damage not only your reputation within the community but also the reputation of your institution. Such actions may hamper the efforts of future researchers as well. If you are ever in doubt about what to say or how to act when engaging with a community, remember to show respect, humility, and sensitivity for their perspectives. Doing so has always served me well.

The act of researching is, in my opinion, an objectively noble venture because it presupposes a finished product—an article, book, lecture, or historical marker—that furthers society's collective knowledge of the subject matter and possesses the potential to inspire continued learning or action. Although both the act of researching and the creation of a finished product are worthwhile, I believe that equal value should also be placed on the relationships that are formed throughout the research process and those formed through sharing the finished product with others.

Historically and currently, individuals tend to hyperfocus on differences rather than similarities, which is particularly detrimental to forging and maintaining meaningful relationships with others and to advancing our understandings of history. In the broadest of terms, this hyperfixation on differences necessitated the publication of the *Green Book* nearly nine decades ago. Although we are no longer bound by segregation laws, one could argue that what the law once did for us we now do ourselves by means of self-segregation on the basis of cultural, religious, and political ideologies. As a result, the challenge of forging meaningful human connections is only compounded when attempting to form relationships with those from diverse backgrounds, as is often the case when engaging in historical work.

Throughout my time researching the *Green Book*, I have been honored to meet and engage with people from many different walks of life, whose livelihoods, zip codes, politics, faith, and skin color all differ from mine. They are people whom I likely would have never encountered had we not shared interest and appreciation for the subject matter and the work which was being done. These connections are where the true fruit of our labor as researchers lies: in our ability to build relationships with others across cultural, religious, and political lines, in uniting together with common interests and goals to bridge generational gaps, and in the strengthening of bonds through history, as a result of history, and even despite history.

As you embark upon your own research journey through the *Green Book*, I encourage you, above all else, to be mindful of the many interactions that you will have with others along the way and of the opportunities that each interaction will hold. Do not take for granted the people you encounter and the circumstances in which you may find yourself, however preplanned, unscheduled, inconvenient, or accidental they may be. History belongs to everyone, and everyone has a role to play in its recovery.

Resources for Research

In addition to the works included in the Works Cited, the following will be especially helpful for those hoping to learn more about *Green Book* businesses.

"African American Heritage." National Parks Service, February 3, 2022. https://www.nps.gov/subjects/africanamericanheritage/visit.htm.

The Architecture of The Negro Travelers' Green Book. Institute for Advanced Technology in the Humanities. University of Virginia, April 20, 2021. https://community.village.virginia.edu/greenbooks/.

Bay, Mia. *Traveling Black: A Story of Race and Resistance.* Harvard University Press, 2023.

Bay, Mia, and Ann Fabian, eds. *Race and Retail: Assumption Across the Color Line.* Rutgers University Press, 2015.

"Capturing History One South Carolina Photograph at a Time." South Carolina Picture Project, accessed September 10, 2025. https://www.scpictureproject.org.

Center for Civil Rights History and Research. University of South Carolina, accessed September 10, 2025. https://civilrights.sc.edu/.

"The Green Book: An Historic Context." National Park Service, accessed September 10, 2025. www.nps.gov.

The Green Book of South Carolina. South Carolina African American Heritage Commission, accessed September 10, 2025. https://greenbookofsc.com.

Hall, Alvin. *Driving the Green Book: A Road Trip through the Living History of Black Resistance.* Harper One, 2023.

Mapping "The Green Book." Tumblr, accessed September 10, 2025. https://mappingthegreenbook.tumblr.com/.

"National Register Database and Research." National Park Service, August 5, 2025. https://www.nps.gov/.

Sorin, Gretchen. *Driving While Black: African American Travel and the Road to Civil Rights.* Liveright Publishing, 2020.

"South Carolina Historic Property Records." South Carolina Department of Archives and History, accessed September 10, 2025. https://schpr.sc.gov/.

Taylor, Candacy. *Overground Railroad: The "Green Book" and the Roots of Black Travel in America.* Abrams Press, 2020.

Cherish Thomas is the Curator of History at the Florence County Museum in Florence, SC. In recent years, she has researched former *Negro Motorist Green Book* sites in both Florence and Darlington Counties and has worked to preserve their stories. She is coauthor of "Intervening in Jim Crow: The *Green Book* and Southern Hospitality," published in the first volume of *Carolina Currents*. Cherish's scholarly interests include race relations in the antebellum South through Reconstruction, the civil rights movement, and the social and political influence of Christianity on the American South.

NOTES

1. Farrelly, dir., *Green Book*.
2. A misspelling of Florence's Cheves Street.
3. Green, *The Negro Motorist Green Book*, 61.
4. For a useful, brief history of the *Green Book*, see Tunnell, "The Negro Motorist Green Book (1936–1964)."
5. "The Green Book," Schomburg Center.
6. "Columbia's Green Book Sites," *Historic Columbia*.
7. See "Green Book Sites," National Trust for Historic Preservation. The South Carolina Department of Archives and History provides an abundance of useful source. See also, Jackson, "Searching for Safe Havens: Rediscovering Extant Green Book Sites in South Carolina."
8. "South Carolina—GIS County Maps." South Carolina's Information Highway.
9. See "Historical Newspapers of South Carolina," University of South Carolina Libraries, Digital Collections.

WORKS CITED

"Columbia's Green Book Sites." *Historic Columbia,* accessed September 10, 2025. https://www.historiccolumbia.org/GreenBook.

Farrelly, Peter, dir. *Green Book*. Universal Pictures, 2018. 130 min.

Green, Victor H. *The Negro Motorist Green Book, Airline Edition*. Victor H. Green & Co., 1953. Available from the Schomburg Center for Research in Black Culture, Manuscripts, Archives and Rare Books Division, The New York Public Library, accessed September 10, 2025. https://digitalcollections.nypl.org/items/2bc86d90-92d0-0132-e771-58d385a7b928.

"The Green Book." Schomburg Center for Research in Black Culture, Manuscripts, Archives and Rare Books Division. The New York Public Library Digital Collections, accessed September 10, 2025. https://digitalcollections.nypl.org/collections/9ea5d5b0-1117-0132-7932-58d385a7b928#/?tab=navigation.

"Green Book Sites." National Trust for Historic Preservation, accessed September 10, 2025. https://savingplaces.org/green-book-sites.

"Historical Newspapers of South Carolina." University of South Carolina Libraries, Digital Collections, accessed September 10, 2025. https://digital.library.sc.edu/collections/historical-newspapers-of-south-carolina.

Jackson, Ramon. "Searching for Safe Havens: Rediscovering Extant Green Book Sites in South Carolina." *The Silver Crescent Standard: The Blog of the South Carolina Department of Archives and History*. SC Department of Archives and History, 2021. https://scdah.sc.gov/.

South Carolina Department of Archives and History, accessed September 10, 2025. https://scdah.sc.gov/.

"South Carolina—GIS County Maps." *South Carolina's Information Highway,* accessed September 10, 2025. https://www.sciway.net/maps/sc-gis-county -maps.html.

Tunnell, Harry. "The Negro Motorist Green Book (1936–1964)." *The Black Past,* July 30, 2014. https://www.blackpast.org/.

Religion, Race, and Revolution

Creating a Biracial Church at Welsh Neck, South Carolina

John Barrington

The American Revolution raised a fundamental issue that haunted the United States for decades: How could white colonists demand liberty from Great Britain while continuing to profit from the labor of enslaved Black men and women?[1] This contradiction spurred discussion and action that varied from region to region. The New England and mid-Atlantic states ended slavery, immediately or gradually, in the quarter century after independence was won. In the Chesapeake region, the Revolution generated soul-searching laments about the economy's dependence on slavery and much wishful thinking about the possibility of one day ending the institution. In the Lower South, however, the contradiction between white liberty and Black slavery seemed to have little impact; at the end of the Revolution, white leaders in the Carolinas and Georgia were chiefly concerned with recovering enslaved people who had defected to the British and ensuring that the national government would not block further imports of enslaved people. The logic of liberty had little effect on the conscience of these southernmost states.

There were, of course, exceptions to the general pattern in the Lower South. This article examines one particular South Carolina community—the Baptist Church of Welsh Neck, in the Pee Dee region—where whites did, in the midst of the Revolution, begin to treat their enslaved neighbors differently. The white church members did not become convinced abolitionists, but after ignoring their Black neighbors for decades, the church suddenly in the summer of 1779 invited enslaved Blacks to join, indicating a willingness to accept at least the spiritual equality of the enslaved. About one hundred enslaved men and women took up the invitation, creating over a three-month period a significant Black component to the Welsh Neck Church. The church remained biracial after the war was over and, by the end of the century, contained a slight majority of Black members.

What led the Whites of the Welsh Neck Church to make this sudden adjustment in their racial attitudes? I argue that three factors brought about this change. First, the heady idealism of the Revolution, translated into

"

religious terms, had an impact on the pastor and perhaps on some of the congregation, impelling them to recognize the humanity of the enslaved people living among them. Second, the British invasion of South Carolina sparked security concerns about slave uprisings. The hope that spiritual fellowship would strengthen loyalty may well explain the timing of the whites' outreach to the Black population. Third, it appears that the enslaved community in the area had reached a point in its acculturation to a white-dominated society, where embracing Protestantism met many of their spiritual and earthly goals. These three factors caused the revolution in this church's membership and ushered in a new chapter in race relations in Welsh Neck.

By the time of the Revolutionary War, the Welsh Neck Church was a well-established and influential institution whose members included important local political leaders. It was founded in 1738 in what was then a frontier region, just opened up for white settlement.[2] The Pee Dee Valley offered good agricultural land and easy communications with the densely populated coast, and it was relatively secure from attack by Native Americans. The founders of the Welsh Neck Church were, indeed, of Welsh origin. The oldest members had left Wales for the Delaware Valley early in the eighteenth century.[3] The next generation was now looking for new lands in a colony that offered a broad toleration to Dissenters.[4] The Welsh Neck Church was one of the earliest Baptist churches in South Carolina, and it became a mother church for a cluster of smaller congregations in the Pee Dee region.[5] During the decades before the Revolution, it was probably the second most influential Baptist church in the colony, yielding in importance only to the church in Charleston. Welsh Neck belonged to the Regular branch of the Baptists, also called Particular Baptists; it adhered to strict Calvinist beliefs, believing that only a small proportion of humanity had been chosen for salvation and requiring all candidates for baptism to relate a personal experience of God's saving grace.[6] The church expected high moral standards from its members and regularly suspended or excommunicated those guilty of sinful behaviors, including sex outside marriage, traveling on the Sabbath, dancing, and drinking to excess. During the 1760s and early 1770s, there were between sixty and eighty members of the church. The church admitted new members infrequently, adding perhaps half a dozen new members per year to roughly balance the number who died or left the area. All members of the church were white.[7]

In the summer of 1779, the stable, all-white membership of the church changed suddenly. The pastor, Elhanan Winchester, who had served the church since 1775, began preaching in what he described as "a more open and general" style and sparked a revival. Over just a few months, one hundred thirty-nine new white members joined the church, more than doubling its size. During this same period, Winchester also began to evangelize the Black population of the area. He later published a detailed account of his first outreach to these Black men and women:

> About this time I began to find uncommon desires for the conversion and salvation of the poor negroes, who were very numerous in that part of the country; but whom none of my predecessors, that I could learn, had ever taken pains to instruct in the principles of Christianity; . . . [O]ne evening seeing a great many of them at the door of the house where I was preaching, I found myself constrained, as it were, to go to the door, and tell them, That Jesus Christ loved them, and died for them, as well as for us white people, and that they might come and believe in him, and welcome. And I gave them as warm and pressing an invitation as I could, to comply with the glorious gospel. This short discourse addressed immediately to them, took greater . . . effect than can well be imagined. There were about thirty from one plantation in the neighborhood present; (besides others). . . . From that very evening they began constantly to pray to the Lord, and so continued; and he was found of them. I continued to instruct them, and within three months of the first of June, I baptized more than thirty blacks belonging to that plantation, besides as many others, as in the whole made up one hundred . . . restoration.[8]

Winchester's description of his first—and very successful—attempt to evangelize enslaved Blacks formed part of a longer story about his journey from strict Calvinism to Universalist beliefs. Born in 1751 in Brookline, Massachusetts, Winchester was largely self-educated. As one of fifteen siblings, his family's financial resources were limited. His parents were New Lights, which is to say, they had adopted the "born-again" Christianity of the Great Awakening, which insisted that churches should only include those who had experienced the tangible working of God's grace in their hearts, indicating that they were chosen for eternal salvation. Winchester underwent this experience in 1769 and became a Baptist. His powerful preaching and knowledge of Scripture earned him a wide reputation in New England, but he was uncompromising in his Calvinist convictions that God had chosen only a small proportion of humanity for eternal bliss and that God's grace alone distinguished the saved from the damned. He fell out with his first congregation at Rehoboth, MA, because of their increasingly Arminian tendencies—their belief that individuals' own efforts to follow God's will could influence their salvation.[9] Winchester's reputation for strict Calvinism helped to secure his place as pastor at Welsh Neck in 1775.[10]

How did this uncompromising Calvinist become not just an Arminian, believing that people could, to some extent, earn their place in heaven, but a Universalist, convinced that God had decided to save all people? According to Winchester's own account, his journey to Universalism started in 1778 with a reading of Paul Siegvolck's *Everlasting Gospel.* Siegvolck's argument that God intended to save all of mankind, not just a tiny elect, intrigued but failed to convince Winchester. However, despite Winchester's intellectual rejection of Siegvolck, he found himself "much stirred up . . . to adopt [the] more open and general method of preaching" referenced in *The Universal Restoration.* Winchester pursued this new method "without considering any thing about its consistency with strict calvinism," following his heart instead of his brain. The success of his new preaching among both whites and Blacks moved him toward a more generous concept of salvation. By the end of the summer of 1779, he was "fully persuaded that the number of the finally saved would equal, if not exceed, the number of the lost." According to his later account, his outreach to the enslaved—and their enthusiastic response— was both an effect and a catalyst of his theological evolution.[11] Winchester traveled back to New England at the end of 1779 to visit family and friends. He intended to return to Welsh Neck, but his journey was delayed, in part by the British invasion of South Carolina and capture of Charleston in 1780. During his northern visit, further reading and reflection pushed him finally to the conclusion that a merciful God would not condemn anyone to hell. Winchester avowed his Universalism at the beginning of 1781 and thereafter became a leading figure in the Universalist movement both in the United States and Great Britain.[12]

Was it a pure coincidence that Winchester's shift to a less elitist view of salvation happened to coincide with the years of the Revolution? Numerous scholars have made convincing arguments that the Revolution's political upheaval often went hand-in-hand with democratic tendencies in religious thought and practice. Certainly, Winchester was not the only Calvinist in this period to abandon a narrow concept of the spiritually elect and to embrace Universalism.[13] It seems probable that the revolution in his ideas about salvation–a revolution that included the enslaved population as fellow children of God–derived from the idealism of the political Revolution that was taking place around him. Winchester's stress on the emotional, over the intellectual, motivation behind his outreach strongly suggests that the spirit of the era influenced him. Winchester's involvement in organizing an ecumenical meeting of Dissenting churches at the High Hills of Santee in 1776 provides a specific link between the political revolution and his theological development. With the Particular Baptists taking the lead, this meeting drafted the "Dissenters' Petition," which was presented to the South Carolina legislature in 1777, demanding that the special privileges of the Church of England be eliminated in the state's new constitution. Working toward a joint political statement of this kind with other Protestants whose theology and criteria for church membership differed radically from Welsh Neck's may have encouraged Winchester's evolving sense that others outside the Particular Baptist world were part of God's family.[14]

Of course, although Winchester was the prime mover in Welsh Neck's outreach to the Black community, he could not have changed the church's racial composition without the consent and support of the white congregation. Because the church "unanimously" renewed its call to Winchester to serve as their pastor at the start of July, after the first baptisms of enslaved Blacks, it seems clear that the congregation espoused his radical new initiative, at least at this early stage. Moreover, enslavers had to consent to the baptism of the enslaved, further suggesting the approval of white congregants. That Winchester found support from his congregation is clear. Less clear is why he found that support. Unlike Winchester, the congregation was not evolving from Calvinism to Universalism. The Welsh Neck Church retained a strict Calvinist creed long after the Revolution. What other factors might have prompted their acceptance of Winchester's transracial initiative?

There are no written accounts describing the views of any Welsh Neck church member about these first baptisms of local enslaved people, but Winchester's memoir provides suggestive details. The crucial statement in his story is that thirty or so enslaved people were standing outside the house where Winchester was preaching, on that day when he decided to reach out to them. Those people were enslaved by Colonel Alexander McIntosh, one of the wealthiest members of the Welsh Neck congregation. McIntosh must at least have given his permission for the enslaved to congregate where Winchester was preaching. Very possibly, he had encouraged or ordered them to attend. In fact, it was not the first time they had attended services in this manner. Church records demonstrated that almost a third of the enslaved ultimately baptized by Winchester belonged to McIntosh, who must, therefore, have been fully in agreement with the pastor in the decision to extend Christianity to the Black community. It may be that McIntosh, like other Americans at this time, was persuaded by the Revolution's rhetoric of freedom to look at his human possessions somewhat differently and to decide that their souls were worth saving. However, there was another possible motive behind his cooperation at this particular moment. At the end of 1778, the British had occupied Savannah, just over the South Carolina border. They used Savannah as a base to make forays into Lowcountry South Carolina throughout 1779, even briefly laying siege to Charleston.[15] During those expeditions, they invited enslaved men and women to join the British cause in return for freedom. This invitation was in accordance with the Philipsburg Proclamation issued in that year by General Henry Clinton, commander-in-chief of British forces in America, who made the freeing of enslaved people a general and permanent policy, rather than an *ad hoc* military tactic. By the end of the Revolution, thousands of enslaved people had accepted the call. In the summer of 1779, when Winchester's outreach to the Black population took place, Welsh Neck enslavers must have realized they could no longer take the enslaved's submission for granted.[16] There was some discussion among South Carolina's leaders of competing with the British for the loyalty of the enslaved by offering them freedom in return for military service, an idea urged by John Laurens, son of prominent planter–merchant Henry.[17] Most of the elite in South Carolina, however, were strongly opposed to the idea, and nothing came of it.[18] Still, the state's leaders recognized the need to counteract British inroads among the enslaved. McIntosh was not in the upper echelons of South Carolina's elite, but he was in its outer circles, rising rapidly through the officer ranks in the state's militia.[19] Courting the enslaved's loyalty by making them brothers and sisters in Christ was perhaps an alternative strategy for averting the mass defections that were occurring at that precise moment in South Carolina's Lowcountry.[20] Baptizing enslaved people for reasons of security was cynical, but it is possible that the pressures of war were mingled with more complex changes in attitudes: Perhaps McIntosh and other enslavers were more easily able to realize that there was a contradiction between their own fight for liberty and their willingness to hold others in bondage, now that enslaved people were potential collaborators with advancing British armies. The enslaved had become decision-making human beings, agents of change, instead of passive chattel.

Whatever the precise mixture of motives that impelled the Welsh Neck congregation to support their minister's evangelization of enslaved people, their efforts would have been in vain had it not been for the readiness of the enslaved converts to accept Christianity. While enslavers could compel their victims to act against their wills, Protestantism placed a great emphasis on the internal faith of the individual believer; conversion was not a simple matter of accepting baptism and submitting to the authority of the Church.[21] Of all Protestant denominations, strict Calvinists, like those of the Welsh Neck Church, were particularly concerned to ensure that all who were baptized not only be willing but also that they could demonstrate clear evidence of God's work on their hearts. A single insincere convert could pollute the purity of the congregation. A central preoccupation of church leaders, as recorded throughout the Welsh Neck Church Book, was to suspend or expel any members whose words or actions indicated that they were not among the spiritually elect. Winchester's criteria for what constituted strong evidence of divine election were perhaps becoming laxer than those of other Church members by 1779, but even so the enslaved people who came forward for baptism must have been willing agents to a significant extent, even if they were experiencing pressures of various kinds from their enslavers.

Winchester's account does emphasize the extraordinary willingness of that first group of Blacks he addressed to accept his invitation. After he had spoken with them, "these returned home, and did not even give sleep to their eyes, as they afterwards informed me, until they had settled every quarrel among themselves, and . . . had married every man to the woman with whom he lived; had restored whatever one had unjustly taken from another; and determined from that time to seek the Lord diligently."[22] Winchester's description of the slaves' reaction to his address suggests two points. First, they seemed already to know what would be required of them if they were to convert to Christianity. Winchester had delivered only a "short discourse" extending a welcome to the Christian faith, yet his audience immediately made some extensive and significant changes to their lives to qualify for baptism. As powerful and inviting as Winchester's preaching might have been, taking such momentous steps strongly suggests that these enslaved converts had been exposed to Christianity before and knew some of what the faith required, certainly in terms of marriage.[23] The most likely source of this knowledge would have been Baptist preachers of the Separate denomination who had been operating in South Carolina for over a decade. The Separate Baptists had emerged in Virginia during the later part of the Great Awakening and then moved south through the Piedmont of North Carolina into South Carolina during the 1750s and 1760s. The Separates, unlike the Regular or Particular Baptists of Welsh Neck, were not strict Calvinists, and they evangelized broadly, reaching out to poor whites and Blacks alike. Those enslaved by Macintosh may have learned about Christianity either directly from a traveling Separate preacher, or indirectly from other Blacks on the Separates' circuit. Whatever the source of the information, it seems clear that the slaves Winchester addressed on June 1, 1779, knew something about the white community's faith and perhaps had already discussed the idea of conversion. Their readiness to convert indicates that they had reached a particular point in the general process whereby the enslaved acculturated to their new American environment. People who had recently arrived from Africa were generally unreceptive to evangelical overtures, as earlier efforts in Lowcountry South Carolina had demonstrated.[24] Lack of English-language skills and strong attachments to African traditions were barriers to conversion. However, Africans who had lived in America for some years and their children who were born here were far more likely to understand white ways and were more willing to conform to them. It seems likely that the Black men and women who accepted Winchester's invitation so quickly had reached this stage in the acculturation process.[25]

The second point that can be gleaned from Winchester's memoir is that the enslaved individuals he addressed acted very much as a group. These Black men and women lived on the McIntosh plantation, and their joint action suggests a phenomenon seen widely in British America: Africans who lived on large plantations often recreated the kin and community groups they had been forced to leave behind by turning other enslaved people on the plantation into a surrogate clan. Those on smaller farms near the large plantations often attached themselves to the group identity of the larger enslaved community.[26] If McIntosh's slaves had, indeed, formed a surrogate kin group of this kind, then acceptance of a Christian identity would have been a group decision, rather than an act by multiple individuals. The first converts to join Welsh Neck, on June 27, 1779, were named Mingo, Plato, Stephen, Darion, and Leannah, all but the first enslaved by McIntosh.[27] It is very possible that one or more of these initial converts were recognized as community leaders on the McIntosh plantation, although there is no certainty that such was the case. Winchester's memoir and other relevant sources provide scant details about the internal social structure or culture of the Pee Dee plantations. However, the African sense of community, adapted to the plantation environment, seems visible in the documents, and it provided the momentum for the large numbers of conversions over a short period of time.

Winchester, in his account of the conversions, makes no mention of his new congregants' previous religious beliefs. As far as he was concerned, those beliefs belonged to the broad category of "heathenism," and the converts were simply leaving those errors behind. However, it is highly likely, given common patterns of slave conversions across the British colonies, that the new converts accepted membership in the Welsh Neck Church because they saw similarities between its practices and their own traditions. When brought to America, enslaved Africans did not abandon the faiths and cultures of their homelands, and those faiths varied.[28] A minority of the enslaved in South Carolina had been Muslim or Catholic, but most had subscribed to one of the many local, animist faiths of sub-Saharan Africa.[29] These faiths differed in many details but shared certain important features that enslaved Africans could recognize in Christianity. Among the Protestant denominations of British America, the evangelical sects and the Baptists were the groups that generally looked most familiar to them.

One important point of familiarity was the nature of evangelical gatherings for worship. As mentioned previously, the enslaved workers on the McIntosh plantation who responded enthusiastically to Winchester's preaching had probably already encountered traveling evangelical preachers who belonged to the Separate Baptists. These preachers often addressed crowds out of doors to reach communities far from churches. They were willing to preach to anyone, be they enslaved Blacks or impoverished whites. Because oral methods of propagating the faith took precedence over study of the Bible or other texts, evangelicalism could be highly effective at reaching people who were nonliterate or semiliterate.[30] Preaching was theatrical and emotional; listeners responded with groans, fainting fits, and even death-like loss of consciousness. People who recalled African religious practice or who had experienced versions of it in the American colonies would find much that they recognized. African worship in animist communities often involved spiritual possession, trances, and enactments of death and rebirth.[31] None of these Separate Baptists settled in the Welsh Neck region to create a permanent congregation. However, when Winchester changed his preaching style, any local enslaved people who had previously been attracted to Christianity through evangelical preaching could now connect with a local church in which they could seek membership.

In contrast to open-air meetings for proselytizing, normal Sunday worship at Welsh Neck was less emotional.[32] Still, Black men and women who decided to join Welsh Neck would find much that was familiar. First, joining the Church involved baptism by total immersion of the convert in a natural body of water, such as a river, a practice common in many African religions.[33] After baptism, new converts would have found themselves in a community that believed fervently in the miraculous. Many white Protestants, especially the wealthier and more educated, were influenced by the Enlightenment, which tended to deny or downplay God's intervention in a world dominated by predictable, measurable, mechanical forces. Welsh

Neck congregants, by contrast, still believed that the supernatural pervaded the earthly sphere. For example, Philip James, one of Winchester's predecessors as pastor at the church, had collapsed while mourning his recently deceased child. He was taken for dead, and his body was laid out next to the corpse of his offspring to be prepared for funeral rites. Suddenly, he awoke and told those gathered that his soul had left his body and journeyed toward heaven. There, a company of angels showed him his child's soul, happy in the afterlife, before bidding him return, for now, to his earthly frame.[34] Such stories of direct contact between ordinary human beings and supernatural powers would have been greeted with skepticism by many of the Charleston elite, brought up in the Church of England. The enslaved members of Welsh Neck, however, would have accepted the interaction of the spiritual and earthly spheres without difficulty, since such experiences were central to many African religions.

Many Black converts would have recognized other practices at Welsh Neck as well. It is important to recall that even Winchester, despite his more passionate preaching, had not abandoned his Calvinist beliefs when he first reached out to the Blacks gathered at the door. Certainly, the rest of his congregation remained firmly convinced that God had saved a tiny segment of the human population. The Welsh Neck congregation, therefore, paid close attention to signs that each member of its congregation had truly been chosen. This practice would also have been familiar to the enslaved converts. African communities commonly watched over the behavior of their members lest any of them break taboos that kept the whole group safe. Those who failed to keep to the rules were admonished, and repeat or serious offenders were expelled, just as happened at Welsh Neck.[35] Such careful sifting of the chosen from the damned would not have been a practice among the Separate Baptists, whose congregations were far less carefully defined. Winchester's "open" preaching, coupled with Welsh Neck's strict Calvinist theology, combined an accessible welcome to the enslaved with membership in a tight, spiritually privileged group.

Overall, the transformation of the Welsh Neck Church into a biracial community during the American Revolution resulted from a concatenation of circumstances. The logic of liberty—that white demands for rights should lead to recognition of enslaved people's humanity—seems to have been in play. However, without the military emergency created by the British invasion and the readiness of the Black community to convert in large numbers, the idealistic impulses of the Revolution would have been unlikely to have had so striking an effect.

The inclusion of Black members in 1779 was not a mere flash in the pan but had a long-term impact on Welsh Neck and other congregations in South Carolina. After the momentous events of that summer of 1779, Winchester took an extended leave of absence and never returned.[36] Soon after he left, the British occupied Charleston, and South Carolina descended into civil war. With the return of stability in 1782, Welsh Neck had to reorganize.[37] Welsh Neck remained a biracial church, even after the new pastor, Edmund Botsford, examined and rejected many of Winchester's converts, white as well as Black, whom the congregation felt had been admitted too hastily. Over the years, Botsford continued to add new enslaved Black as well as white converts. By the time Botsford left Welsh Neck for Georgetown in 1796, Blacks were a slight majority in the church. The biracial community thus survived the particular wartime circumstances that had created it.

Furthermore, Welsh Neck's inclusion of Black members had an impact beyond its local area. During the war, the Regular Baptist congregation in Charleston had been scattered. When peace returned, Botsford played a leading role in reconstituting the Charleston church. He included new Black members as well as former white members.[38] The change in race relations wrought by the Revolution at Welsh Neck thus spread to the most important Baptist church in South Carolina. The Welsh Neck and Charleston churches went on to influence beliefs and practices throughout the state, thanks to their prominent roles in the Charleston Association, a body with persuasive authority over many individual congregations.[39]

Of course, enslaved church members remained enslaved. In most essentials, the condition of the Black population had not changed even after admission to Welsh Neck or other Baptist churches. Had whites at Welsh Neck altered their views of the enslaved in any significant way? The whites' acceptance of certain Blacks' spiritual equality is worth emphasizing. Welsh Neck and the other Regular Baptist congregations with which it was associated continued to adhere to a very restricted, traditionally Calvinist view of salvation.[40] The inclusion of African and African-American members was, therefore, particularly significant, more so than in the case of evangelical sects in the South that had incorporated Black members between the 1760s and the end of the century. Evangelicals like the Separate Baptists and Methodists, who were avowedly or at least *de facto* Arminians, offered a salvation to Blacks that was widely on offer to all humans. The Calvinists of Welsh Neck and the Charleston Association offered their Black neighbors a very restricted privilege that elevated them, in spiritual terms, above the majority of the white community, who, they believed, were condemned to eternal torment. Inclusion among the spiritually elect might seem small compensation, given the continuation of slavery and all of its abuses, but to the members of these Regular Baptist congregations, there was no greater privilege than election to eternal life.

With regard to this world, there are some indications that Black membership in Welsh Neck impelled white owners to treat enslaved people more humanely. The revision to the Welsh Neck Church Covenant in 1785 imposed, for the first time, assorted duties on enslaving church members:

> We promise that if we should be possessed of negro or other slaves, that we will act a truly christian part by them; by giving them good advice, laying our commands on them to attend the worship of God in public on Lord's days & in private in our families when convenient & we also promise, that we will not treat them with cruelty, nor prevent their obtaining religious knowledge, & will endeavour to prevent their rambling: and will encourage those who can read, at proper times to instruct others; & in all things endeavour to act in our families, as to obtain the blessing of God.[41]

The commands in this covenant to act a "christian part" toward the enslaved, to provide them with what white members felt to be constructive guidance, and to abstain from what the white community regarded as "cruelty" represented an important extension of the Church's moral regulation into the private affairs of its white congregation. At no point before the Revolution had Church members been chastised for ill treatment of the enslaved. Among the practices entailed in the 1785 covenant, teaching enslaved people to read was an unusual, even daring, act, as was encouraging the enslaved to instruct others in their community, a practice consistent with allowing Black preaching on the plantations. A limited recognition of Black leadership in spreading God's word was thus embedded in this new covenant. Although the overall picture of race relations in this document is one of white paternalism, there was an improved recognition of Black humanity and agency. It is important to note that the commands laid on whites in this covenant not only affected those Black men and women who became full members of the Church, but also the wider group of people enslaved by Welsh Neck members.

The *Baptist Register* provides an interesting insight into the relationship between religion and race among Welsh Neck congregants after the Revolution. Reverend Botsford and others at Welsh Neck during the 1790s eagerly sought this biannual publication, compiled by the Reverend John Rippon of the Carter Lane Baptist church in London. The *Register* was relatively expensive: After trans-Atlantic postage, it cost five shillings an issue, yet leading members of Welsh Neck purchased three dozen subscriptions, even as they eschewed other books and published sermons.[42] The *Register* provided a forum where Baptists across the world could share information about the progress of the denomination and the exemplary lives of some of its practitioners. Articles came from Britain, Ireland, the United States, the British Caribbean, the Netherlands, France, Switzerland, Poland, Prussia, Russia, India, and Sierra Leone. Botsford contributed news items about Welsh Neck and other churches in South Carolina. The Welsh Neck readers of those three dozen subscriptions were able to envisage their backwoods church in the Pee Dee district as part of a vibrant, global "imagined community" of Baptists who were spreading the faith to ever-growing numbers.[43]

This global community was multiracial, with Black members sometimes holding leadership roles. The *Register* featured stories about Black pastors who were enjoying success in several places, such as Georgia, Nova Scotia, and Jamaica. These stories not only showed Blacks working alongside whites to spread God's word but presented these figures as complex individuals whose life stories invited an empathetic understanding of what it was like to be enslaved. For example, George Liele, who had been born into slavery in Virginia and then sold to an enslaver in Georgia, had experienced a deep sense of his sinfulness as a young man and became convinced that he was bound for hell after hearing the preaching of a Reverend Matthew Moore. An inpouring of God's grace to his heart then demonstrated that he was among the Chosen, and he was formally received into the Baptist faith. During the Revolutionary War, he was enslaved by a Loyalist, Henry Sharp, a deacon at the Reverend Moore's church. Sharp freed him before the British evacuation of Savannah, but Liele did not leave with the British and had to prove that he had been freed. Fortunately, he had the right documents and succeeded in avoiding re-enslavement. He then worked for two years as an indentured servant to earn freedom for his family. As a free man, he began preaching to the enslaved people on his plantation, using singing as an effective means of evangelization. He so impressed local Baptist leaders that he was sent to preach at other plantations and even addressed the white congregation on occasion. Liele and his family (at the time of publication of the article in the *Register*, he had a wife, three sons, and a daughter) then emigrated to Jamaica. There, he founded his own church and, after overcoming the hostility of the local white community, managed to convert about four hundred fifty people, including some whites, as part of a larger effort to spread the Baptist faith on the island. Like many born into slavery, Liele had no precise sense of his age but believed that he was around forty at the time he founded his ministry.[44] Stories like Liele's humanized enslaved Blacks and presented them to Welsh Neck readers as anything but passive chattel.

In addition to individual biographies of this kind, readers of the *Register* at Welsh Neck encountered a range of opinions about the compatibility of slavery and Baptist Christianity. Letters from Baptists in London and some of the northern states were openly critical of both the slave trade and slavery. For example, minutes of the Shaftesbury, NY, Baptist Association included an exhortation to prayer "for that auspicious day, when the Ethiopian, with all the human race, shall enjoy all that liberty due to every good citizen of the commonwealth; and the name of Slave be extirpated from the earth."[45] One of the Reverend Botsford's own contributions to the *Register* struck a different note, celebrating the fact that the "owners [of enslaved converts] begin to discover that their slaves are of increasing value to them when they become religious" though Botsford also went on to praise Virginia planter Robert Carter for freeing his enslaved people, stressing that Carter did so after leaving the Church of England for the Baptists. Rippon, the *Register*'s editor, added a statement from Carter that "the toleration of slavery indicates VERY GREAT DEPRAVITY of mind."[46] Although the *Register*'s contents were not unambiguously abolitionist, certainly Welsh Neck readers would have encountered regular antislavery statements in its pages.

Neither their reading of the *Register* nor the new church covenant, nor the fact that whites and Blacks worshiped in the same building meant that the white members of Welsh Neck had become ardent abolitionists or that they believed in racial equality. Black members of the church sat in a separate wing during services. The church covenant's exhortation to behave humanely only discouraged, but did not forbid, breaking up enslaved families by selling individuals far from home. At their best, whites' attitudes toward Black church members were patronizing. However, these limitations, serious as they were, should not obscure the fact that the Revolutionary War period had witnessed a significant improvement in the way that the whites of Welsh Neck looked at the Blacks in their community. Although that improvement stalled and then lost ground during the early nineteenth century, the Welsh Neck story should remind us that there were multiple possibilities in the development of race relations and that even the Lower South was not entirely immune from the logic of liberty unleashed by the Revolution.

John Barrington was born in New York City but grew up largely in Great Britain. He has been teaching at Furman University for close to thirty years. His focus is on the American Revolution, especially on its religious and trans-Atlantic aspects.

NOTES

1. Some of the research for this article was originally conducted for *Baptists in Colonial America*. Mercer University Press has graciously consented to the reuse of this material here.
2. Brackney, *Baptists in North America*, 16–17.
3. Dunaway, "Early Welsh Settlers of Pennsylvania," 251–54, 263–67.
4. *Dissenters* was a general term that included all Protestants who did not belong to the Church of England. The Church of England was the established, government-supported church in South Carolina, but other Protestant denominations were allowed to worship freely. For a history of Dissenting factions in America, see Young, *Dissent*.
5. Townsend, *South Carolina Baptists*, 62–63.
6. A key component of Calvinist theology was the idea of predestination: All humans were sinful and deserving of eternal punishment in hell, but God had decided to save a small number of people and grant them eternal joy in heaven. Those chosen for salvation had not earned it through their own efforts; God arbitrarily decided to save particular individuals to show how merciful He was. Those so chosen were then given the grace to conduct themselves decently (certainly not perfectly). A key point in Calvinism was that an individual's good behavior was the product, rather than the cause, of being chosen by God for eternal happiness. For a history of Calvinism and predestination, see McNeill, *The History and Character of Calvinism*.
7. Barrington, "The Welsh Neck Church Book," 9–29; henceforth "WNCB."
8. Winchester, *The Universal Restoration*, ix–x.
9. Arminians did not believe that anyone could earn eternal happiness entirely through their own efforts but taught that God had generously decreed a set of less-than-perfect standards for salvation that humans were capable of reaching by themselves. Arminians thus retained the Calvinist contention of a merciful God who saved the undeserving while creating scope for human free will. See Olson, *Arminian Theology*.
10. Stone, *Biography of Reverend Elhanan Winchester*, 13–25. The Charleston Baptist Association, of which Welsh Neck was a member, had in 1767 formally embraced the 1689 London Confession of Faith, placing the Regular or Particular Baptists of South Carolina firmly in the Calvinist camp. See Furman, *A History of the Charleston Association of Baptist Churches*, 1811.
11. Winchester, *Universal Restoration*, viii.
12. Stone, *Biography of Reverend Elhanan Winchester*, 126–46.
13. Stone, *Biography of Reverend Elhanan Winchester*, 77–80, 102–04; Lindman, "Bad Men and Angels from Hell," 261–62; Bressler, *The Universalist Movement in America*, 14–15.

14. "WNCB," 20; Townsend, *South Carolina Baptists*, 276–78.

15. This first siege was unsuccessful, as British General Augustine Prevost withdrew in the face of reinforcements from the Continental Army, under General Benjamin Lincoln. A second siege took place in the spring of the following year, when the British, under General Clinton, succeeded in capturing the city. See "The Siege of Charleston."

16. By the end of the war, one quarter of Lowcountry slaves had defected to the British. See Morgan, *Slave Counterpoint*, 283–85, 492–95, 666.

17. Henry Laurens served as the fifth president of the Continental Congress, from November 1777 to December 1778. See Kelly, "Henry Laurens," 82–123.

18. Massey, *John Laurens and the American Revolution*, 140.

19. McIntosh was one of the first major slaveholders of the Pee Dee region. He entered the South Carolina militia during the Regulator agitations of the 1760s and continued to serve during the Revolutionary War, rising to the rank of brigadier general. See Gregg. *History of the Old Cheraws*, 119–20, 289.

20. On a smaller scale, a similar reaction to a security threat from the enslaved had occurred back in 1739 and 1740. At the start of the War of Jenkins' Ear, Spain, ensconced in Florida, had invited South Carolina slaves to rise up in what became known as the Stono Rebellion and flee to San Agustín to support the Spanish cause in return for freedom. Alexander Garden, head of the Church of England in South Carolina, had responded by intensifying efforts to convert slaves and by establishing a school that provided a religious education to slaves whose owners consented. See Barrington, "Suppressing the Great Awakening," 5–10.

21. Sobel, *Trabelin' On*, 59–64; Frey and Wood, *Come Shouting to Zion*, 52–53.

22. Winchester, *Universal Restoration*, x.

23. Many of the enslaved in America retained versions of marriage customs in Africa, which often tolerated a series of short-term relationships as well as polygyny. Wood, *Slavery in Colonial America*, 48–51.

24. Even the great George Whitefield, who attracted crowds of up to twenty thousand during his 1739–40 preaching tour in the colonies, made little headway among the enslaved Blacks of South Carolina's Lowcountry, converting a mere twelve during his 1740 visit. His listeners likely spoke little English and were still wedded to the faiths of their homelands. See Raboteau, *Slave Religion*, 114–20.

25. Unfortunately, little information is available about the enslaved individuals who joined Welsh Neck. We do know the names of the first seventy-two Black converts, and the majority of those were Anglo or Classical names or the names of places in the English-speaking world, rather than African ones. Such evidence is inconclusive but suggests that these individuals were either born in America or had long been residents here. See Mullin, *Africa in America*, 22–27.

26. Sobel, *Trabelin' On*, 31–34.

27. "WNCB," 41.

28. Some scholars, notably Frazier in *The Negro Church in America* and Butler in *Awash in a Sea of Faith*, have argued that the traumatic removal of the enslaved from their home communities and the horrors of the voyage across the Atlantic shattered Africans' beliefs in the religions of their homelands, creating a

spiritual vacuum that could be filled by one version or another of Christianity. Other scholars, including Frey and Wood (*Shouting to Zion*) stress the ability of the enslaved to reconstitute their traditional faiths in America, despite the many challenges. Arguably, the reality was somewhere in the middle, with some elements of belief—those that depended on institutions or on specific locations back in Africa—being lost, whereas versions of others could be recreated in New World conditions. Raboteau (*Slave Religion*), Sobel (*Trabelin' On*), Mullin (*Africa in America*), and Morgan (*Slave Counterpoint*) espouse this middle ground.

29. See Thornton, "African Dimensions of the Stono Rebellion," 1101–13, for a discussion of the significant minority of Catholic slaves, mostly from the Kongo, where Portuguese missionaries had been active for two and a half centuries.

30. Raboteau, *Slave Religion*, 114–20; Frey and Wood, *Shouting to Zion*, 82–83.

31. Raboteau, *Slave Religion*, 131–35.

32. Although the standard religious service at Welsh Neck was more sedate, there were exceptions. After the war, Winchester's successor as pastor, Edmund Botsford, introduced revival meetings on a regular basis to recruit new members. It may be that he was influenced in this decision by the Black members of Welsh Neck; certainly, the revivals seem to have been more effective at recruiting new Black than new white members. See "WNCB," 62–63.

33. Sobel, *Trabelin' On*, 128–31, 139–40; Raboteau, *Slave Religion*, 43, 55–59.

34. Edwards, "Materials Towards a History of the Baptists," 19–20.

35. Sobel, *Trabelin' On*, 14–21, 82–83, 88.

36. "WNCB," 45.

37. Among the disruptions was the loss of leading church member Alexander McIntosh. He had been captured at the fall of Charleston in May 1780 and died later that year. See Gregg, *History of Old Cheraws*, 234, 236, 254, 256, 285.

38. "WNCB," 34.

39. Mallary, *Memoirs of Edmund Botsford*, 63–67; Rogers, *Richard Furman*, 54.

40. The renewed Church covenant adopted on June 18, 1785, made the traditional Calvinist beliefs of the reconstituted Welsh Neck Church very clear. See "WNCB," 55–57.

41. "WNCB," 56. By talking of "negro or other slaves," the Welsh Neck covenant was probably recognizing that some of the enslaved were Native American. About one quarter of those enslaved in South Carolina in 1700 were Native Americans, and the colony in its early years exported Indian slaves to the West Indies. The Native American slave trade, although dwarfed by the importation of slaves from Africa, continued through the eighteenth century, albeit at a reduced level, so that a significant minority of slaves were either Native American or mixed race. See Morgan, *Slave Counterpoint*, 481–85.

42. Letter from Edmund Botsford to Richard Furman, December 12, 1791, in Barrington, *Baptists in Early North America*, 87–88.

43. The concept of an "imagined community" was developed by Benedict Anderson to explain the origins of modern nationalism, but it works well for other types of community that existed in print, rather than as face-to-face groupings. See Anderson, *Imagined Communities*, 5–7.

44. Rippon, *The Baptist Annual Register for 1790, 1791, 1792, and part of 1793*, 332. Liele's evangelization work in Savannah resulted in two permanent Black congregations: First Bryan and First African Baptist.
45. Rippon, *The Baptist Annual Register for 1794, 1795, 1796–7*, 198.
46. Rippon, *Baptist Register, 1790, 1791, 1792, and part of 1793*, 105–7.

WORKS CITED

Anderson, Benedict. *Imagined Communities: Reflections on the Origin and Spread of Nationalism*. Verso Books, 1983.

Barrington, John P., ed. *Baptists in Colonial America*, Vol. V: *Welsh Neck, South Carolina*. Mercer University Press, 2018.

Barrington, John P. "Suppressing the Great Awakening: Alexander Garden's Use of Anti-Popery against George Whitefield." *Proceedings of the South Carolina Historical Association* (2003): 1–14.

Barrington, John P., ed. "The Welsh Neck Church Book." In *Baptists in Early North America*, vol. 5 of *Welsh Neck, South Carolina*. Mercer University, 2018.

Brackney, William H. *Baptists in North America*. Blackwell Publishing, 2006.

Bressler, Ann Lee. *The Universalist Movement in America, 1770–1880*. Oxford University Press, 2001.

Butler, Jon. *Awash in a Sea of Faith: Christianizing the African People*. Harvard University, 1990.

Dunaway, Wayland F. "Early Welsh Settlers of Pennsylvania," *Pennsylvania History: A Journal of Mid-Atlantic Studies* 12, no. 4 (1945): 251–69.

Edwards, Morgan. "Materials Towards a History of the Baptists in the Province of South-Carolina." Unpublished manuscript, N.D., typescript. Baptist Historical Collections Oversized. James B. Duke Library, Special Collections and Archives. Furman University.

Frazier, Edward Franklin. *The Negro Church in America*. Liverpool University Press, 1964.

Frey, Sylvia R., and Betty Wood. *Come Shouting to Zion: African American Protestantism in the American South and British Caribbean to 1830*. University of North Carolina, 1998.

Furman, Wood. *A History of the Charleston Association of Baptist Churches in the State of South Carolina*. Charleston, SC: J. Hoff, 1811.

Gregg, Alexander. *History of the Old Cheraws, Containing an Account of the Aborigines of the Pedee, the First White Settlements, Their Subsequent Progress, Civil Changes, the Struggle of the Revolution, and Growth of the Country Afterward, Extending from about A.D. 1730 to 1810. With notices of families and sketches of individuals*. The State Co., 1925.

Kelly, Joseph P. "Henry Laurens: The Southern Man of Conscience in History." *South Carolina Historical Magazine* 107, no. 2 (2006): 82–123.

Lindman, Janet Moore. "'Bad Men and Angels from Hell:' The Discourse of Universalism in Early National Philadelphia." *Journal of the Early Republic* 31, no. 2 (2011): 259–83.

Mallary, Charles Dutton. *Memoirs of Edmund Botsford*. Charleston, SC: W. Riley, 1832.

Massey, Gregory D. *John Laurens and the American Revolution*. University of South Carolina Press, 2000.

McNeill, J. T. *The History and Character of Calvinism*. Oxford University Press, 1967.

Morgan, Philip D. *Slave Counterpoint: Black Culture in the Eighteenth-Century Chesapeake and Lowcountry*. University of North Carolina Press, 1998.

Mullin, Michael. *Africa in America: Slave Acculturation and Resistance in the American South and the British Caribbean, 1736–1831*. University of Illinois Press, 1992.

Olson. Roger E. *Arminian Theology: Myths and Realities*. InterVarsity Press, 2009.

Raboteau, Albert J. *Slave Religion: The "Invisible Institution" in the Antebellum South*. Oxford University Press, 1978.

Rippon, John. *The Baptist Annual Register for 1790, 1791, 1792, and part of 1793. Including Sketches of the State of Religion Among Different Denominations of Good Men at Home and Abroad*. London: Dilly, Button, and Thomas, 1793. Reprint, *Eighteenth-Century Collections Online*. Gale Cengage Learning, 2003. https://www.gale.com/primary-sources/eighteenth-century-collections-online.

Rippon, John. "The Baptist Annual Register for 1794, 1795, 1796–7. Including Sketches of the State of Religion Among Different Denominations of Good Men at Home and Abroad." London: Dilly, Button, and Thomas, 1793. Reprint, *Eighteenth-Century Collections Online*. Gale Cengage Learning, 2003. https://www.gale.com/primary-sources/eighteenth-century-collections-online.

Rogers, James A. *Richard Furman: Life and Legacy*. Mercer University Press, 1985.

"Siege of Charleston." *The American Revolution in South Carolina*, 2021. http://www.carolana.com/SC/Revolution/revolution_siege_of_charleston.html.

Sobel, Mechel. *Trabelin' On: The Slave Journey to an Afro-Baptist Faith*. Greenwood Press, 1979.

Stone, Edwin Martin. *Biography of Reverend Elhanan Winchester*. Boston: H. B. Brewster, 1836.

Thornton, John K. "African Dimensions of the Stono Rebellion." *American Historical Review* 96, no. 4 (1991): 1101–13.

Townsend, Leah. *South Carolina Baptists, 1670–1805*. Florence Printing, 1935.

Winchester, Elhanan. *The Universal Restoration: Exhibited in Four Dialogues between a Minister and his Friend, Comprehending the Substance of Several Real Conversations which the Author Hath Had with Various Persons, Both in America and Europe, on that Interesting Subject, Chiefly Designed Fully to State, and Fairly to Answer the Most Common Objections that are Brought Against it from the Scriptures. The Second Edition, with Additions. By Elhanan Winchester. To this Edition is Prefixed, a Brief Account of the Means and Manner of the Author's Embracing These Sentiments, Intermixed with Some Sketches of His Life During Four Years*. Philadelphia, PA: T. Dobson, 1792.

Wood, Betty. *Slavery in Colonial America, 1619–1776*. Wayne State University Press, 1984.

Young, Ralph. *Dissent: The History of an American Idea*. New York University Press, 2015.

Presbyterianism, Slavery, and the Settlement of South Carolina's Pee Dee Region

Erica Johnson

Presbyterians were among the first Europeans to settle in South Carolina's Pee Dee region in the 1700s. The Pee Dee consists of twelve counties stretching from the vast pines of the Sandhills to the shores of the Outer Coastal Plain. The region is defined by its rivers—the Great Pee Dee, the Little Pee Dee, and the Waccamaw—its vast pine forests and farms of the interior, and the tourist hotspots along the coast. The region got its name from the Pee Dee Indians, one of at least seven Indigenous tribes that lived in the area before European colonization. After the Interregnum and Restoration in England, King Charles II established the Carolinas, and the proprietors charged with populating the colonies used the promise of religious freedom and land as enticements. Scots–Irish Presbyterians acquired land in the Pee Dee, and they established plantations worked by enslaved laborers. These settlers also founded Presbyterian churches, including Aimwell, Hopewell, Indiantown, Salem, and Williamsburg.[1] For more than a century, the ministers at these churches helped to establish, reinforce, and sometimes reconcile the Presbyterian stance on slavery and the interests of local enslavers. The enslaved peoples who attended these churches in the Pee Dee experienced Presbyterianism as a part of the institution of slavery. This article is about them.

Although scholars have explored the relationship between slavery and Presbyterianism, the historiography has yet to center on the enslaved and their perspectives. White Presbyterians have led the efforts to examine the church's connections to slavery, often misrepresenting the experiences of the enslaved. In 1966, for example, Presbyterian minister Andrew E. Murray glorified white Christianity in his extensive study, writing, "unlike his white counterpart, who had been nurtured in the Christianized culture of Europe, the American negro came out of a non-Christian culture of Africa."[2] Quite the contrary! Historians studying African history have shown that a majority of African societies involved in the Atlantic trade in human beings had been exposed to and even adopted Christianity.[3] Murray's broad claims evidence a disregard of accurate Black history. Other scholars have explored how American Presbyterians reconciled revolutionary and republican ide-ologies with slavery, concentrating primarily on antislavery Presbyterian clergy, such as Samuel Davies.[4] In more recent years, authors have started to highlight how Princeton University benefited from Presbyterianism's ties to slavery.[5] Although these studies provide significant contributions to the his-toriography of Presbyterianism and slavery, the authors similarly omit the perspectives of the enslaved in these histories. This article seeks to empha-size their voices and begin to rectify their historiographical silence.

Various methodologies help to recover enslaved experiences despite limited sources. Ethnohistory combines historical and anthropological approaches to preliterate groups, including the enslaved. Enslaved peoples living in the Pee Dee did not leave written records of their lives, religious or otherwise. There are no diaries or letters.[6] However, four individuals enslaved in the Pee Dee during the nineteenth century recounted their experiences within the Hopewell Presbyterian Church to interviewers who were part of the Federal Writers' Project in the 1930s.[7] Using methodology from ethnohistory, I am able to "upstream" from these later accounts to make inferences about how enslaved peoples from the late eighteenth cen-tury and throughout the nineteenth century experienced Presbyterianism.[8] Upstreaming involves "explaining the unknown from the known, hence the past from the present."[9] In this case, I use the available oral histories from formerly enslaved peoples in the 1930s to understand the experiences of enslaved peoples between the 1770s and the 1860s. I contextualize these accounts with other primary sources available for the Pee Dee in the eigh-teenth and nineteenth centuries.

Although enslaved peoples left no written and limited oral accounts, white South Carolinians created numerous records related to slavery and Presbyterianism. Presbyteries, synods, ministers, legislators, and enslav-ers in the late eighteenth century and early nineteenth century published many sources. I have read against the grain of these documents to glimpse the encounters of the enslaved with the religion and its white practitioners.[10] Social theorist Walter Benjamin claimed, "there is no document of civiliza-tion which is not at the same time a document of barbarism. And just as such a document is not free of barbarism, barbarism taints also the man-ner in which it was transmitted from one owner to another."[11] Therefore, he urged historians to "brush history against the grain."[12] In other words, historians are to separate the history within the source from the "barba-rism" of the author. The author was often the assumed "victor" in the story.[13] Indeed, until the American Civil War and the ratification of the Thirteenth

Amendment, the enslavers were the victors in the Pee Dee's history. In this way, I read against the grain of the white sources, against the authors' primary intentions, to grasp all the perspectives within a document, even those of the enslaved.

During the early years of South Carolina settlement, there was tension between Presbyterian enslavers and the Church of England, also known as the Anglican Church. The missionary arm of the Church of England, the Society for the Propagation of the Gospel, proposed converting the growing enslaved population in British American colonies, including South Carolina. Enslavers in South Carolina quickly rebuffed their efforts.[14] Although the enslavers may have been opposed to providing Christian instruction to the enslaved people of South Carolina in the early years of settlement, they also bucked such interference by Anglicans specifically. Presbyterianism originated in the Puritan movement that challenged the Church of England for much of the seventeenth century. Whereas the Anglican Church relied on a hierarchical governance structure, the Presbyterians favored a more democratic form of church governance. This disagreement came to a head during the English Civil War (1642–1652) and Interregnum (1649–1660). When Charles II regained the monarchy in 1660, he embraced the Church of England and its episcopal system, and Presbyterians looked to the Carolinas as a place to freely practice and govern their religion as well as develop plantation agriculture.[15] The imposition of Anglicanism upon the enslaved would have been especially unwelcome.

Notably, Presbyterians continued to embrace democratic principles within religious and political structures but did not extend them to the system of slavery. Ministers and elders of Hopewell Presbyterian Church were active patriots during the American Revolution, fighting for freedom from British hierarchal rule. For instance, James Gregg was a founder and elder of Hopewell. He served as a military captain and provided horses, saddles, and bridles for American forces.[16] British forces burned his home and destroyed much of his property.[17] However, after the war, Gregg obtained over one thousand acres of land, and, according to the 1790 census, enslaved sixteen people.[18] Another Revolutionary War veteran, Reverend Humphrey Hunter, was the first full-time pastor at Hopewell, taking up the call in April 1790. He came to North America by way of Charleston at age four in 1759, and he grew up in Mecklenburg, North Carolina. He was present for the Mecklenburg convention in 1775, which people from that region call "the first American Declaration of Independence."[19] The Mecklenburg Declaration of Independence claimed the British crown had "wantonly trampled" the "rights and liberties" of American colonists and "inhumanly shed the innocent blood of Americans." Its authors declared themselves "a free and independent people . . . a sovereign and self-governing people under the power of God and the general Congress; to the maintenance of which independence we solemnly pledge to each other our mutual co-operation, our lives, our fortunes, and our most sacred honor."[20] This document scorned the British crown for trampling their rights—those of white, propertied men—while they did the same to the people they enslaved. During his five years ministering at Hopewell, Hunter led a congregation of enslavers, despite having fought in a war for liberty against the English. South Carolina Presbyterians, like those at Hopewell, fought for democratic governance religiously and politically, but only for white people.

There are two main governing bodies within Presbyterianism, the presbytery and the synod.[21] A presbytery consists of ministers (known as teaching elders) and elected laymen (known as ruling elders) from churches within an outlined spiritual jurisdiction. The primary role of each presbytery was to ensure that its churches have ministers. In the eighteenth century, the Carolinas were part of the Presbytery of Hanover and then the Presbytery of Orange. South Carolina founded its own presbytery in 1785.[22] The Presbytery of South Carolina divided into the First and Second Presbyteries of South Carolina in 1799, and Hopewell became a member of the First Presbytery. In 1810, Hopewell joined the newly formed Harmony Presbytery.[23]

A synod is a Presbyterian council that meets to decide matters of doctrine, administration, and discipline. Like the presbytery, it consists of elected ministers and elders. Synods approve the creation of new presbyteries and make doctrinal decisions, such as the church's stance on slavery. The Synod of the Carolinas formed in 1788.[24] Neither presbyteries nor synods in South Carolina included free or enslaved Black members. Presbyterian ideals of religious liberty and democratic governance conflicted with the realities of the plantation hierarchy based on race and subjugation.

Many white Presbyterian settlers in the Pee Dee–owned plantations worked by enslaved laborers. Immigrants to South Carolina from Barbados brought experience and knowledge of how to run a society based on slavery.[25] South Carolina, in fact, adopted the *Negro Act of 1740*, which was almost identical to the one enacted in Barbados nearly a century earlier. It remained in place through the American Revolution, and the legislature for the new state of South Carolina recodified it in the late eighteenth century.[26] Although the code focused primarily on prohibitions and punishments for the enslaved, Article Twenty-Two referenced the religious lives of the enslaved. The article did not require enslavers to provide Christian instruction, but it forbade enslavers from working enslaved individuals on Sundays. Of course, there was an exception for "works of absolute necessity and the necessary occasions of the family."[27] Enslavers, undoubtedly, may not have observed the law or felt any obligation to take those whom they enslaved to church. However, accounts from the formerly enslaved suggest that many white Presbyterians did so in the Pee Dee.[28]

Narratives provided by formerly enslaved individuals living in Marion, South Carolina, which is in the Pee Dee, shed light on their perceptions of their enslavers and the Hopewell Presbyterian Church. When talking about Hopewell, Mom Sara Brown remarked, "Dat a slavery church."[29] Similarly, Mom Ryer Emmanuel described Hopewell as "dat sho a old, old slavery time church."[30] Both women associated the church with the institution of slavery first and foremost. They did not suggest that it was just a church that white people attended. Instead, they suggested that the church was a pillar in the institution of slavery. In addition, they each mentioned the cemetery at the church. Emmanuel noted, "Dat dey slavery graveyard settin right dere in front de church," and Brown explained, "Oh, my Lord, dere a big slavery graveyard dere at Hopewell Church."[31] Brown and Emmanuel remembered those buried there for their roles in a society centered on slavery. Although not everyone buried in the cemetery was an enslaver, connecting the cemetery to slavery suggests a perceived white racial unity in the region.[32] For the formerly enslaved, the church and cemetery reflected the racial hierarchies of Pee Dee society.

The enslaved were not the only ones who connected those buried at the cemetery to slavery. Intriguingly, one of the earliest markers still visible in the Hopewell cemetery is that of Elizabeth Gregg. The men of the Gregg family, including her husband James, were founders of Hopewell as well as enslavers on nearby plantations.[33] Buried in 1799, Elizabeth's marker states that she was "a humane and benevolent Mistress to those under her care and a devout Christian."[34] The family did not deny her role as an enslaver, instead focusing on her kindness and religion. This reflects Article Thirty-Seven of the *Negro Act of 1740*, as it stated, "Cruelty is not only highly unbecoming those who profess themselves Christians but is odious in the eyes of all men who have any sense of virtue and humanity." It is important, however, to clarify what the law deemed as cruelty. Of course, the law forbade murder. Cutting out the tongue, putting out an eye, castration, scalding, burning, and depriving of a limb were also punishable with a fine. However, "whipping or beating with a horsewhip, cowskin, switch or small stick" was acceptable.[35]

This is not to suggest that Elizabeth Gregg did these things, but she would have been within her legal and religious rights if she had and might still have been considered benevolent by her family and congregation.

It is highly likely that some of those buried in the Hopewell cemetery physically punished the people they enslaved. Charlie Grant recalled how the overseer on his enslaver's plantation whipped the enslaved: "De overseer, he pretty rough sometimes. . . . Had to go to work fore daybreak en if dey didn' be dere on time en work like de out to, de overseer so whip dem. Tie de slaves clear de ground by dey thumbs wid nigger cord en make dem tiptoe en draw it tight as could be. Pull clothes off dem fore tie dem up. Dey didn' care nothin about it. Let everybody look at it."[36] The enslavers humiliated African-descended peoples by removing the enslaved person's clothing before whipping them and putting them on display for others to see. Grant also explained that his mother had been whipped, but no men had whipped him. However, women had whipped him "wid four plaitted raw cowhide whip."[37] Grant did not name anyone who whipped the enslaved, so we cannot be certain any of them attended Hopewell. Washington Dozier recounted hearing about enslaved people running away because of "bad treatment." When captured, they were tortured: "[D]ey'ud buff em en gag em en hoss whip em." However, he stated that his enslaver, Wiles Gregg, did not punish those enslaved along with him.[38] Whether the enslaved suffered whippings or worse at the hands of their enslavers and white overseers or just heard about these actions, the memories associated the church's "slavery graveyard" and its interred white Christians with systematic abuse.

Many of the formerly enslaved described funerals for enslaved individuals, shedding further light on their associating the church cemetery with enslavers and slavery. Significantly, none of the accounts indicates that the enslaved received a Christian burial near the church. Dozier recounted how funerals for the enslaved were like those after slavery, except they "ne'er hab no preacher 'bout."[39] This was likely because they typically had to bury enslaved individuals after dark. Emmanuel explained how the enslaved "'couldn' bury dem in de day cause dey wouldn' have time.'"[40] If they had wanted a proper Christian funeral, the enslavers denied the enslaved that opportunity, prioritizing work during the day. On the other hand, it is possible that the enslaved did not want a Christian burial, and the nighttime burials afforded them privacy and agency in burying their dead, perhaps even observing customs preserved through the African diaspora.[41]

For the enslaved, Presbyterianism may have appeared to be more an instrument of oppression than a spiritual community. From a modern perspective, it appears to be a deeply flawed, even hypocritical institution, one predicated on liberty but complicit in cruelty and domination. These dynamics become especially evident in the church's theological tracts. Presbyterian ministers offered guidance on how enslavers should provide Christian instruction to the enslaved. In 1787, North Carolina Presbyterian Reverend Henry Pattillo wrote *The Plain Planter's Family Assistant,* which claimed that enslavers likely felt "a kind of brotherly or paternal affection" for enslaved people and that "the slaves of my *Plain Planter,* are among the happiest human beings."[42] A charitable reading of Pattillo's work might suggest that he used the rhetorical technique of *paraenesis*—advice through praise. In other words, he encouraged good treatment of the enslaved by praising enslavers for already providing it. A closer reading of the text, however, suggests that he was more focused on defending slavery and easing the consciences of those engaged in its horrors. Writing just after the American Revolution, he blamed the British for starting slavery, absolving Americans for continuing it. He commended enslavers for their patience in managing enslaved people because of their "real, or pretended ignorance; their obstinacy, and laziness; their endeavors to evade, or flight their work, under his eye; the universal practice of lying, to conceal or lessen their offenses; their provoking or petulant answers, when reproved, or moderately corrected; with a countless train of other faults and deficiencies."[43] He attributed these perceived negative characteristics and behaviors to the coming from "the unenlightened regions of *Africa.*"[44] Pattillo believed that religious instruction could deliver the enslaved from these supposed flaws and to not teach them about Christianity would be "a great national evil."[45] Pattillo encouraged enslavers to also serve as an example to the enslaved of good Christians. He suggested that the children of enslavers teach the enslaved to prevent "the Negroes" from "corrupting" the white children.[46] Because both Carolinas belonged to the same synod, it is likely that enslavers in the Pee Dee region of South Carolina utilized Pattillo's guide. Religious instruction, for theologians such as Pattillo, becomes a means of reinforcing toxic racial stereotypes and diminishing white complicity in an evil practice.

In addition to the extensive explanation and justification for teaching enslaved peoples about Christianity, *The Plain Planter's Family Assistant* also provided a catechism and prayer for the enslaved. Pattillo's "The Negroes Catechism" asked, "How can you be free and bound both?" The expected answer was: "If Jesus Christ has broke the chain of sin, and freed me from the curse of the law, and the slavery of the devil, I am free indeed, although my body and services may be at the command of another."[47] Pattillo and

Presbyterian enslavers expected the enslaved to reconcile their spiritual freedom through God with their lived enslavement. Christianity, in fact, became a defense for their persecution. The forty-eighth question of the catechism asked, "Is there the same heaven and hell for white and black?" The answer was: "Yes: there will be no difference there, but what more holiness or more sin makes."[48] For the enslaved, this may have offered some hope through faith that racial slavery ended after death, but it also suggests that obedience will lead to eternal salvation. Enslavement was a price to pay for redemption. The "Prayer for Negroes" continued these sentiments:

> O Thou great God, the Maker and Lord of all creatures, I, a poor sinner, black in body, and full blacker with sin, would humbly try to worship thee . . . and make the land of my slavery, the place of my true freedom. Lord pity the poor Negroes, that are living without God in the world, and turn and convert them to thee. Bless my master, and all that are his. Make me a faithful servant; and teach me to remember, that what good thing forever any man doth; the same shall receive of the Lord, whether he bound or free.[49]

In the prayer, "true freedom" would come through faith in God. The catechism and prayer sought to reinforce slavery through Presbyterianism, even implying that God was the ultimate enslaver, an idea found in the Apostle Paul's claim that the saved, having been "made free from sin" become the "servants of righteousness."[50] An African-descended person, the prayer suggests, could enjoy their freedom in the next world, only by sacrificing it in this world.

Accounts of the formerly enslaved also provide glimpses into their experiences with Presbyterian teachings. For instance, Emmanuel stated that her enslaver, Anthony Ross made the enslaved go "to preachin every Sunday en dey was mighty strict about us gwine to prayer service, too."[51] This does not mean that Emmanuel did not embrace Presbyterianism or Christianity more broadly, just that she had no choice as to where to attend. However, she explained that her enslaver told all the enslaved on his land to "carry dey chillum up dere en get dem baptized."[52] The enslaver ordered the adults to have their children baptized, regardless of their beliefs. Grant recounted how his enslaver's daughter, Lizzie Johnson, had a "catechism what dey teach," where she asked him repeatedly who made him until he answered God (instead of his parents), with the threat that if he "didn't change" his "chat," the enslaver would whip him.[53] The first two questions of Pattillo's

"The Negroes Catechism" allude to Grant's experiences with Johnson. The first question read: "Do you know who made the Negroes?" The second question continued: "Do you think white folks and negroes all come from one father?"[54] In both scripted responses, the enslaved person was to refer to God as the creator of everyone. However, Pattillo did not suggest whipping or threatening to whip an enslaved person for not properly reciting the catechism, as Johnson did. This suggests a level of coercion in the conversion of enslaved peoples. The enslaved experienced Presbyterian teachings through the physical and psychological brutality of enslavement.

Enslaved people in the Pee Dee also experienced Christianity outside of the church and away from enslavers. Dozier, for example, recalled a "spiritual hymn" that angels sang to him in his "slumberin' hours," so that he "might gi'e it to de libin' heah on dis earth."[55] He explained that angels communicated with him directly in his dreams, so he could share their messages with others when he woke. It was about Revelation 10:2.[56] The angels sang, "Chillun, wha' yuh gwinna do in de judgment mornin' when old Gable [Gabriel] go down on de seashores? He gwinna place one foot in de sea end de udder on de land, en declare tha' time would be no more."[57] The song is about the end of times and God's Day of Judgment. The angel Gabriel would come to earth and stop time. The angels were questioning whether Dozier and those around him would be ready for God's judgment and their eternal fate: Were they right with God? Dozier received this message from the angels, not a minister or child catechist. He also perceived himself as a catechist or lay minister, as he was not allowed to become an elder or ordained minister. His account suggests that enslaved people fellowshipped together as Christians outside of the church. Despite being enslaved by a member of Hopewell Presbyterian Church, Dozier experienced Christian faith on his own terms, and there were likely many others like him.

Formerly enslaved people also gave accounts of their experiences attending Hopewell Church. For instance, they recounted wearing special clothing for services. Emmanuel recalled her baptism and how "oh, my happy, dey been fix us up dat day." She got to wear "clean homespuns en long drawers" and a new bonnet."[58] Similarly, Grant reminisced about his enslaver giving them a "cotton suit to wear on Sunday en de nicest leather shoes dat dey make right dere at home."[59] Church afforded the enslaved access to nicer garments. Despite wearing their "Sunday best," enslaved people had to sit in a segregated upper gallery during services for the most part. Emmanuel, Grant, and Dozier mentioned having to sit up in the gallery.[60] However, Brown noted that she sat right beside her female enslaver on a "lil chair wid a cowhide bottom."[61] It is possible that Brown's enslaver kept her with them during church in case they needed her assistance. On the other hand, Brown was only around eight years old, and she may not have had other enslaved family members to attend to her behavior during services. Last, Brown's enslaver could have favored her, as she noted elsewhere in her narrative that her enslaver had her learning to be a nurse from a local doctor and lived in the house "wid her all de time."[62] These accounts, once again, show how these individuals perceived Hopewell as a part of their enslavement.

In addition to the accounts from these enslaved individuals, some religious leaders in the Pee Dee published sermons that enslaved people likely heard. Reverend Thomas Reese is one example. Although he was the official minister at Salem Presbyterian Church, he also preached at Hopewell numerous times in the 1780s and delivered the ordination sermon for Hopewell's first full-time minister, Reverend Hunter, in 1790. Reese was also a charter member of the Presbytery of South Carolina. Most significantly for this study, he was involved a debate with Reverend W. C. Davis about slavery and Presbyterianism in the mid-1790s. Davis denounced slavery and called out enslavers, whereas Reese defended the institution. Reese maintained that slavery was a "local custom" that did not threaten society's overall moral order.[63] The Presbytery of South Carolina and Synod of the Carolinas chose to adopt "a policy of pulpit silence concerning emancipation."[64] It is with this in mind, as well as the fact that Reese enslaved people himself, that I read against the grain of his sermons to understand how the enslaved might have received his teachings.[65]

One of Reese's sermons, "Death the Christian's Gain" is particularly relevant here considering the accounts of the enslaved about funerals and the Hopewell cemetery. Using words from the Apostle Paul, he explained how Christians should comfort themselves in knowing that death would deliver them from sin. He stated, "He is then freed, fully and completely freed, from all the remains of sin."[66] He clarified that all people have sinned, and he repeated the word *free* half a dozen times throughout the sermon. In another place, he noted how in death the Christian could "rest from his labors and be free from all distress and tribulation. In the blessed state, he shall no longer be subject to pain, sickness or disease."[67] This message must have resonated with the enslaved as they labored most days on plantations. The idea of living an eternity free from forced labor and the physical hardships that came with it would have likely offered some hope for the enslaved. Several lines later, Reese exclaimed, "O what a happy exchange does the poor, afflicted, persecuted Christian make, when released from his house of clay! . . . from bondage to freedom!"[68] These words would have meant something completely different to a free white person than to an enslaved Black person. Like Patillo, Reese hoped to justify the suffering of the enslaved by positing that affliction and persecution are intrinsic to the Christian experience, necessary preconditions for salvation. Suffering was cosmic design, not earthly oppression.

Reese also published a sermon about Haman and Mordecai from the Old Testament story of Esther.[69] An official under the Persian king, Haman was full of pride and expected everyone to bow to him, much like enslavers required of peoples of African descent. However, in the story, a Jewish man named Mordecai refused to bow to Haman. Filled with anger, Haman asked the Persian king to kill thousands of Jews, not knowing that Queen Esther was also a Jew. In the end, Haman is hanged on the gallows intended for Mordecai. At the conclusion of the sermon, Reese declared, "Mordecai in a state of poverty and captivity, enjoyed more genuine satisfaction and tranquility of mind, than Haman in the midst of all his riches and honors."[70] Perhaps white Presbyterians saw Mordecai as themselves and Haman as King George III's ministers George Grenville and William Pitt.[71] To his enslaved listeners, Reese undoubtedly hoped to communicate that their positions of poverty and captivity were happier than those of their enslavers, once again using Christianity to support slavery. Reese reinforced this idea when he added, "reprobates all the malignant passions, and inculcates a benevolent, meek, gentle, and forgiving spirit," and "the command and example of our Redeemer, not only to love our friends, but even our enemies."[72] Although white colonists fought against the English for their independence, Reese's words encouraged trusting God, remaining peaceful, and being forgiving. Enslaved peoples, however, likely saw themselves in Mordecai and the plantation overseers in Haman.

Reese addressed his farewell sermon to the Aimwell, Hopewell, Indiantown, Salem, and Williamsburg churches, all of which had white and Black congregants. Toward the middle of the sermon, Reese delved into the issue of religious liberty in "an age of revolutions."[73] While highlighting the importance of freedom of religion, as Presbyterians had broken away from the Anglican Church, he also cautioned the congregants against quickly accepting new sects or doctrines. He wrote this sermon just before the beginning of the Second Great Awakening and during a time when revivalists such as Methodists and Baptists had begun to move into the South and increasingly more religious leaders throughout the United States were advocating for abolition.[74] Even within South Carolina, Presbyterian Reverend

James Gilliland's opposition to slavery led the Synod of the Carolinas to intervene. The Synod would only ordain him if he agreed not to speak publicly on the issue. He attempted to honor the Synod's ruling for a brief time, but he eventually moved to Ohio where he could freely advocate for the end of slavery.[75] Although enslaved peoples may not have known about the inner religious politics, they would have been aware of abolitionist religious leaders.[76] Peoples of African descent may have seen Reese's warnings as worth consideration so as to not be filled with false hope. On the other hand, his sermon may have sounded like a desperate appeal by an enslaver to try to perpetuate the idea of Christian slavery.

There were divisions in Presbyterianism over slavery, and Southerners protected the institution through their churches. In 1818, the General Assembly of the Presbyterian Church issued a statement on slavery that represented a compromise: It condemned slavery as immoral without damning enslavers or calling for immediate abolition. The statement acknowledged how slavery violated God's law while not calling enslavers sinners. The church vowed to promote more humane treatment of enslaved peoples and gradual abolition.[77] However, the church did not portray African-descended peoples as equal to white people and called for the relocation of formerly enslaved peoples to Africa by means of colonization societies.[78] The statement in 1818 was an effort to keep the church unified, but it did not last. In 1837, the church divided itself into the New School and the Old School. Although not all members of the New School were abolitionists, it was predominantly Northern and Midwestern. Southerners gravitated toward the Old School.[79] Joseph Brown became the minister of Hopewell in 1838, and he served there until his passing in 1859.[80] According to the 1850 census, Reverend Brown enslaved nineteen people.[81] It is likely that Brown included the people he enslaved in the church's numbers of Black congregants during his twenty-one year tenure as minister at Hopewell. According to church records of congregants, there were one hundred fifteen white and one hundred thirty-nine Black congregants in 1841; one hundred twenty-six white and forty-six Black congregants in 1849; and one hundred and twenty white and one hundred Black congregants in 1852.[82] Having an enslaver as head of the church was sure to keep Presbyterianism and slavery intertwined in the area.

The Presbyterian Church included enslaved peoples in their numbers of congregants in the 1850s, but the church assumed membership through a Presbyterian enslaver. In an 1852 report, Reverend John Robinson provided numbers as well as his logic in calculating them. He claimed that members of the Presbyterian Church likely enslaved around seventy thousand people.

He did not assert that all members of the church were enslavers; instead, he believed that "one-third of the ministers, and one-half of the members of the Church, who are heads of families, own slaves."[83] He determined that Presbyterians enslaved approximately thirty thousand adults in the South, and over twenty percent of those enslaved adults were "professors of religion." He listed Hopewell's sister churches—Salem, Indiantown, and Williamsburg—as having more Black congregants than white.[84] Hopewell reported having one hundred twenty white and one hundred Black members in 1858, one year before Reverend Brown died.[85] Robinson and the Pee Dee's Presbyterian churches assumed that an enslaved person accompanying an enslaver to church meant the enslaved person had adopted the religion and accepted membership in the church. However, he neglected to acknowledge that enslaved people would not have had a choice in attendance or baptism. This is not to deny their agency in professing a religion, but it highlights that going to church was a part of their enslavement.

Presbyterian churches in the Pee Dee supported the Confederacy during the American Civil War. In 1861, members of the Old School in Southern states broke away from the rest of Presbyterians in the United States, and they formed the Presbyterian Church of the Confederate States of America.[86] Dozier recounted attending Hopewell with his enslaver Wiles Gregg while David Ethan Frierson preached there.[87] Frierson served Hopewell during the American Civil War and Reconstruction (1859–1871), and he made contributions to the Confederate war effort through the South Carolina Tract Society.[88] Although he did not publish any of his sermons, they likely reflected the numerous religious pamphlets the society published during the war. One such pamphlet, *An Appeal to Young Soldiers*, suggested, "This war is waged for the establishment of Truth, Justice, and Mercy—for the rescue of the gracious King's subjects from the tyranny of a cruel oppressor, who seeks to delude them into serving him—and if they do not leave him, he will lead them into a place where they will be tortured for ever and ever."[89] The author continued, "Will you resign yourself to 'everlasting chains and slavery,' when the great 'Captain of our salvation' is willing to admit to you 'the glorious liberty of the children of God?'"[90] With unintentional irony, the pamphlet uses the metaphor of slavery as well as the threat of eternal damnation to encourage Confederates to fight against the Union. Although white Confederates, including those in the Pee Dee, were making claims that the North would oppress and enslave them, they were doing just that to the African-descended peoples who attended Presbyterian churches with them and whom they claimed as fellow congregants.

There are numerous men and women buried at Hopewell Presbyterian Church Cemetery who aided and fought for the Confederacy. There are as many as thirty-eight Confederate soldiers buried in the Hopewell cemetery. One of those was Anthony Ross, Mom Ryer Emmanuel's enslaver.[91] Another Confederate soldier buried there is Wilds Gregg, Washington Dozier's enslaver.[92] There are fourteen other Gregg men who fought for the Confederacy buried alongside him. Even the founder of Florence, General William Wallace Harllee, signatory of the South Carolina Ordinance of Secession, rests in the Hopewell cemetery.[93] For enslaved people such as Emmanuel and Dozier, the Hopewell cemetery represented their enslavers' determination to preserve slavery, so much so that they broke from the United States and fought in a war. Emmanuel even recounted how the Ross family hid rations under the houses of the enslaved and fled to the swamp to hide from "dem Yankees."[94] The women of Hopewell Presbyterian Church also contributed to the Confederate war effort. They formed the Ladies' Aid Society, raising funds and collecting supplies for Confederate soldiers. The first president of the society was Amelia Harllee, wife of Dr. Robert Harllee, General W. W. Harllee's brother. Their son, Robert Armstrong Harllee was a Confederate soldier who died in 1862. All three rest at Hopewell cemetery.[95] In 1860, Robert Harllee enslaved one hundred fourteen people, and W. W. Harllee enslaved thirty-five people.[96] Although these enslaved peoples would have been listed among the church's congregants, they would not have been a part of the church's democratic form of governance, and they would have known that their enslavers were fighting a war to keep them enslaved.

Enslaved peoples in the Pee Dee experienced Presbyterianism as a part of slavery. Many of the people who founded the Pee Dee's Presbyterian churches also established the region's plantations. Later accounts from four formerly enslaved individuals revealed how they associated churches with slavery above all else. They did not simply describe the churches as somewhere they attended during slavery but as "slavery churches." This would have weighed heavily on how they received sermons and perceived ministers. It is likely that they did not associate Christianity with slavery, as certain sects and other denominations opposed their enslavement and many Black churches appeared in the Pee Dee after abolition. In white Presbyterian churches, Black congregants had to worship from segregated galleries under "white paternal leadership."[97] The Presbyterian Church would not permit Black congregants to establish Black Presbyterian churches or have Black church leadership. After the American Civil War and the abolition of slavery, Black Christians preferred to start their own churches or join another denomination to "second-class membership" in a Presbyterian church.[98] African-descended peoples did not just want freedom in death, as Reese had preached. Once they got that freedom, they continued to find hope and comfort in Christianity, but not in slavery's churches.

Erica Johnson is associate professor of history and codirector of African and African American Studies at Francis Marion University (FMU). A native of Oklahoma, she specializes in the history of the Atlantic World. She is author of a monograph, *Philanthropy and Race in the Haitian Revolution*, part of the Cambridge Imperial and Post-Colonial Studies Series (Palgrave Macmillan, 2018). She has published articles in *The History Teacher, Southern Quarterly, Journal of Transnational American Studies,* and *Journal of Western Society for French History.* Her research interests include race, religion, and revolution in the greater Atlantic World. She is the faculty coordinator for FMU's Universities Studying Slavery initiative.

NOTES

1. Boddie, *History of Williamsburg,* 48–51. On the basis of modern county lines, Hopewell and Aimwell fall within Florence County, whereas Williamsburg and Indiantown are in Williamsburg County, and Salem Black River is in Sumter County.
2. Murray, *Presbyterians and the Negro,* 29.
3. See, e.g., Thornton, "The Development of an African Catholic Church in the Kingdom of Kongo," 47–167; Thornton, "On the Trail of Voodoo: African Christianity in Africa and the Americas," 261–78; Law, "Religion, Trade and Politics on the 'Slave Coast': Roman Catholic Missions in Allada and Whydah in the Seventeenth Century," 42–77; Ryde, "Missionary Activity in the Kingdom of Warri to the Early Nineteenth Century," 1–26; Isichei, *A History of Christianity in Africa;* and Pawliková-Vilhanová, "Christian Missions in Africa and Their Role in the Transformations of African Societies," 249–60.
4. See, e.g., Daniel, "Southern Presbyterians and the Negro in the Early National Period," 291–312; Thompson, "Slavery and Presbyterianism in the Revolutionary Era," 121–41; and Smith, "'The Necessary Result of Piety,'" 1–15. For more on Davies, see Richards, "Samuel Davies and the Transatlantic Campaign for Slave Literacy in Virginia," 333–78.
5. Innis, "'A Southern College Slipped from Its Geographical Moorings,'" 236–50 and Darity Mullen, "Who Reaped the Fruits of Slavery?" 51–68.
6. This is especially true as the *Negro Act of 1740* prohibited teaching the enslaved to write. See Campbell, "Article XLV," https://ushistoryscene.com/article/excerpts -south-carolina-slave-code-1740-no-670-1740/.
7. For more on the WPA narratives, see Schwartz, "The WPA Narratives as Historical Sources," 89–100.

8. Axtell, "Ethnohistory: An Historian's Viewpoint," 5.

9. Grana-Behrens, "The Past by the Present," 45.

10. My methodology aligns with that of the many scholars who center the enslaved despite the evidentiary difficulties. See, e.g., Trouillot, *Silencing the Past*; Hartman, "The Dead Book Revisited," 208–15; Smallwood, "The Politics of the Archive and History's Accountability to the Enslaved," 117–32; Fuentes, *Dispossessed Lives*; and Holden, *Surviving Southampton*.

11. Benjamin, *Illuminations*, 256.

12. Benjamin, *Illuminations*, 257.

13. Benjamin, *Illuminations*, 256–57.

14. Little, "The Origins of Southern Evangelicalism," 780.

15. Leyburn, "Presbyterian Immigrants and the American Revolution," 9–32.

16. Gregg, *Accounts Audited of Claims Growing Out of the American Revolution*.

17. Readling, *History of Hopewell Presbyterian Church*, 4.

18. James Gregg, Plat for 477 Acres on East Side of Poke Swamp, Georgetown District, Surveyed by John Henderson, 19 February 1788 State Plat Books (Charleston Series), South Carolina Department of Archives and History (SCDAH); James Gregg, Plat for 248 Acres on Waters of Pee Dee River, Georgetown District, Surveyed by John McCottry, 22 July 1789, State Plat Books (Charleston Series), SCDAH; James Gregg, Plat for 388 Acres on Branch of Jeffries Creek, Georgetown District, Surveyed by James Gregg, 3 December 1793, State Plat Books (Charleston Series), SCDAH.

19. Rogers, "First Hopewell Pastor Veteran of Revolution," 4.

20. *The Mecklenburg Declaration of Independence*.

21. For more on the origins of Presbyterianism, presbyteries, and synods, see Hansen, "Sixteenth-Century Origins," 9–28.

22. Stone, *A History of Orange Presbytery*, 5–7, 11.

23. Readling, *History of Hopewell Presbyterian Church*, 6.

24. Howe, *History of the Presbyterian Church in South Carolina*, 681–83.

25. For more on this immigration, see Waterhouse, "England, the Caribbean, and the Settlement of Carolina," 259–81; Navin, *The Grim Years: Settling South Carolina, 1670–1720*; and Dunn, "The English Sugar Islands and the Founding of South Carolina," 81–93.

26. Jennings, "Slave Codes, 1690–1865."

27. Article XXII, *Excerpts from South Carolina Slave Code of 1740 No. 670 (1740)*.

28. Alex Gregg was an exception. He was enslaved on the Gregg plantation, and he told his son that he had not "went to church in a church building when he was a slave." See Vernon, *African Americans at Mars Bluff*, 39.

29. Brown, 139.

30. Emmanuel, 18. Emmanuel's first name was likely Moriah, and Ryer was a nickname or what the interviewer heard. There is a Moriah Emmanuel in the 1930 census in Jeffreys, SC. She was a seventy-year-old widow living with her grandsons.

31. Brown, 18.

32. See Merritt, *Masterless Men*; and Coombs, "'Poor, Deluded, Ignorant Masses,'" 285–302.

33. According to the 1790 census for Prince Frederick's Parish of the Georgetown District, James Gregg enslaved sixteen people. In his 1802 will from Marion District, James Gregg bequeathed at least six enslaved individuals to his descendants. For information on the role of the Greggs in the founding of the church, see Howe, *History of the Presbyterian Church in South Carolina*, 413; and Readling, *History of Hopewell Presbyterian Church, Claussen*, 4.
34. Elizabeth "Mary" Wilson Gregg (1744–1799).
35. Article XXXVII.
36. Grant, 174.
37. Grant, 173.
38. Dozier, 333. This is most likely Wilds Gregg, not Wiles Gregg.
39. Dozier, 334.
40. Quoted in Vernon, *African Americans at Mars Bluff*, 37.
41. See, e.g., Orser Jr., "The Archaeology of African-American Slave Religion in the Antebellum South," 33–45; Jamieson, "Material Culture and Social Death: African-American Burial Practices," 39–58; Samford, "The Archaeology of African-American Slavery and Material Culture," 119–40; Early, "Sacred Ground," 331–42.
42. Patillo, *The Plain Planter's Family Assistant*, 22.
43. Patillo, *The Plain Planter's Family Assistant*, 23. All these are examples of what Scott calls "infrapolitics," or ways of subtly resisting the system of slavery. See *Domination and the Arts of Resistance*, 183–201.
44. Patillo, *The Plain Planter's Family Assistant*, 25.
45. Patillo, *The Plain Planter's Family Assistant*, 25.
46. Patillo, *The Plain Planter's Family Assistant*, 26–27.
47. Patillo, *The Plain Planter's Family Assistant*, 50.
48. Patillo, *The Plain Planter's Family Assistant*, 51.
49. Patillo, *The Plain Planter's Family Assistant*, 51–52.
50. Romans 6:18. KJV.
51. Emmanuel, 18.
52. Emmanuel, 19.
53. Grant, *Slave Narratives*, 174. William Rogers Johnson enslaved Grant. Grant names him in his interview. Johnson owned a plantation on sixteen hundred ninety acres, where he built a Greek Revival home, now on the National Register as the Rankin-Harwell House, also known as "The Columns." See William R. Johnson, Plat for 1,690 Acres on Back Swamp and Black Creek, Marion District, Surveyed by Levi Leggett, 30 May 1845, State Plat Books (Charleston Series), SCDAH.
54. Patillo, *The Plain Planter's Family Assistant*, 46.
55. Dozier, 332.
56. "And he had in his hand a little book open: and he set his right foot upon the sea, and *his* left *foot* on the earth," Revelation 10:2, KJV.
57. Dozier, 332.
58. Emmanuel, 19.
59. Grant, 172.
60. Emmanuel, 18; Grant, 174; Dozier, 331.

61. Brown, 139. It is likely that A. W. Cusack enslaved Brown. A. W. Cusack appears in the 1860 census for Marion as the female head of household as well as the 1860 Slave Schedule for Marion. In the Slave Schedule, there is an enslaved female listed as ten years old, most likely Sara.

62. Brown, 137, 140.

63. Smith, 'The Necessary Result of Piety,'" 2–3.

64. Daniel, "Southern Presbyterians and the Negro in the Early National Period," 298–9.

65. Stokes and Dease, "Thomas Reese."

66. Reese, "Death the Christian's Gain," 378.

67. Reese, "Death the Christian's Gain," 382.

68. Reese, "Death the Christian's Gain," 382.

69. Esther 7: 1–10, KJV.

70. Reese, "The Character of Haman," 342.

71. Some authors have linked this sermon to anti-British and anticrown sentiments. See, e.g., Stokes, "Thomas Reese in South Carolina," 137.

72. Reese, "The Character of Haman," 341–42.

73. Reese, *Steadfastness in Religion*, 17.

74. See, e.g., Mathews, *Slavery and Methodism*; and Kellison, *Forging a Christian Order*.

75. Murray, *Presbyterians and the Negro*, 299.

76. Enslaved peoples were aware of what was going on in much of the Atlantic World. See Scott, *The Common Wind*.

77. Moorehead, "Between Hope and Fear," 49.

78. Moorehead, "Between Hope and Fear," 59.

79. Adams, "Divided Nation, Divided Church," 687–86.

80. Jones and Mills, eds., *The History of the Presbyterian Church in South Carolina*, 888.

81. Joseph Brown, US Federal Census, 1950.

82. Readling, *History of Hopewell Presbyterian Church*, 9.

83. Robinson, *The Testimony and Practice of the Presbyterian Church*, 168.

84. Robinson, *The Testimony and Practice of the Presbyterian Church*, 168.

85. Jones and Mills, eds., *The History of the Presbyterian Church in South Carolina*, 892.

86. Ramey, "Salvation Black or White," 7.

87. Dozier, 331.

88. He donated fifteen dollars to the cause. See "South Carolina Tract Society," 1.

89. *An Appeal to Young Soldiers*, 2.

90. *An Appeal to Young Soldiers*, 3.

91. Emmanuel, 18, and Readling, *History of Hopewell Presbyterian Church*, 11.

92. Dozier, 330, and Readling, *History of Hopewell Presbyterian Church*, 12.

93. Readling, *History of Hopewell Presbyterian Church*, 9–10.

94. Emmanuel, 20.

95. Readling, *History of Hopewell Presbyterian Church*, 11, 39, 88.

96. Both men are listed as enslavers in the Marion District. See US Federal Census, 1850.

97. Murray, *Presbyterians and the Negro*, 31.
98. Murray, *Presbyterians and the Negro*, 62.

WORKS CITED

Adams, Elizabeth T. "Divided Nation, Divided Church: The Presbyterian Schism, 1837–1838." *The Historian* 54, no. 4 (1992): 687–86.

An Appeal to Young Soldiers by a Young Lady. Charleston: South Carolina Tract Society, 1863.

Axtell, James. "Ethnohistory: An Historian's Viewpoint." *Ethnohistory* 26, no. 1 (1979): 1–13.

Benjamin, Walter. *Illuminations*, edited by Hannah Arendt. Shocken Books, 1968.

Boddie, William Willis. *History of Williamsburg: Something About the People of Williamsburg County, South Carolina, From the First Settlement by Europeans About 1705 Until 1923.* The State Company, 1923.

Brown, Mom Sarah. 1937. Interview by Annie Ruth Davis. In *Slave Narratives: A Folk History of Slavery in the United States from Interviews with Former Slaves*, vol. 14, part 1, of *South Carolina Narratives*. Federal Writers' Project, 1941.

Campbell, Annie. *Excerpts From South Carolina Slave Code of 1740 No. 670 (1740).* US History Scene, accessed September 10, 2025. https://ushistoryscene.com/article/excerpts-south-carolina-slave-code-1740-no-670-1740/.

Coombs, Harriet. "'Poor, Deluded, Ignorant Masses': Revisiting Poor Non-Slaveholding Whites of the Antebellum South." *American Nineteenth Century History* 23, no. 3 (2022): 285–302.

Darity, William, and A. Kirsten Mullen. *From Here to Equality: Reparations for Black Americans in the Twenty-First Century.* University of North Carolina Press, 2020.

Dozier, Washington. 1937. Interview by Annie Ruth Davis. In *Slave Narratives: A Folk History of Slavery in the United States from Interviews with Former Slaves*, vol. 14, part 1, of *South Carolina Narratives*. Federal Writers' Project, 1941.

Dunn, Richard S. "The English Sugar Islands and the Founding of South Carolina." In *The Atlantic Slave Trade*, vol. 2, edited by Jeremy Black. Routledge, 2002.

Early, Bradley. "Sacred Ground: Enslaved African Americans and the US Religious Freedom Paradigm." *Journal of Church and State* 65, no. 3 (2023): 331–42.

Emmanuel, Mom Reyer. Interview by Annie Ruth Davis. In *Slave Narratives: A Folk History of Slavery in the United States from Interviews with Former Slaves*, vol. 14, part 2, of *South Carolina Narratives*. Federal Writers' Project, 1941.

Fuentes, Marisa J. *Dispossessed Lives: Enslaved Women, Violence, and the Archive.* University of Pennsylvania Press, 2016.

Grana-Behrens, Daniel. "The Past by the Present: Ethnography as a Means to Explain Ancient Maya." *Acta Mesoamericana* 28 (2012): 47–64.

Grant, Charlie. Interview by Annie Ruth Davis. In *Slave Narratives: A Folk History of Slavery in the United States from Interviews with Former Slaves*, vol. 14, part 2, of *South Carolina Narratives*. Federal Writers' Project, 1941.

Gregg, Elizabeth "Mary" Wilson (1744–1799). *Find a Grave*, accessed September 8, 2025. https://www.findagrave.com/memorial/83719308/elizabeth-gregg.

Gregg, James. *Accounts Audited of Claims Growing out of the American Revolution*, South Carolina Department of Archives and History, File No. 309.

Hansen, Gary Neal. "Sixteenth-Century Origins." In *The Oxford Handbook of Presbyterianism*, edited by Gary Scott Smith and P. C. Kemeny. Oxford University Press, 2019.

Harrison, Daniel W. "Southern Presbyterians and the Negro in the Early National Period." *Journal of Negro History* 58, no. 3 (1973): 291–312.

Hartman, Saidiya. "The Dead Book Revisited." *History of the Present* 6, no. 2 (2016): 208–15.

Holden, Vanessa. *Surviving Southampton: African American Women and Resistance in Nat Turner's Community*. University of Illinois Press, 2021.

Howe, George. *History of the Presbyterian Church in South Carolina*, vol. 1. Columbia, SC: Duffie and Chapman, 1870.

Innis, Lolita Buckner. "'A Southern College Slipped from Its Geographical Moorings': Slavery at Princeton." *Slavery & Abolition* 39, no. 2 (2018): 236–50.

Isichei, Elizabeth. *A History of Christianity in Africa: From Antiquity to the Present*. Wm. B. Eerdmans Publishing, 1995.

Jamieson, Ross W. "Material Culture and Social Death: African-American Burial Practices." *Historical Archaeology* 29 (1995): 39–58.

Jennings, Matthew H. "Slave Codes, 1690–1865." *South Carolina Encyclopedia*, August 23, 2022. https://www.scencyclopedia.org/.

Jones, F. D., and W. H. Mills, eds. *The History of the Presbyterian Church in South Carolina Since 1850*. R. L. Bryan Company, 1926.

Kellison, Kimberly R. *Forging a Christian Order: South Carolina Baptists, Race, and Slavery, 1696–1860*. University of Tennessee Press, 2023.

Law, Robin. "Religion, Trade and Politics on the 'Slave Coast': Roman Catholic Missions in Allada and Whydah in the Seventeenth Century." *Journal of Religion in Africa* 21 (1991): 42–77.

Leyburn, James G. "Presbyterian Immigrants and the American Revolution." *Journal of Presbyterian History* 54, no. 1 (1976): 9–32.

Little, Thomas J. "The Origins of Southern Evangelicalism: Revivalism in South Carolina, 1700–1740." *Church History* 75, no. 4 (2006): 768–808.

Matthews, Donald G. *Slavery and Methodism: A Chapter in American Morality, 1780–1845*. Princeton University Press, 1965.

The Mecklenburg Declaration of Independence Charlotte North Carolina May 20th. Reprint, 1775. https://www.loc.gov/item/2020775438/.

Merritt, Keri Leigh. *Masterless Men: Poor Whites and Slavery in the Antebellum South*. Cambridge University Press, 2017.

Moorehead, James H. "Between Hope and Fear: Presbyterians and the 1818 Statement on Slavery." *Journal of Presbyterian History* 96, no. 2 (2018): 48–61.

Murray, Andrew E. *Presbyterians and the Negro—A History*. Presbyterian Historical Society, 1966.

Navin, John J. *The Grim Years: Settling South Carolina, 1670–1720*. University of South Carolina Press, 2019.

Orser, Charles E. Jr. "The Archaeology of African-American Slave Religion in the Antebellum South." *Cambridge Archaeological Journal* 4, no. 1 (1994): 33–45.

Pattillo, Henry. *The Plain Planter's Family Assistant; Containing an Address to Husbands and Wives, and Children and Servants.* Wilmington, DE: James Adams, 1787.

Pawliková-Vilhanová, Viera. "Christian Missions in Africa and Their Role in the Transformations of African Societies." *Asian and African Studies* 16, no. 2 (2007): 249–60.

Ramey, Susan E. "Salvation Black or White: Presbyterian Rationale and Protestant Support for the Religious Instruction of Slaves in South Carolina." Master's thesis, University of Nevada, Las Vegas, 1994.

Readling, Rev. James M. *History of Hopewell Presbyterian Church, Claussen, South Carolina, 1770–1970.* R. L. Bryan Company, 1970.

Reese, Thomas. "Death the Christian's Gain." In *The American Preacher; or a Collection of Sermons from Some of the Most Eminent Preachers Now Living in the United States of Different Denominations in the Christian Church,* vol. 1. Elizabethtown, NJ: Shepard Kollock, 1791.

Reese, Thomas. *Steadfastness in Religion.* Philadelphia, PA: Young, 1793.

Richards, Jeffrey H. "Samuel Davies and the Transatlantic Campaign for Slave Literacy in Virginia." *Virginia Magazine of History & Biography* 111, no. 4 (2003): 333–78.

Robinson, Rev. John. *The Testimony and Practice of the Presbyterian Church in Reference to American Slavery with an Appendix.* Cincinnati, OH: John D. Thorpe, 1852.

Rogers, James A. "First Hopewell Pastor Veteran of Revolution." *Florence Morning News,* 8 May 1977, 4.

Ryde, Alan. "Missionary Activity in the Kingdom of Warri to the Early Nineteenth Century." *Journal of the Historical Society of Nigeria* 2, no. 1 (1960): 1–26.

Samford, Patricia. "The Archaeology of African-American Slavery and Material Culture." *The Archaeology of Slavery in North America* 24 (1995): 119–40.

Scott, Julius S. *The Common Wind: Afro-American Currents in the Age of Revolutions.* Verso Books, 2018.

Scott, James C. *Domination and the Arts of Resistance: Hidden Transcripts.* Yale University Press, 2008.

Smallwood, Stephanie E. "The Politics of the Archive and History's Accountability to the Enslaved." *History of the Present* 6, no. 2 (2016): 117–32.

Smith, Miles. "'The Necessary Result of Piety': Slavery and Religious Establishments in South Carolina Presbyterianism, 1800–1840." *Religions* 8 (2017): 1–15.

Schwartz, Marie Jenkins. "The WPA Narratives as Historical Sources." In *The Oxford Handbook of the African American Slave Narrative,* edited by John Ernest. Oxford University Press, 2014.

Stokes, Durward T. "Thomas Reese in South Carolina." *The South Carolina Historical Magazine* 74, no. 3 (July 1973): 128–46.

Stokes, Duward T., and Jared Dease. "Thomas Reese." *North Carolina Encyclopedia,* 1994. https://www.ncpedia.org/biography/reese-thomas.

Stone, Robert Hamlin. *A History of Orange Presbytery.* Greensboro, NC: Heritage Printers, 1790.

Thompson, J. Earl, Jr. "Slavery and Presbyterianism in the Revolutionary Era." *Presbyterian Historical Society* 54, no. 1 (1976): 121–14.

Thornton, John K. "The Development of an African Catholic Church in the Kingdom of Kongo, 1491–1750." *The Journal of African History* 25, no. 2 (1994): 147–67.

Thornton, John K. "On the Trail of Voodoo: African Christianity in Africa and the Americas." *The Americas* 44, no. 3 (1988): 261–78.

Trouillot, Michel-Rolph. *Silencing the Past: Power and the Production of History.* Beacon Press, 1995.

US Federal Census, 1850, accessed September 8, 2025. https://ancestry.com.

Wallace Vernon, Amelia. *African Americans at Mars Bluff, South Carolina.* Louisiana State University Press, 1993.

Waterhouse, Richard. "England, the Caribbean, and the Settlement of Carolina." *Journal of American Studies* 9, no. 3 (1975): 259–81.

Two Murders in Marion

Stories of the Enslaved in South Carolina Criminal Prosecutions

Stan Barnett

Historical archives provide an abundance of information concerning slavery but less about the actual lives of the enslaved. There are, of course, slave narratives, most famously those by Olaudah Equiano, Frederick Douglass, Harriet Jacobs, and Solomon Northup.[1] Collectively, these narratives provide vital information about the lives of enslaved people. Readers should remember, however, that these accounts focus largely on the lives of those who escaped enslavement, which is to say, they record the exceptional rather than the typical. Moreover, the authors of those autobiographies often wrote to shape opinion. Their narratives focus on events that strengthen their themes and promote the noble cause of abolition, sometimes subordinating completeness to purpose. Other narratives—such as *Sketches of the Life of Joseph Mountain, a Negro Who Was Executed at New-Haven, on the 20th Day of October, 1790* and *Dying Confession of Pomp, A Negro Man, Who Was Executed at Ipswich*—follow familiar patterns of criminal biography.[2] Often written by white observers, these accounts sacrifice authenticity to literary convention and sensationalism.

Contemporaneous biographical narratives will always be essential for our understanding of Black life in America. They cannot, however, provide a complete account. They remain necessary, but never sufficient. Recent scholarship—such as, notably, Tiya Alicia Miles's brilliant *All that She Carried: The Journey of Ashley's Sack, a Black Family Keepsake*—seeks to fill gaps by using material history to recover voices that have been lost or erased.[3] The following essay contributes to this essential work. Examining the criminal trials of two enslaved people charged with murder in the Pee Dee region, it uses court records to recreate the experiences of enslaved families in poor rural communities. In doing so, it provides glimpses into the complicated and contradictory ways enslaved people interacted with the criminal justice system. The trials of these enslaved men were two of one thousand thirty-three similar cases in South Carolina for which records survive. Readers may be surprised to discover that courts provided a level of due process for the enslaved. More surprising is the fact that statewide conviction rate for the enslaved was only forty-eight percent. In comparison, the overall conviction rate today in South Carolina is seventy-seven percent.[4] The protections afforded to enslaved individuals originated both in a belief in the "unalienable rights" of all human beings, including the enslaved, and in the legally articulated property rights of the enslavers. The men tried and convicted of murder in these two cases exist both as individuals responsible for their actions and as assets that cannot be seized without compensation. The Magistrates and Freeholders Courts that tried the enslaved individuals reflected many of the inherent contradictions in America's founding principle of freedom. These courts and South Carolina's appellate courts both affirmed and denied the humanity of the enslaved.[5]

Like all historical documents, the court records are imperfect and were sometimes doubtlessly affected by bias. We have no way of knowing whether the testimony was coerced or, unlike today's verbatim transcriptions, accurately recorded. Shaped by attorneys' questions and memorialized by a court reporter, these words remain forever encased in the oppression of antebellum culture. Despite these limitations, the records provide compelling and important narratives of real people. They offer glimpses into the interactions of enslaved families, the daily lives of those who toiled without freedom, and the slight, tenuous, and evanescent claims that enslaved people had for justice.

South Carolina law categorized African-descended peoples as the property of other human beings and subject to rigid control and punishment. Enslavers or their family members could sell enslaved people. Enslavers, overseers, "slave drivers," members of a "slave patrol," or any white man who had "justification" could physically punish the enslaved.[6] However, the system of slavery in South Carolina also regarded enslaved people as human beings. The law considered them as people capable of committing crimes—everything from murder or theft to those crimes peculiar to slavery, like "impudence to a white man."[7] South Carolina provided specific courts for the trial of enslaved people who were accused of crimes. The courts that tried enslaved and free Black people were the Magistrates and Freeholders Courts.

Until the eighteenth century, the system provided few protections for enslaved defendants. In 1740, South Carolina lawmakers passed statutes that overlaid many, but not nearly all, of the protections guaranteed to white defendants. South Carolina's legal system required the following:

1. An enslaved person could only be charged with a crime after a warrant was issued on the basis of probable cause.

2. At the commencement of a proceeding, an enslaved person was entitled to be specifically and accurately informed of the charge against them.
3. An enslaved defendant was given the chance to plead guilty or not guilty and told that in the event of a not-guilty plea, a trial would be held at which they would be entitled to call witnesses in their defense.
4. An enslaved person was entitled to be represented by a lawyer.
5. If convicted of a capital offense, an enslaved person was entitled to appeal the conviction to Circuit Court.[8]

These legally recognized rights provided protections on the basis of the understanding that the enslaved were human beings, albeit human beings held in a condition of slavery. Judges referred to them in exactly those words. With varying success, lawyers for the enslaved also argued that their defendants had other rights as well, including the following:

1. They were not subject to double jeopardy.[9]
2. No one could force them to testify against themselves.
3. They had the right to protection from punishment for something their enslavers ordered them to do.
4. They had "benefit of the clergy," meaning that they could claim they were ministers of the Gospel who were entitled to a narrower application of criminal law.[10]

Enslaved people convicted of capital crimes such as murder, arson, or burglary had the right to appeal a conviction and ordered punishment. Lawyers for enslaved individuals made many arguments on appeal to the Circuit Court. Some were based on well-founded principles, whereas others advanced premises that were more creative. To a surprising extent, these appeals were successful. In many cases, judges ordered new trials. In others, the punishment ordered was set aside pursuant to a "motion for avoidance" if the court accepted the argument that the punishment was not justified by the facts at trial.

South Carolina laws forbade enslaved people from testifying except in support of the State's prosecution of another enslaved person, and the enslaved could never contradict the testimony of a white person.[11] In reality, in every district from which case files survive, the enslaved did exactly that. They testified on behalf of enslaved defendants and very often directly contradicted the testimony of white people. In many cases, juries relied on the testimony of enslaved witnesses to acquit other enslaved individuals, even in the face of conflicting testimony by white people.

The psychological and physical abuse that enslavers inflicted on enslaved individuals inevitably led to untrue coerced testimony and even false confessions.[12] Many case files show elaborate efforts by white men to convince the enslaved to confess. In nearly every case, the white men testifying about these efforts went to extreme lengths to explain that there was no undue pressure, no promises made, no threats brandished, and, most significantly, that the enslaved person was not whipped to force testimony or a confession. Jurors were alert to what they all knew very well was possible: testimony coerced, "under the lash" as it was called, or the threat of it.[13] Sometimes the jury disregarded evidence that an enslaved person's statement was coerced, but they often rejected testimony they concluded was coerced.

Throughout the nineteenth century, individuals in positions of power roundly criticized the courts for not providing fair trials for the enslaved. For example, Judge John Belton O'Neall described American justice as "the worst system which could be devised."[14] In 1833, Governor Robert Y. Hayne wrote that, "the law ought ... to afford complete protection against injustice" and added that "the courts before which slaves must now be tried, for crimes of every description, are liable to be so arranged as to deprive them of an impartial trial." He went on to complain that "capital offenses committed by slaves ... are often tried by courts composed of persons ignorant of the law and left without the aid of counsel."[15] Governor John Peter Richardson II in 1841 and Governor James Hopkins Adams in 1855 noted that many cases came to them that did not comply with law, often leading them to issue pardons for enslaved people who were convicted of crimes.[16] It is important to remember that all these men were vocal defenders of slavery.

Although scholars have written about the prosecutions of enslaved individuals elsewhere in the South, there is still a great deal to learn about this history in South Carolina.[17] The two cases discussed in the following text took place in Marion District, and both resulted in convictions. Using the extant court records and transcripts of testimony, I have tried to let the witnesses tell the stories of each case and not tell it for them.

The Murder of William B. Haselden

In 1844, William B. and Sarah Haselden lived in Marion District on their plantation. Along with six children younger than fifteen years of age, they lived in a community among many relatives between the Lynches and Pee Dee Rivers near Mars Bluff. They did not own a grand plantation; they only had a single cabin for the people whom they enslaved.[18] The individuals whom Haselden enslaved worked under the "task system," wherein Haselden assigned specific tasks to each laborer for the day.[19] Once those tasks were completed, the rest of the day belonged to the enslaved to use any way they wished, consistent with the restrictions of slavery. As was common, Haselden often rented enslaved laborers from other nearby enslavers to work for him.[20] From the perspective of those rented out to him, Haselden remained bound by the rules of the task system.

On Friday, July 12, 1844, the enslaved people working for Haselden worked a full day and completed the tasks assigned to them. Haselden enslaved two of them: Harry, who was in his late thirties, and Scipio, called "Sip," in his midtwenties. Neighbors enslaved other workers and rented them to Haselden for specific work. One of the enslaved women Haselden hired was Risbe, Harry's sister. Hepsa also worked that day. Haselden's son John previously owned Hepsa, but by 1844, she was enslaved by Isabella Gregg, a sixty-year-old widow and neighbor.[21] Hepsa was in her late twenties and was the mother of several children, also enslaved by Gregg.[22]

As late afternoon turned to evening, the enslaved people working for Haselden gathered at his sole "negro house" for supper. It rained not only that day but also the night before, and the ground was wet. The wet soil was ideal, and the season was right to plant slips for sweet potatoes. These were cuttings from the sweet potato plant used to speed the growth of new vines. Haselden wanted the enslaved laborers to plant these slips after their supper. Haselden sent his son James to order the workers to come back out and plant the slips. Harry told James, "They were not done eating." James went back to Haselden's house and waited a while, then returned. All the enslaved people were inside. James ordered them out repeatedly. Harry insisted that they were still eating. When James told him this, Haselden became enraged and took matters into his own hands. He went to the enslaved workers himself to demand they come out and plant the sweet potato slips. As soon as he entered the dwelling, Sip killed him.[23]

In the trial that followed, conducted in Haselden's own house, nine whites and three enslaved people testified. There was no conflict in their stories. Harry and Risbe described what happened in the "negro house" after James demanded that they continue work after supper. Immediately, Sip refused to go. Sip and Hepsa said that it "*was a pretty come off* to have to plant slips after doing their tasks." She meant that the order was unfair and oppressive. Hepsa was adamant that the tasks assigned to her were "too large." She was furious with Haselden for violating the task system by ordering her to do more work beyond her assigned tasks in the hours of remaining daylight after supper.[24]

After James's first trip to the laborers' cabin, Harry and Risbe started to get their hoes. Sip and Hepsa told them to put them down in the "negro house yard." Hepsa dared Harry "to touch them." Hepsa said she was going to leave and go to Reese Gregg's for the night.[25] She sent her children off the Haselden property, telling them she would meet up with them later. Harry, the oldest of the enslaved, ordered the rest to obey James's second demand that they plant the slips, but Sip and Hepsa angrily refused.[26] The excuse that Harry gave twice to James was his way of attempting to delay and diffuse a dangerous confrontation. He knew he was in the middle of a firestorm.

Harry and Risbe's testimony made it clear that Sip and Hepsa were very close. They never quarreled, Harry said, and "they were mostly in company" with each other. Sip and Hepsa already harbored intense animosity toward Haselden. Hepsa was open about her contempt for Haselden, his family, and whites in general. She told Harry, "That she would not take a whipping from Haselden or any other Buckra"—*buckra* being an insulting term for white people that was common among the enslaved. She told Risbe "that Haselden should not whip her" and "that her own people did not whip her and if anybody else tried it, she would fight till she died." Hepsa said, "She did not like any of the [Haselden] family."[27] They "were the meanest people she had ever lived with in her life," she told Risbe. Haselden's wife, Sarah, testified, "Hepsa's general conduct has not been that of a faithful slave and [she] has been pretty stubborn" and "disobedient," once telling Sarah, "Not to bother her." Sip told Harry and Risbe that he was not going to sleep in the warehouse anymore. This was a one-room storehouse and, unlike the house for the enslaved, it had no beds or fireplace, making it a miserable place to rest. Hepsa urged him to refuse. James Haselden testified that Sip told him the previous week, "that if I have to lie in that warehouse any more, there will be war."[28]

Harry and Risbe left the "negro house" and headed to the kitchen house.[29] William Haselden met them there, holding a walking stick with a pewter tip. His wife and two of his daughters saw him beat Harry and Risbe when he met them in the kitchen. Sarah called it "correcting them lightly," adding that "he gave them a cut or two." Thirteen-year-old Elizabeth, "Betsy," was more graphic, saying her father was, "whipping Harry and Risbe." Nineteen-year-old Mary agreed with Betsy. After Haselden beat them in the kitchen,

Harry and Risbe headed for the "big gate" at the entry to the lane that led to the public road. At the gate, they heard, but could not see, what happened next. Haselden's daughters, Betsy and Mary, saw it all.[30]

After beating Harry and Risbe at the kitchen house, Haselden, wearing his hat and carrying his walking stick and a whip, marched to the "negro house," only fifteen steps away. As he reached the house, Hepsa's children left and headed to the cornfield where Hepsa had spent the day working. Betsy saw Hepsa in the house and said she moved from the fireplace to the other end of the house. Sip was standing at the fireplace.[31]

As soon as Haselden entered the house, Sip struck him several blows with the blade of an axe. The girls yelled for their mother to come, Betsy shrieking, "Ma, I saw Sip strike Pa!" Sarah ran to the "negro house" and screamed. She saw Haselden lying on the floor and confronted Sip, gasping, "Oh Sip, have you killed my poor husband?" Sip was still holding the axe, tossing it from his left hand to his right. He turned the blade toward Sarah and yelled back, "Yes, damn you, I hope I have!" James heard her screams and ran to the "negro house." He saw his mother cradling his father's head in her arms. Blows from the axe left gashes on Haselden's right jaw, two above his right ear, on his arm and on his leg. His right eye was swollen badly. They carried Haselden to their house and laid him in a bed.[32]

As the family moved Haselden into their house, Sip and Hepsa fled. On their way off the property, Sip cut Haselden's walking stick with the axe, and Hepsa threw his hat and whip into the yard. They joined Harry and Risbe in the cornfield near the road outside the big gate. Hepsa told Harry how Sip struck Haselden with the axe. Sip confirmed that he cut Haselden with the axe. Clearly excited, Hepsa said that if she had struck Haselden, "she would have knocked him so dead, he would not have blowed," meaning that he would not have breathed. Sip and Hepsa warned the other two enslaved people not to go back to Haselden's. They told Harry, "If he went back, they would shoot him." Hepsa told Risbe that if they stayed there, the Haseldens "would kill her or whip her or burn her things." Hepsa, Harry, and Risbe returned to the "slave cabin" for their belongings. Hepsa collected a bundle of her clothes and left it with her children in the cornfield. Once the others gathered their property, Harry used his lock to secure the door of the "slave cabin," and they all left Haselden's farm.[33]

Hepsa and Sip did not go, as she originally planned, to Reese Gregg's place, but to the house where Ephraim Gregg, his younger brother, lived. Harry said he was afraid to go back to the "negro house" and went with them. He stayed that night at Gregg's place. After dark, Hepsa and her children went to the house of Joe, one of the people Gregg owned. Joe asked her, "Why are you here this time of the week?" She answered, "I gained the time," meaning that she had done her assigned tasks and earned the free time. Then she told him about the murder of William Haselden earlier that evening. She said that "after the rain, they were ordered to plant slips" and "they refused to." She said that she "saw Mr. Haselden whip Harry and Risbe near the kitchen," that Sip struck him, and that "I heard groans."[34]

Haselden's wife summoned Dr. James H. Jarret, who lived nearby. He arrived at the house at sundown, around eight thirty. Dr. Jarret examined Haselden and concluded that the wounds to his head were fatal. He described "compression of the brain," caused by the axe blows. He concluded that the injuries to Haselden's leg and arm were not from the blade of an axe but from a blunt object like a stick. It was difficult to rouse Haselden, Jarret said, but Haselden finally became conscious and answered Jarret's questions after asking for water. He told Jarret and his son John that Hepsa also struck him with a stick. However, neither Jarret nor John Haselden was certain that William Haselden was competent at that point. Jarret's opinion was that he was "insensible." Significantly, John testified that he had no opinion as to Hepsa's guilt. John further testified that he sat with his father that night after Jarret left. After midnight, Haselden called out and "worked his hand toward him." He took John's hand. William Haselden died the next night.[35]

Two days later, William R. Johnson held a coroner's inquest at the Haselden house. Johnson and his jury determined that Haselden's death resulted from the blows to his head. Magistrate A. L. Gregg, Haselden's son-in-law, issued a warrant for the arrest of Sip and Hepsa arrest for murder. Gregg went on to preside at the trial of Sip and Hepsa. For Gregg to act as the judge in a trial for murder of his father-in-law was not as much of a conflict of interest then as it would be today. At the trial, Hepsa's enslaver, Isabella Gregg, paid E. A. Law to represent her. Gregg also sent her son-in-law, John Foxworth, a riverboat captain, to serve as her agent.[36] Some of the pages of the trial record are missing. The extant record shows that Law argued that enslaved people were permitted to testify in South Carolina. The prosecutor, General William W. Harrell, agreed that this was the practice throughout the state. The magistrate accepted Law's argument and ruled that enslaved people could testify for the defense. When the state finished presenting its case, Law and Foxworth chose to present no evidence in Hepsa's defense. There is no indication whether counsel represented Sip, but it is doubtful. After all, his enslaver, the only man who might have paid for a lawyer, was dead.[37]

On August 3, the jury found both Sip and Hepsa guilty and sentenced them both to "suffer death by hanging by their necks until they are both dead."[38] Magistrate Gregg ordered the hanging to take place at "the crossroads near Mars Bluff on the west side of the Great Pee Dee River." Their bodies were to be buried under the gallows. An appraisal was conducted of the value of both. The jury of white men found that each was worth two hundred dollars.[39] The purpose of this valuation was so the state could properly compensate their enslavers for putting them to death.[40] The two hundred dollars for Sip, of course, was to be paid to the estate of William Haselden.

On the day the jury found both defendants guilty and sentenced them to death, Sip made an impassioned statement that Hepsa was in no way responsible for the murder. The magistrate noted that Sip "cleared the culprit Hepsa from any participation in the murder." On the basis of Sip's statement, the jury unanimously granted attorney Law's motion and recommended that the governor grant Hepsa executive clemency. On August 14, 1844, Governor James H. Hammond did not merely commute her sentence: He pardoned Hepsa. He adopted the same condition requested by the jury that "she be removed beyond the bounds of this state on or before the 6th of September never to return on penalty of the immediate execution of the penalty." This meant that if she came back, the authorities would hang her. Having saved Hepsa's life, Sip went to his death on the gallows at the Wolf Trap crossroads in Mars Bluff on August 16, knowing that the governor, in an extraordinary act, had spared Hepsa the same fate. The magistrate annotated the record confirming that authorities hanged Sip, and "he died with indifference like a dog."[41] It is not likely that Sip was indifferent; he simply refused to show any fear or remorse for killing Haselden.[42]

As with any political act, there is the temptation to look for a political motivation. Isabella Gregg, Hepsa's enslaver, was not poor, but she was by no means rich. Her family had been in Marion District for many years, but she could not be classed as politically influential.[43] Governor Hammond was not from the Pee Dee region. His roots were in Newberry District. The lack of any obvious political tie to explain the governor's pardon of an enslaved woman convicted on strong evidence of complicity in the murder of a white man makes his act even more remarkable.

There is no mystery, however, about what led to the murder. Already strong resentment from the enslaved people who worked for him was inflamed into violent rage by a single act. Haselden demanded that they continue working after their tasks for that Friday were complete. His order to keep working after supper was an egregious affront to what they considered as their right. They had already worked all day in the rain. They completed their tasks and considered the rest of the day their time. They were having their supper when he tried to make them keep working. His attempt to coerce them into working more than their assigned tasks, in violation of the task system's rules, cost him his life.[44] The public narrative suggests that enslaved people were subject to control without any tangible limitation. This case is a window into a far more complex reality.

The Murder of Rhoda Etherton

No case is more tragic and none illustrates more strongly the burning desire to escape the bonds of slavery than the murder of Rhoda Etherton.[45] Etherton was a widow around forty years old who lived alone. She never enslaved anyone. Woods near the crossroads of Wahee Road and Moore's Mill Road four miles west of the village of Marion surrounded her home of many years.[46] It was just west of Catfish Creek, a small house with a central hallway and two bedrooms.[47]

On the evening of Friday, May 17, 1850, Etherton prepared herself for bed. She laid her bonnet and a basket on the table next to the bed and pulled on a nightcap. Before she could remove her blue homespun frock, an intruder burst into the room, swung the blunt end of an axe, crushing her skull, and killing her with a single blow. There were no dogs to warn her of the attacker. The murderer turned the bed over searching for valuables. He took Etherton's two trunks outside to her collard patch and broke the larger one open. He left a dress and other personal items in the trunk before making his way down Wahee Road in the quiet spring night. All he took was a switchblade knife.[48]

As the killer passed the home of Job Foxworth, a half mile away, the family's dogs began barking loudly. It was nine o'clock at night. The man ran back toward Etherton's house chased by the dogs. This aroused Etherton's neighbors, who came to her house, and there they found her body. Marion's Sheriff, Elly Godbold, attended a coroner's inquest the next day. The scene that Godbold and another participant, twenty-nine-year-old Wesley Gregg, described was gruesome. Blood pooled around Etherton, and brain tissue was splattered on the floor. The blunt end of the axe was still embedded in her head.[49]

The murder was widely reported in newspapers from Wilmington to Georgetown. It was the most frightening kind—a random killing by a total stranger. The *Marion Star* described Etherton as, "a mild inoffensive being who disturbed or meddled with no one." The paper noted that the murder could not have been for "plunder, for she certainly had nothing which could have [been] an inducement."[50] Coroner John McMillan led an investigation. On Wednesday, May 22, he issued an affidavit charging Garrett, a man no more than twenty years old, who was enslaved by Sanders McCall, with the murder.[51] By the middle of June, authorities detained Garrett in the Georgetown jail. Elly Godbold's twenty-two-year-old son, Hugh, took charge of him and returned him to Marion. On July 11, a jury trial began. Seventeen witnesses testified: nine white men and eight enslaved individuals. There was no evidence that raised any doubt about Garrett's guilt.[52] The jury found him guilty and sentenced him to death. Garrett was hanged in Marion on Friday, August 2, in front of a crowd of two thousand observers, most of them enslaved people sent to witness the hanging by their owners.[53] News of the hanging was reported not only by papers in the region but also by the leading abolitionist paper in the country, *The Liberator.*[54]

The swiftness of the investigation was the result of the close ties of people living in Etherton's community. The enslaved and white people knew each other very well. One of those neighbors knew exactly who planned to kill Etherton and why. Many others described Garrett's movements before and after the killing and corroborated his motivation. The key witness identifying the killer was Barnabas Powell, a thirty-eight-year-old white laborer who lived close to Etherton. A week before her murder, Powell was in the Marlboro District jail in Bennettsville with seven other men, including a white man named "Truman" and two enslaved men, Grantham, enslaved by the McRae family, and Garrett, enslaved by Moses Sanders McCall (called "Sanders"), who lived in eastern Darlington District.[55] Powell did not enslave anyone or own land and was illiterate. At trial, Powell explained that Garrett confided in Clark, another prisoner, and later to Powell that Truman had promised him one hundred twenty dollars to kill Etherton, twenty of which was to be in paper currency.[56] Powell, who knew Etherton, was emphatic with Garrett in a conversation on May 10, "I told him for God's sake not to do it."[57] Powell was not on speaking terms with Truman, having "fallen out about a knife." He described Truman as often speaking to Black people outside from the window of the jail and noted that Truman and Garrett had many private talks.[58]

The same day Powell told Garrett not to kill Etherton, Garrett learned that Sanders McCall was coming to take him from the jail and back to his plantation. Garrett was "very excited" and feared that McCall would "use him badly." He knew from the other times he ran away that McCall would have him whipped. In rejecting Powell's advice, Garrett ominously said, "I would rather do it and be hung for it than to live with McCall." As he left the jail on Saturday, May 11, Garrett asked Powell if "Truman was good to do what he promised." Powell testified, "I told Garrett that Truman was worth nothing and that the $20 bill was counterfeit." As Garrett left, Truman said, "Good bye Garrett. I am sorry you are going to leave us." The following Tuesday night, May 14, Truman tried unsuccessfully to "break jail." Powell admitted that he did not ask the sheriff in Marlboro to report the plan to murder Etherton "down to Marion."[59] Not only could he have told the Marion sheriff of the plot, he also could have warned Etherton directly, but he did neither.

One of Marion's lawyers, forty-seven-year-old E. B. Wheeler, explained why Truman would want to have Etherton killed. At the previous term of court, Truman was tried and convicted of beating his wife. Etherton testified against Truman as a prosecution witness. Convicted for assault and battery, Truman was sentenced to six months in jail. The testimony of other witnesses indicated that Truman expected to be released from jail in October. As Powell described it, the murder was a "hit" procured by Truman to get even for Etherton's testimony.[60]

Etherton knew the threat posed by Truman's anger. In the days before the murder, she visited several of her neighbors. A week earlier, Sarah, a woman enslaved by Willis G. Smith, asked Etherton about the knife in a basket she was carrying, "I asked her what she was going to do with it." She said, "Guard herself and that she had a pistol at home well loaded." Sarah did not pursue the matter. The fact that Sarah so freely asked Etherton about the knife, however, suggests a degree of familiarity between the two women. Authorities took the same knife from Garrett when they arrested him in Georgetown, and a series of witnesses in addition to Sarah identified it. Etherton's neighbors, Cyrus Bassett, John Turbeville, and Stephen Martin all identified the knife, a switchblade, as the property of Etherton's late husband.[61]

Garrett arrived in the Marion area by May 14, the Wednesday before the murder, having absconded from McCall's plantation only four days after being returned to it. He met two enslaved individuals that day on different plantations, both of whom he knew—Aaron, whose enslaver was not listed in the case file, and Fran, one of thirty people enslaved by Charles Reaves. Garrett told both men the same thing: While in jail in Marlboro District, near where he lived, a white man promised that he would pay him and "carry me to one of the free countries" if Garrett "took care of a piece of business" near the courthouse in Marion. Garrett told Aaron that he was on his way to the Burroughs plantation where he would see his brother. He refused to tell either man what "business" the man hired him to do. If Barnabas Powell's testimony was truthful, the "business" was killing a woman not just for one hundred twenty dollars but also to be taken out of slavery to a place where he would be free.[62]

On the night of the murder and in the days after, Garrett met many people. The white people did not know him. All but two of the enslaved did. Marion is thirty-eight miles from Bennettsville, the area where Garrett grew up. It is thirty-two miles from the Sanders McCall plantation. For travel on foot, these were not small distances. However, Garrett knew most of the enslaved he visited during those weeks in May. The distances are even more impressive because Garrett was barefoot. All the witnesses who ran into him that week recalled that he wore no shoes. They also remembered in consistent detail his clothes—dark pantaloons, a dark green overcoat with outside pockets, and a black high crowned hat with the bill damaged. He stuttered, so that when he encountered a stranger, he spoke very slowly.[63]

Garrett did not know where Etherton lived. The night of the murder, he encountered Lige, a man enslaved by Elly Godbold, on the road. Lige did not know Garrett but said that the man he encountered was coming from Catfish Creek and asked him where Etherton lived. Lige said he did not know but directed him to the Foxworth's property where he could get directions. It was sundown. At eight o'clock that evening, Garrett passed Hugh Godbold, the twenty-two-year-old son of the sheriff who later picked him up in Georgetown. Godbold said he spoke to Garrett, whom he did not know, which was itself strange for the community. Godbold thought it even stranger that the Black man did not answer him but only laughed.[64]

Sometime between eight and nine o'clock, Garrett found Etherton's house, entered it, and killed her with an axe he found outside. Either Etherton did not know he was in the house or she did not perceive him to be the threat she feared, because she did not put up a fight. After all, it was Truman who, she thought, would come after her. In either case, her knife and pistol were no protection. Garrett did not have any wounds from a knife, and no one heard a gunshot that night.[65]

At nine o'clock, Chesly Foxworth, the twenty-six-year-old son of Job Foxworth who lived a half mile from Etherton, was preparing for bed when his dogs alerted him to a "young man" who ran from them back toward Etherton's house. At ten o'clock, Garrett came up behind Jim, a man enslaved by Nathan Evans, traveling west in a wagon on the road from Catfish Creek. Jim explained that he did not know the man, who said his name was "Tom

Dickinson" and talked very slowly.[66] Garrett took the fork in the road toward the house of "Uncle Cuff," a seventy-five-year-old man and one of ten people enslaved by Jane Evans. Cuff testified that Garrett arrived at his house around ten o'clock. He was suffering from a toothache and was sitting up when Garrett called to him from outside. Cuff's dogs were barking loudly.[67] He knew Garrett and offered him shelter for the night as well as food. Garrett slept all night by the fire until Cuff awoke him at daybreak. At noon on Saturday, Garrett saw Jim, a man in his thirties enslaved by William Hodge. Jim knew Garrett and went to "Abrams" to get food for him. When leaving, Garrett said he planned to meet a man from Marlboro and would be back a half hour after dark, but Garrett did not return.[68]

That night, Garrett again visited Aaron and Fran. He said that he had to leave the area, as a white woman had been killed and there was "a cry about it." The "white people made such a fuss about it I could not stay." He said he had to hide ("lie concealed") until the man came to take him "to the free countries."[69] On May 23, the Thursday after the murder, Garrett showed up at the house of Frederick, a man enslaved by Peter Evans, during supper. Frederick said he "knew him well." When Frederick asked why he was there, Garrett explained that he had been in Charleston but was recognized getting off a boat by "a colored man." He was then apprehended and returned to his owner, where he was "put in stocks." Garrett questioned Frederick about Truman and his wife—"what made Truman hurt her?" Frederick explained that Truman "punished" his wife and when they came to get him, "he would not submit." Frederick said that he had not seen Etherton since court, referring to the trial of Truman for assault and battery of his wife. It may be that Etherton witnessed Truman beating his wife or was told about the beating by her. Frederick told Garrett that Truman was "a bloodthirsty man," who had been in jail three times. Frederick added, "He was there any time I was." Frederick showed Garrett the way to Back Swamp, which runs east of Marion between the town and the Little Pee Dee River.[70]

Garrett also visited another enslaved person who is not named in the court record, part of the record having been lost, but the testimony that survives is poignant. The meeting took place at a plantation where Garrett lived and worked for a year east of Marion. He said that he traveled with a white man he did not identify whom he claimed had killed Etherton. Still, Garrett was afraid that if he was caught, they would "make me touch her." He said, "If you murder anyone and touch it, it will make the body bleed. If they are to catch me and dig her up and make me touch her and she was to bleed, it would not be because I killed her, but because I was knowing to it. My

God. I'm clear of it."[71] Garrett was terrified that someone would ask him who he belonged to and "was pestered in mind." He said he had taken the road from the Evans plantation "and came into the road at Smith's Swamp"—a stream between Marion and Back Swamp—"and took the road to the Back Swamp."[72] Garrett, with his fear and perhaps guilt infused with superstition weighing heavily on his mind, headed across the Little Pee Dee and to his capture in Georgetown in June. Six weeks later, authorities hanged Garrett before a crowd of thousands.

When Garrett walked up the steps of the gallows in Marion, the crowd of enslaved people ordered to witness his hanging believed they knew why this was happening to Garrett. Society had found that he killed Etherton, a woman he did not know and from whom he took nothing except a switchblade. They knew he was desperate to escape from Sanders McCall and from slavery. He spent a good deal of time as a runaway and was frequently jailed and whipped for it, leaving his back badly scarred.[73] The enslaved people who knew the young man always began his greeting when he showed up at their houses at night the same way: "Why are you here?" "Where have you been?" They unfailingly took care of the tortured teenager, giving him shelter, food, and directions. They did not ask too many questions, and they let him talk. They knew they were committing a crime by "harboring a runaway slave" and could be severely punished, but they helped him anyway.[74] In the wake of Etherton's brutal murder, however, they did not hesitate to tell the full truth about Garrett's acts and his intent, perhaps to save themselves from punishment.[75]

Garrett was comfortable dealing with white men, even befriending them. Powell tried to save him, whereas Truman trapped him in an evil scheme to commit murder. Garrett's burning desire to be free made him easy prey for the smooth-talking reprobate. Like many murders over time, this one asks the same question: Was Garrett the real murderer? No jail records for a "Truman" survive to confirm whether he succeeded in escaping before the murder. It is certainly possible that Truman paid someone else to commit the murder. Even Powell, who strangely failed to warn his neighbor of a threat on her life, is a little suspect.

The detailed record leaves little to the imagination. The images of Etherton in her blue homespun frock and nightcap and Garrett in his green overcoat and high crowned hat are vividly overlaid in this tragedy that cost both their lives. Powell moved to North Carolina soon after Etherton's murder. His admission that he failed to warn her attracted too much disgust in the community for him to remain.

Conclusion

The society depicted in these prosecutions is mostly familiar to us. It was overwhelmingly rural and agricultural. In these closely intertwined communities, Black and white people knew each other, as people would in any rural area. They recognized each other's voices. When someone did not attend church, others noticed. They knew each other's personalities. Both white and Black people knew the husbands and wives of enslaved people and where they lived. This picture of a close-knit rural society is very recognizable.

Over one hundred sixty years separates us from slavery, and American society has undergone fundamental changes since then. Laws have banned racial discrimination in government and businesses for more than sixty years. The concept of one person owning another seems horribly alien to us. For the most part, the testimony by enslaved people in these cases provides the only contemporary statements by the enslaved in South Carolina describing their lives. They did not write diaries or journals, and the New Deal–era interviews with the surviving formerly enslaved people were conducted seventy years after slavery ended.[76] These case testimonies in South Carolina, on the other hand, contain the words of men and women in the very middle of it. These witnesses were not elderly survivors; they were mostly young. Their testimonies are not fictionalized dialogues, secondhand quotes, or autobiographies written much later. Their words were taken down as they were spoken in open court, testimony by witnesses describing places, people, and events that were important to the fate of the enslaved people on trial, sometimes for their lives. They are the voices of the enslaved who are speaking to us from the other side of Jordan, in the words of the old spiritual, before they crossed over to freedom.[77] If we want to try to understand the reality of slavery, we should listen to them.

Stan Barnett graduated from The Citadel in 1974 and the University of South Carolina School of Law in 1977. His practice focuses on contract litigation and environmental regulation. He served in the Army on active duty and in the Reserves for twenty-five years and has taught political science courses at The Citadel as an adjunct professor. In 2003, he published *A Single Star* (Corinthian Books), an action-suspense novel set primarily in South Carolina. He has also written history, including *Rivers in Time*, a history of associated families in northeastern South Carolina, and a history of the southern half of Williamsburg County, *A Brave, Honest and Industrious People.*

NOTES

1. Equiano, *The Interesting Narrative of the Life of Olaudah Equiano*; Douglass, *Narrative of the Life of Frederick Douglass, an American Slave*; Jacobs, *Incidents in the Life of a Slave Girl*; Northup, *Twelve Years a Slave*.

2. *Sketches of the Life of Joseph Mountain*; Plummer, *Dying Confession*. For a useful discussion of the impact of *Sketches in the Life of Joesph Mountain*, see Baaki, "Circulating the Black Rapist."

3. Miles, *All that She Carried*.

4. Chien, "America's Paper Prisons," 592.

5. See, e.g., the ruling of a circuit court judge in Anderson, SC, who reversed an enslaved man's conviction and death sentence for burglary because the confession that formed the basis for the conviction was clearly coerced: "The prisoner's own confession made under circumstances such as these, to be of that free and voluntary character which is deemed sufficient to consign *a human being* to the extreme penalty of the law, handled here to say the least of it, willfully to ignore all those humane principles which pervade every deportment of our code of criminal jurisprudence." The State v. Sam, a Slave, Anderson District (1861).

6. For more on slave patrols, see Hadden, *Slave Patrols*.

7. "Impudence to a white man" was a common charge. In Anderson District, there were twenty-one such cases, of which thirteen resulted in convictions. See Trial Papers of Magistrates and Freeholders (Anderson District).

8. *An Act for the Better Ordering and Governing Negroes and Other Slaves In this Province*, Province of South Carolina, no, 670, 1740, cited as *Negro Act of 1740* in O'Neall, *The Negro Law of South Carolina*, 33, 34.

9. The Court of Appeals recognized this right in *Ex Parte Brown*, 2d Bail. 323, cited in O'Neall, *The Negro Law of South Carolina*, 36.

10. See Black, "Benefit of Clergy," *Black's Law Dictionary*, 200.

11. *Negro Act of 1740*, Sec. 13 and 14, cited in O'Neall, *The Negro Law of South Carolina*, 14.

12. For more on abuse, see Fede, "Legitimized Violent Slave Abuse in the American South"; and Wyatt-Brown, "The Mask of Obedience."

13. See case records for "The State v. Richmond, A Slave," Anderson District (1852); and "The State v. Jerry, Andy, Sam, Anderson, Steven and Ellis," Slaves, Spartanburg District (1860).

14. O'Neall, *The Negro Law of South Carolina*, 35, quoted in Henry, *Police Control of the Slave in South Carolina*, 59.

15. Hayne, "Annual Message to Legislature, 1833," quoted in Henry, *Police Control of the Slave in South Carolina*, 59, 65.

16. Pardon documents from two other governors survive, one from Governor J. H. Hammond in 1844 and one from Governor R. F. W. Allston in 1858.

17. See, e.g., Hindus, "Black Justice under White Law"; Wood, "'Until He Shall Be Dead, Dead, Dead'"; Schwarz, *Twice Condemned*; Frazier, *Slavery and Crime in Missouri*; and Hindus, *Prison and Plantation*.

18. William Haselden, Plat for 132 Acres on the Big Pee Dee River, Marion District, Surveyed by John Harllee, 28 July 1817. State Plat Books.

19. For more on the task system, see Morgan, "Work and Culture."

20. For more on how enslavers hired enslaved laborers see Martin, *Divided Mastery*.

21. The State vs. Sip or Scipio and Hepsa, Slaves, Marion District (1844).

22. According to the US Census,1840, Gregg enslaved fourteen people. Isabella Gregg, Marion, US Census, 1840.

23. The State vs. Sip or Scipio and Hepsa, Slaves, Marion District (1844).

24. The State vs. Sip or Scipio and Hepsa, Slaves, Marion District (1844).

25. David Reese Gregg was the thirty-two-year-old nephew of Isabella Gregg and lived next door to her on his own farm. In 1840, he enslaved twenty-four people. US Census, 1840.

26. The State vs. Sip or Scipio and Hepsa, Slaves, Marion District (1844).

27. The clerks making notes and summarizing testimony in these cases often alternated between first and third person. Their summaries were not word-for-word transcriptions, which would have been beyond the technology of the time and beyond the abilities of most clerks to take down in handwriting.

28. The State vs. Sip or Scipio and Hepsa, Slaves, Marion District (1844).

29. Kitchens were separate buildings that were close but not joined to the main house to reduce the risk of fire.

30. The State vs. Sip or Scipio and Hepsa, Slaves, Marion District (1844).

31. The State vs. Sip or Scipio and Hepsa, Slaves, Marion District (1844).

32. The State vs. Sip or Scipio and Hepsa, Slaves, Marion District (1844).

33. The State vs. Sip or Scipio and Hepsa, Slaves, Marion District (1844).

34. The State vs. Sip or Scipio and Hepsa, Slaves, Marion District (1844).

35. The State vs. Sip or Scipio and Hepsa, Slaves, Marion District (1844).

36. There are several possible motivations for Gregg paying a lawyer to represent the woman accused of cooperating in the murder of her daughter-in-law's father. First, Hepsa was valuable property. Second, she also was seen by the community as part of Gregg's "household," so Gregg's reputation would be affected by her conviction for murder. For more on lawyers who represented enslaved individuals, see Gillmer, "Lawyers and Slaves."

37. The State vs. Sip or Scipio and Hepsa, Slaves, Marion District (1844).

38. The jurors for the trial were Nat McCall, Joseph Gregg, Christopher Bailey, H. Singletary, and J. C. Legette.

39. The State v. Sip or Scipio and Hepsa, Slaves, Marion District (1844).

40. For more on the valuation of enslaved people, see Berry, *The Price of Their Pound of Flesh*.

41. The State v. Sip or Scipio and Hepsa, Slaves, Marion District (1844).

42. Scott refers to such action as *infrapolitics*, a way of subtly resisting the system of slavery. What white onlookers perceived as a lack of remorse may have been his resistance against their expectations of him. See *Domination and the Arts*, 183–201.

43. In the US Census, 1840, there are at least twelve Greggs in Marion. For more on the Greggs in Marion County, see Gregg, *History of the Old Cheraws*.

44. Their resistance, first through continuing to eat and then through violence, are examples of agency. Enslaved people did not passively exist within slavery. Each day, they accommodated and resisted their circumstances. For more on agency, see Maza, *Thinking about History*, 33–34.

45. The State v. Garret, a Slave, Marion District (1850).

46. The US Census, 1840, shows Etherton living alone and between twenty and thirty years old, already a widow. She may have been the daughter of David Leggett Sr., who lived nearby.

47. According to the US Census,1840, Etherton's home was also only four farms away from the house where William B. Haselden had been murdered six years before.

48. The State v. Garret, a Slave, Marion District (1850).

49. The State v. Garret, a Slave, Marion District (1850).

50. "Murder," *Marion Star*, reprinted in the *Wilmington Journal*, 7 June 1850, 4.

51. The marriage contract of Moses S. McCall and Catherine F. McRoe, dated May 6, 1847, was filed in Darlington District and lists fourteen enslaved people McRoe brought into the marriage, including "boys," one of whom was Garrett. See "Separate Property of Married Women 1849–1872."

52. The State v. Garret, a Slave, Marion District (1850).

53. *Marion Star*, reprinted in *Weekly Commercial*, 23 August 1850, 4.

54. "Execution," *The Liberator*, 30 August 1850, 4.

55. The other prisoners were men named Sias, Peter, and George; Barnabas Powell on redirect testimony, The State vs. Garret, a Slave, Marion District (1850).

56. Wertheimer discusses another case of such "criminal bargaining" in South Carolina. See *Race and the Law in South Carolina*, 6–7.

57. Powell is noted in the summary of his testimony as referring to Truman as Etherton's husband. This is probably an error in the note taking. Etherton is referred to by news accounts as a widow, a fact confirmed by her probate record in Marion County. Powell knew and lived close to her, so he was certainly aware that she was not married to Truman.

58. The State v. Garret, a Slave, Marion District (1850).

59. The State v. Garret, a Slave, Marion District (1850).

60. The State v. Garret, a Slave, Marion District (1850).

61. The State v. Garret, a Slave, Marion District (1850).

62. The State v. Garret, a Slave, Marion District (1850).

63. The State v. Garret, a Slave, Marion District (1850).

64. The State v. Garret, a Slave, Marion District (1850).

65. The State v. Garret, a Slave, Marion District (1850).

66. This is another instance of agency. Garrett gave a false name in hopes of evading capture.

67. South Carolina law forbade the enslaved from owning personal property, and what property they had was really the property of their enslaver. However, these case files clearly show that, regardless of the law, enslaved people were understood to own property, and many cases revolved around their ownership of animals, guns, watches, jewelry, and money.

68. The State v. Garret, a Slave, Marion District (1850).

69. There are many references in cases across South Carolina to an enslaved person longing to be taken to "a free country." The reference is almost certainly to states that had outlawed slavery, such as Pennsylvania and New York.

70. The State v. Garret, a Slave, Marion District (1850).

71. This refers to a practice called *cruentation* that can be traced back to medieval Europe. Authorities would place a murder suspect in front of their supposed victim with the expectation that the body would bleed in front of the actual killer. See, e.g., Brittain, "Cruentation: In Legal Medicine and in Literature"; Peterson, *Involuntary Confessions of the Flesh in Early Modern France*; De Ceglia, ed. *The Body of Evidence*; Rosen, "'The Voice of the Innocent Blood Cries Aloud from the Ground to Heaven'"; and Rosen, "Framing Mark: Reading Africanist Presence in Early American Broadsides."

72. The State v. Garret, a Slave, Marion District (1850).

73. For more on enslaved people running away in South Carolina, see Johnson, "Runaway Slaves and Slave Communities in South Carolina"; Morgan, "Colonial South Carolina Runaways"; Schweninger, "Counting the Costs"; and Marshall, "'They Will Endeavor to Pass for Free.'"

74. There are many of these case files where enslaved people were prosecuted for exactly that crime. As with all categories of crime, they were often acquitted, but when there were convictions, the punishment could be harsh.

75. The State v. Garret, a Slave, Marion District (1850).

76. Beginning in 1937, the Federal Writers' Project, which was part of the Work Projects Administration, began collecting the oral histories of people who had been enslaved. Transcriptions of those histories are available through the Library of Congress. See "Born in Slavery."

77. Numerous Negro spirituals associate crossing the Jordan River with escaping slavery. Bradford reports that, while escaping slavery, Harriet Tubman sang, "I'm sorry, frien's, to lebe you,/Farewell! Oh, farewell!/But I'll meet you in de morning',/Farewell! Oh, farewell!/I'll meet you in de mornin'/When you reach de promised land;/On de oder side of Jordan,/For I'm boun' for de promised land." See *Harriet, The Moses of Her People*, 28.

WORKS CITED

Baaki, Brian. "Circulating the Black Rapist: *Sketches in the Life of Joesph Mountain* and Early American Networks of Print." *New England Quarterly* 90, no. 1 (2017): 36–68.

Berry, Diana Ramey. *The Price of Their Pound of Flesh: The Value of the Enslaved from Womb to Grave in the Building of a Nation*. Beacon Press, 2017.

Black, Henry Campbell. "Benefit of Clergy." In *Black's Law Dictionary*, Revised Fourth Edition. West Publishing, 1968.

"Born in Slavery: Slave Narratives from the Federal Writers' Project, 1936 to 1938." Library of Congress, accessed September 10, 2025. https://www.loc.gov/collections/slave-narratives-from-the-federal-writers-project-1936-to-1938/about-this-collection/.

Bradford, Sarah H. *Harriet, The Moses of Her People*. New York: Geo. R. Lockwood & Son, 1886. https://docsouth.unc.edu/neh/harriet/harriet.html.

Brittain, R. P. "Cruentation: In Legal Medicine and in Literature." *Medical History* 9, no. 1 (1965): 82–88.

Chien, Colleen. "America's Paper Prisons: The Second Chance Gap." *Michigan Law Review* 119, no. 3 (2020): 519–612.

De Ceglia, Francesco Paolo, ed. *The Body of Evidence: Corpses and Proofs in Early Modern European Medicine*. Brill, 2020.

Douglass, Frederick. *Narrative of the Life of Frederick Douglass, an American Slave*. Boston: Anti-Slavery Office, 1845.

Equiano, Olaudah. *The Interesting Narrative of the Life of Olaudah Equiano, or Gustavus Vassa, The African. Written by Himself*. London: Olaudah Equiano, 1789.

Fede, Andrew. "Legitimized Violent Slave Abuse in the American South, 1619–1865: A Case Study of Law and Social Change in Six Southern States." *American Journal of Legal History* 29 (1985): 93–150.

Frazier, Harriet C. *Slavery and Crime in Missouri, 1773–1865*. McFarland and Company, 2001.

Gillmer, Jason A. "Lawyers and Slaves: A Remarkable Case of Representation from the Antebellum South." *University of Miami Race and Social Justice Law Review* 1 (2011): 37–65.

Gregg, Alexander. *History of the Old Cheraws*. New York: Richardson and Company, 1867.

Hadden, Sally E. *Slave Patrols: Law and Violence in Virginia and South Carolina*. Harvard University Press, 2001.

Henry, H. M. *The Police Control of the Slave in South Carolina*. Emory and Henry College, 1914. Reprint, Forgotten Books, 2018.

Hindus, Michale S. "Black Justice Under White Law: Criminal Prosecutions of Blacks in Antebellum South Carolina." *Journal of American History* 63, no. 3 (1976): 575–99.

Hindus, Michale S. *Prison and Plantation: Crime, Justice, and Authority in Massachusetts and South Carolina, 1767–1878*. University of North Carolina Press, 2017.

Jacobs, Harriet. *Incidents in the Life of a Slave Girl, Written by Herself*. Boston, 1861.

Johnson, Michael P. "Runaway Slaves and Slave Communities in South Carolina, 1799 to 1830." *The William and Mary Quarterly* 38, no. 3 (1981): 418–41.

Marshall, Amani. "'They Will Endeavor to Pass for Free': Enslaved Runaways' Performances of Freedom in Antebellum South Carolina." *Slavery & Abolition* 31, no. 2 (2010): 161–80.

Martin, Jonathan D. *Divided Mastery: Hiring in the American South*. Harvard University Press, 2004.

Maza, Sara. *Thinking About History*. University of Chicago Press, 2017.

Miles, Tiya Alicia. *All that She Carried: The Journey of Ashley's Sack, A Black Family Keepsake*. Random House, 2021.

Morgan, Philip D. "Colonial South Carolina Runaways: Their Significance for Slave Culture." *Slavery & Abolition* 6, no. 3 (1985): 57–78.

Morgan, Philip D. "Work and Culture: The Task System and the World of Lowcountry Blacks, 1700 to 1880." *The William and Mary Quarterly* 39, no. 4 (1982): 563–99.

Northup, Solomon. *Twelve Years a Slave*. Buffalo, NY: Derby, Orton and Mulligan, 1853.

O'Neall, John Belton. *The Negro Law of South Carolina*. Columbia, SC: John G. Bowman, 1848.

Peterson, Nora Martin. *Involuntary Confessions of the Flesh in Early Modern France*. University of Delaware Press, 2016.

Plummer, Jonathan. *Dying Confession of Pomp, A Negro Man, Who Was Executed at Ipswich*. Newburyport, MA: Jonathan Plummer, 1795.

Rosen, Rebecca M. "Framing Mark: Reading Africanist Presence in Early American Broadsides." *Early American Literature* 59, no. 2 (2024): 419–29.

Rosen, Rebecca M. "'The Voice of the Innocent Blood Cries Aloud from the Ground to Heaven': Speaking and Discovering Infanticide in the Early American Northeast." *Early American Literature* 57, no. 1 (2022): 85–122.

Schweninger, Loren. "Counting the Costs: Southern Planters and the Problem of Runaway Slaves, 1790–1860." *Business and Economic History* 28, no. 2 (1999): 267–75.

Scott, James C. *Domination and the Arts of Resistance: Hidden Transcripts*. Yale University Press, 2008.

"Separate Property of Married Women 1849–1872." *Polk County, Texas, Record Book B*. Liberty, Texas: Sam Houston Library and Research Center.

Sketches of the Life of Joseph Mountain, a Negro Who Was Executed at New-Haven, on the 20th Day of October, 1790. New Haven, CT: T. and S. Green, 1790.

State Plat Books (Columbia Series). S 213192. South Carolina Department of Archives and History.

The State v. Garrett, a Slave. Marion District Magistrate and Freeholders Court (1844).

The State v. Sam, a Slave. Anderson District Magistrate and Freeholders Court (1861).

The State v. Sip or Scipio and Hepsa, Slaves. Marion District Magistrate and Freeholders Court, Marion, SC (1850).

Schwarz, Philip J. *Twice Condemned: Slaves and the Criminal Laws of Virginia, 1705–1865*. Lawbook Exchange Ltd., 1998.

Trial Papers of Magistrates and Freeholders. Anderson District, microfilm. OCLC 866493242. South Carolina Department of Archives and History.

US Census, 1840. *Family Search*, accessed September 10, 2025. https://www .familysearch.org/ark:/61903/1:1:XHRY-Z7S.

Wertheimer, John W. *Race and the Law in South Carolina: From Slavery to Jim Crow*. Amherst College Press, 2023.

Wood, Betty. "'Until He Shall Be Dead, Dead, Dead,': The Judicial Treatment of Slaves in Eighteenth-Century Georgia." *The Georgia Historical Quarterly* 71, no. 3 (1987): 377–98.

Wyatt-Brown, Bertram. "The Mask of Obedience: Male Slave Psychology in the Old South." *The American Historical Review* 93, no. 5 (1988): 1228–52.

Community Commitment

A Key to Recruitment and Retention at South Carolina's Rural-Serving Institutions

Todd C. Couch

In recent years, higher education has faced increased public scrutiny. Various factors, including heightened political polarization, economic challenges, and skyrocketing student debt, have fueled demands for colleges and universities to demonstrate their value to the public. A recent Pew Research Center report reveals that only twenty-five percent of adults in the United States view a four-year degree as very important. Furthermore, forty-nine percent believe a four-year degree is less valuable today than twenty years ago, and only twenty-two percent consider it worth the financial investment.[1] Adding to this skepticism is the perception that institutions prioritize ideological agendas over equipping students with practical skills for the future.[2] Given the public's attitudes toward higher education, industry consultants have described the contemporary academy as experiencing a "reckoning with relevance."[3]

Despite the public's suspicion, evidence consistently shows that earning a four-year degree significantly enhances life opportunities. Increased career stability, access to diverse professional networks, and eligibility for roles requiring advanced qualifications are among the benefits afforded to degree holders.[4] Additionally, college graduates benefit from higher lifelong earnings, improved health outcomes, and increased self-esteem.[5] For instance, the 2023 annual report of the Association of Public & Land-Grant Universities notes that individuals with a four-year degree earn, on average, $1.2 million more over their lifetimes than those without.[6] Furthermore, individuals with four-year degrees experience better physical and mental health compared with those without.[6] These benefits are especially pronounced for students attending rural or rural-serving institutions, including many in South Carolina. These colleges and universities exist within dynamic contexts that must be analyzed to fully unearth the life-changing benefits these institutions offer their students, employees, and the communities they serve.

Rural-Serving Institutions

Rural-serving institutions address the critical needs of rural communities, such as economic development, health care, and education by partnering with local governments, businesses, and nonprofit organizations to drive regional growth.[7] Students who attend these institutions often come from geographically isolated communities and have limited access to educational resources.[8] For these students, attending a rural institution frequently offers a pathway out of poverty and toward financial stability.[9] The Alliance for Research on Regional Colleges (ARRC) identifies thirty-two of South Carolina's thirty-three public and twenty-seven private colleges and universities as either rural located or rural serving.[10] Together, these institutions support approximately 109,484 students, with 100,473 learners pursuing undergraduate degrees and 9,011 enrolled in advanced graduate studies. Of note is the socioeconomic background of the learners at these institutions.

According to the Alliance for Research on Regional Colleges (ARRC), 57.2% of South Carolina's rural learners are Pell eligible, meaning that they demonstrate significant financial need to pursue higher education. This datum highlights that the Pell eligibility of students attending rural and rural-serving institutions in South Carolina is twenty-seven percent higher than the state's total average if institutions in larger urban and suburban areas are included.[11] This observation highlights the economic disparity experienced by the residents of rural South Carolina. Students among the state's rural populations are intellectually capable but frequently lack the financial resources to support their education. Fortunately, the Pell program allows these students to experience the social mobility commonly provided by a four-year degree.

In addition to the socioeconomic background of South Carolina's rural students, the ARRC found that sixteen percent of the state's rural learners may be classified as nontraditional or adult learners, meaning that they are students twenty-five years of age or older.[12] These students often enter higher education later in life as a result of delaying their education for military service, losing access to a recent job or career path, or needing to upskill for a promotion at their existing place of employment.[13] The nontraditional rural learner's pursuit of higher education is frequently connected to the changing economic opportunities available in their community. As the blue-collar jobs that once defined much of rural South Carolina continue to evolve, community members are seeking higher education as a means of competing in a hypercompetitive and globalized marketplace.[14] South

Carolina's rural-located and rural-serving institutions provide the state's rural residents with improved economic prospects and the ability to pivot careers as the demands of the modern workplace continue to shift. By bridging gaps in education and resources, these institutions play a vital role in sustaining rural communities.

The success of South Carolina's rural-serving institutions and their students is closely tied to their personalized, community-focused culture. At these institutions, students experience small class sizes, faculty who are deeply involved in community activities, and a campus focused on addressing local economic and social challenges. Additionally, the faculty and staff at South Carolina's rural institutions frequently hold influential roles within their communities, providing them with opportunities to form supportive relationships with students external to the college or university campus.[15] Together, the elements of this community-focused culture create an uplifting environment where students are seen not just as learners but as fellow community members contributing to the town's well-being.

The deep connections established within rural institutions also create personal investments for faculty and staff in students' success.[16] The significance of campus relationships can be observed in the individualized mentorship provided to students in South Carolina's rural institutions. Unlike the broad-stroke approach often seen at larger institutions, mentorship at rural-serving colleges across the state is tailored to each student's unique goals and circumstances.[17] This personalized guidance leads to higher persistence, shorter time to degree, and improved graduation rates among South Carolina's rural learners.[18] For these students, the promise of higher education becomes a tangible reality through intentional mentorship. The relationships created on rural campuses are not merely transactional. Rather, they are often deep and last well beyond graduation.

Rural-serving institutions' community-facing culture extends beyond the college and university campus. Frequently hosting community events, such as job fairs and health clinics, South Carolina's rural institutions actively work to bring students, faculty, and local residents together. These activities help students see the practical impact of their education while simultaneously fostering a sense of pride and belonging.[19] Additionally, these efforts by rural colleges across the state provide opportunities for rural institutions to learn more about the needs facing their communities and explore how best they may be of service.[20]

Rural-serving institutions play an indispensable role in fostering the well-being of rural communities by addressing the unique challenges faced by students and industry in these areas. These institutions serve not only as pathways to education and social mobility but also as engines of economic growth and community engagement. The personalized support systems, mentorship programs, and community-focused cultures that they foster enable students to thrive despite financial and geographic barriers. By bridging educational gaps and adapting to the shifting demands of the workforce, South Carolina's rural-serving colleges and universities empower and uplift the rural populations they serve.

Despite the critical roles they occupy within rural communities, rural-serving institutions face significant challenges in recruiting and retaining faculty and staff. Among these challenges are difficulty in offering competitive salaries, limited professional development opportunities, and geographic isolation, all of which can deter prospective candidates.[21] Low educational attainment levels in rural communities further complicate recruitment efforts, as qualified candidates are often reluctant to relocate to areas lacking cultural and recreational amenities.[22] Even when candidates accept positions, many struggle to adjust to the rural lifestyle and report high turnover intentions.[23] Brantley and Shomaker's recent report for the College and University Professional Association for Human Resources documents the difficulty of adjusting to rural life and its impact on staff turnover rates, noting that colleges in rural areas experience thirteen percent higher attrition rates compared with their urban counterparts.[24]

Because of the community-centric culture fostered at rural-serving institutions, the consequences of their recruitment and retention challenges are felt directly by students, faculty, and the local community. As institutions experience increased faculty and staff attrition and prolonged position vacancies, students lose trust in the institution's commitment to their academic and professional success. Adequate staffing is crucial for addressing the mental health issues, food and housing insecurity, and postpandemic learning loss that many rural learners face.[25] Additionally, faculty and staff shortages lead to larger class sizes, reduced course offerings, and diminished opportunities for individualized support, affecting many of rural institutions' fundamental points of value. Furthermore, as their colleagues exit the institution, faculty and staff lose critical institutional knowledge, and collaborative efforts between the institution and the broader community are disrupted.[26] These issues underscore the urgent need for creative solutions to recruit and retain talented faculty and staff in rural higher education. Without strategic innovation, the future of South Carolina's rural-serving institutions, along with all of the promise they provide for the state's rural communities, may fall into question.

A More Holistic Strategy

Improving faculty recruitment and retention at South Carolina's rural-serving institutions requires strategies tailored to the unique qualities of rural colleges and the communities they serve. Unfortunately, most existing research focuses on metropolitan contexts and fails to address rural-specific challenges and opportunities.[27] To address the recruitment and retention obstacles faced by the state's rural institutions, a strategy must be developed that approaches the context of rural-serving institutions holistically. Special attention should be given to efforts that increase employees' connection to both the campus and the larger community. Examples may include mentorship opportunities for new hires, exposing job candidates as well as new hires to local cultural experiences, and highlighting the institution's deep community involvement. A successful strategy must explore how South Carolina's rural colleges may utilize internal and external resources and relationships to construct a well-rounded approach to increasing recruitment and retention.

Organizational Commitment

Beginning the process of developing a more holistic recruitment strategy may be informed by the existing research on organizational commitment, which explores employees' dedication to their organization. According to Allen and Meyer, employees develop a sense of commitment to their organization that is based on connecting to the organization's mission and goals, feelings of personal obligation, workplace benefits, and relationships with coworkers.[28] These types of commitment may be referred to as affective, normative, and continuance commitment. Collectively, the three styles of commitment construct a significant internal instrument for evaluating and increasing faculty and staff retention. South Carolina's rural institutions can use this mechanism to develop strategies for enhancing internal efforts to decrease employee attrition. The following paragraphs offer recommendations for the practical application of each form of organizational commitment with respect to the state's rural-serving institutions.

Increasing affective commitment within South Carolina's rural colleges and universities requires institutions to maintain clear communication about their mission and values. Frequently, candidates and new hires are exposed to these items during the recruitment and orientation processes but are provided decreasing opportunities to explicitly engage with them as they settle into new positions. This creates an increased perceived distance between the employee and the organization's values, which contributes to burnout and turnover intentions.[29] If they are to develop a sense of belonging and commitment to the organization, new faculty and staff must understand the larger impact that their work has on students and how it furthers the college's mission. To aid in this process, rural institutions may explore hosting regular town hall meetings in which senior leadership clearly articulates institutional values and communicates to employees how their work directly contributes to accomplishing institutional milestones, such as improved graduation rates and community projects. By increasing opportunities for employees to engage explicitly with their institutional mission and values, South Carolina's rural colleges create an intentional context for improving levels of affective commitment among their employees and reducing turnover intentions.

As faculty and staff experience an increased resonance with their college's mission and values, their connection often develops into a sense of obligation to the organization. This normative commitment frequently emerges as employees encounter roles with elevated responsibility within the organization.[30] South Carolina's rural institutions may explore implementing *formalized* mentorship structures within their organizations, in which experienced faculty serve as advisors for their less experienced colleagues as a means of bolstering normative commitment. Many rural colleges have informal mentorship programs, but unless the mentor is already intrinsically motivated to guide less experienced faculty, the informal nature of these relationships does not necessarily communicate a level of increased responsibility on behalf of the mentor.[31] A more formalized approach to mentorship at rural institutions, however, may increase normative commitment among more experienced employees, as they would be explicitly given a stake in the success of their less experienced colleagues, thereby formally increasing their responsibility within the organization.

Cultivating campus relationships and, where possible, increasing workplace benefits can not only increase employees' connection with institutional values and their sense of obligation to the organization but also decrease faculty and staff attrition at South Carolina's rural institutions. Continuance commitment's power to reduce turnover lies in an organization's ability to foster positive interpersonal relationships and invest in the holistic well-being of its employees.[32] South Carolina's rural-serving institutions would benefit from offering more dedicated team-building opportunities. Research has long recognized the positive impact of staff retreats on increasing team morale and providing a context for interpersonal relationships to develop.[33] As organizations intentionally invest in cultivating these personal bonds between coworkers, they observe improved group cohesion, an increase in team productivity, and a heightened sense of commitment to the organization.[34] Should the state's rural institutions dedicate a portion of their limited resources to campus-wide retreats, evidence suggests that it will likely be a worthwhile expenditure for the return it provides in increased continuance commitment and reduced employee turnover.

Strategically investing in the organizational commitment of their employees is something that South Carolina's rural-serving institutions must seriously consider as they seek to reduce faculty and staff attrition. Vacant positions on campus erode trust in the organization and directly affect the college's ability to fulfill its obligations to students and the broader community. However, the research on organizational commitment provides a set of valuable mechanisms for increasing employee retention and fortifying rural institutions against the loss of talented faculty and staff. Through clear, frequent communication of the institution's mission and values, colleges can increase the affective commitment of their employees. The development of formalized mentorship structures offers valuable opportunities for experienced faculty and staff to guide less experienced colleagues and develop an increased sense of responsibility within the organization. As this normative commitment increases, attrition will begin to decline. Furthermore, by intentionally creating contexts to cultivate interpersonal relationships with coworkers such as campus-wide retreats, rural institutions can increase continuance commitment, which is shown to positively affect employees' desire to remain at an organization. Through using the three tools of organizational commitment, South Carolina's rural-serving institutions can empower themselves to continue providing valuable service to the state's rural communities.

Community Commitment

As noted previously, research on organizational commitment provides rural institutions with mechanisms for increasing faculty and staff retention.

These largely internally focused efforts emphasize steps organizations can take within the context of their campus to improve employee commitment. Although these strategies are proven to be impactful, they ignore the fact that South Carolina's rural institutions exist within a larger community context and that it is this specific context that contributes to faculty and staff attrition.[35] If the state's rural-serving institutions are to minimize turnover and increase recruitment efforts, they must develop a reasonable strategy for integrating employees into the communities they serve. Expanding the fundamental ideas offered by research on organizational commitment to explore methods of increasing employees' commitment to the community in which they live may provide such a strategy. This expanded framework is referred to as *community commitment*, the extension of the fundamentals of organizational commitment beyond the workplace and into the larger communities in which organizations exist. Applying the principles of affective, normative, and continuance commitment to a community context may provide a framework for South Carolina's rural institutions to increase faculty and staff retention.

Improving affective commitment relies on increasing employees' resonance with an organization's mission and values. An extension of this concept to the community context would assert that affective commitment may be observed in a resident's connection to the larger community's mission and values. In the recruitment process, rural institutions can work to establish affective commitment with the community by providing job candidates with opportunities to meet with local government and community leaders. During these meetings, applicants have a chance to become familiar with the community's aspirations and values. A candidate who connects with these issues has a higher likelihood of being a future employee who is invested in the success of the larger community. Their investment, which is based on resonance with community values, would reflect the faculty and staff members' affective community commitment. Thus, if South Carolina's rural institutions are intentional about incorporating local community leaders into the recruitment process, they will provide an opportunity to establish affective community commitment, which would positively affect retention.

To further strengthen their recruitment and retention efforts, rural institutions should seek to establish normative commitment between employees and the larger community. An investment based on a personal sense of obligation, often in the form of increased responsibility, directly improves faculty and staff's commitment to their organization.[36] Extending this idea to the community context would imply that a personal sense of obligation to the larger community would reduce a resident's desire to relocate. Beginning with the recruitment process, rural institutions can take an active role in helping employees identify local needs and connecting them with community organizations. Traditionally, this type of networking has been left up to the faculty or staff members to navigate themselves. If South Carolina's rural institutions took an active role in making these connections for their employees, they would provide a context for establishing normative community commitment. Community-facing activities such as neighborhood cleanups and other volunteer opportunities can be useful in making the connections needed to establish a sense of obligation, thereby increasing employees' desire to live in the local community and reducing turnover intention for rural institutions.

Continuance commitment relies on institutional benefits and interpersonal relationships' ability to increase an employee's commitment to the organization. Extending this concept to the community context would assert that residents will desire to stay within their community if personal relationships and community benefits are strong enough. If rural institutions strategically partnered with local businesses to offer dual-career opportunities for the spouses or partners of college employees, they could offer a significant benefit to prospective employees and strengthen the local workforce. This approach would not require additional financial resources on behalf of the institution in the same way a traditional university spousal hire does, but it would offer the benefit of addressing the employee's familial needs while providing an additional context for interpersonal relationships to develop. Rural institutions may also invest in sponsoring the many local cultural festivals that are ever present across South Carolina's rural communities. These events serve as cultural hubs, frequently cultivating personal relationships in rural communities.[37] Through establishing intentional partnerships with the local community, rural institutions have an opportunity to increase employment benefits and create contexts for employees to develop meaningful relationships within the community. If this opportunity is taken, South Carolina's rural colleges should observe enhanced community commitment among their employees and reduced turnover.

Although the data consistently show that increasing employees' organizational commitment reduces turnover intentions, South Carolina's rural-serving institutions must explore a holistic approach to improving recruitment and retention efforts. In addition to the more internally focused strategies frequently used by rural colleges, an attempt must be made to integrate external efforts into their endeavors at reducing attrition.

Extending the principles of organizational commitment to the community context in the form of "community commitment" may provide a meaningful starting point. If South Carolina's rural institutions invest in cultivating affective, normative, and continuance community commitment, they have an opportunity to increase employees' desire to live within the communities they serve. Integrating the framework of community commitment into their recruitment and retention strategy, alongside long-standing efforts at increasing organizational commitment, will provide South Carolina's rural colleges and universities with a more holistic approach to attracting talented faculty and staff, enabling them to better fulfill their critical role in rural communities.

Conclusion

As higher education finds itself at a crossroads in terms of its perceived value to the public, it has never been more important that South Carolina's colleges and universities be able to communicate the life-changing opportunities they offer students effectively. This conversation must emphasize the social mobility experienced by rural learners and the impact of rural institutions on local economic development. However, for the state's rural colleges to continue to serve as vital resources for rural communities and their residents, they must develop holistic approaches to employee recruitment and retention. Traditional efforts aligned with strengthening organizational commitment only address half of the retention issues facing South Carolina's rural institutions. In addition to these internally directed endeavors, rural colleges must invest in integrating faculty and staff into the larger community as early as during the recruitment process. By increasing the campus' connection to the surrounding community, rural-serving institutions have an opportunity to increase the community commitment of their employees. Combining this community-focused approach with institutional efforts to increase organizational commitment will provide South Carolina's rural colleges with a holistic approach to recruitment and retention that empowers them to continue offering life-changing opportunities to rural communities for years to come.

Todd C. Couch is an associate professor of sociology and codirector of African and African American Studies at Francis Marion University. He is professionally interested in applied sociological research focused on creating, promoting, and maintaining equitable communities and organizations.

NOTES

1. Fry et al., "Is College Worth It?"
2. Parker, "The Growing Partisan Divide."
3. Workman, "Higher Ed's Reckoning with Relevance."
4. Workman, "Higher Ed's Reckoning with Relevance."
5. Fry et al., "Is College Worth It?"; Horowitz and Parker, "How Americans View Their Jobs."
6. "2023 Annual Report," Association of Public & Land-Grant Universities.
7. Koricich, "Crafting Better Rural-Focused Postsecondary Policy, 67–69"; McNamee, "Rural-Located Institutions and Rural-Serving Institutions."
8. Manly et al., "Who Are Rural Students?" 1–5.
9. Iselm and Boatman, "Exploring Economic Returns Across Rural-Serving Colleges."
10. Koricich et al., "Introducing Our Nation's Rural-Serving Postsecondary Institutions."
11. Koricich et al., "Introducing Our Nation's Rural-Serving Postsecondary Institutions."
12. Koricich et al., "Introducing Our Nation's Rural-Serving Postsecondary Institutions."
13. Kenner and Weinerman, "Adult Learning Theory," 88.
14. Bellare et al., "Motivations and Barriers for Adult Learners," 31.
15. Mitchell et al., "Recruiting and Retaining Higher Education Leaders," 30–34.
16. Schulte and Schreder, "Rural Students Find Their Voice," 71–72.
17. See Martinez et al., "Landscape of Mentorship Programs," and Anderson et al., "Experiences of Students in Recovery," 1; 3–6.
18. Islem and Boatman, "Exploring Economics Returns Across Rural-Serving Colleges."
19. Olcoń et al., "No University Without Community," 2004–2006.
20. Olcoń et al., "No University Without Community," 2009–2010.
21. Wood et al., "If We Get You, How Can We Keep You?" 6–12.
22. See Leist, "Exemplary Rural Community College Presidents," and Murray, "Recruiting and Retaining Rural Community College Faculty," 3–7; 57–61.
23. Mitchell et al., "Recruiting and Retaining Higher Education Leaders for the Rural Community College," 26–27.
24. Brantley and Shomaker, "What's Next for the Higher Education Workforce?"
25. Weissman, "The Great Resignation at Community Colleges."
26. Menzies, "Continuity and Churn," 5.
27. Mitchell et al., "Recruiting and Retaining Higher Education Leaders," 26–27.
28. Allen and Meyer, "The Measurement and Antecedents of Affective, Continuance, and Normative Commitment," 13–14.
29. See Bucklin et al., "Predictors of Early Faculty Attrition," 4–6.
30. Meyer and Parfyonova, "Normative Commitment in the Workplace," 290–92.
31. Herrbach et al., "Undesired Side Effect?" 1562–66.
32. Vandenberghe et al., "Continuance Commitment and Turnover," 404–5.
33. Traba and Yoo, "Staff Retreats," 55–56.
34. Schrank et al., "Institution-Wide Retreats," 372–73.

35. Mitchell et al., "Recruiting and Retaining Higher Education Leaders," 26–28.
36. Verma and Kaur, "Faculty Retention Dynamics."
37. Hjalager and Kwiatkowski, "Entrepreneurial Implications, Prospects and Dilemmas in Rural Festivals," 3–6.

WORKS CITED

"2023 APLU Annual Report." Association of Public & Land-Grant Universities, accessed September 10, 2025. https://www.aplu.org/wp-content/uploads/APLU_AR23_F.pdf.

Allen, Natalie J., and John P. Meyer. "The Measurement and Antecedents of Affective, Continuance, and Normative Commitment to the Organization." *Journal of Occupational Psychology* 63, no. 1 (1990): 1–18. https://doi.org/10.1111/j.2044-8325.1990.tb00506.x.

Bellare, Yamini, Adam Smith, Kelcee Cochran, and Samuel Garcia Lopez. "Motivations and Barriers for Adult Learner Achievement: Recommendations for Institutions of Higher Education." *Adult Learning* 34, no. 1 (2023): 30–39.

Brantley, Andy, and Rob Shomaker. "What's Next for the Higher Education Workforce? A Look at the Challenges and Opportunities That Lie Ahead." College and University Professional Association for Human Resources, Spring 2021. https://www.cupahr.org/.

Bucklin, Brenda, Morgan Valley, Cheryl Welch, V. Tran Zung, and Steven R. Lowenstein. "Predictors of Early Faculty Attrition at One Academic Medical Center." *BMC Medical Education* 14, no. 1 (2014): 1–7. https://dx.doi.org/10.1186/1472-6920-14-27.

Fry, Richard, Dana Braga, and Kim Parker. "Is College Worth It?" Pew Research Center, May 23, 2024. https://www.pewresearch.org/social-trends/2024/05/23/is-college-worth-it-2.

Herrbach, Oliver, and Karim Mignonac. "Undesired Side Effect? The Promotion of Non-Commitment in Formal vs. Informal Mentorships." *International Journal of Human Resource Management* 22, no. 7 (2011): 1554–69. https://doi.org/10.1080/09585192.2011.561965.

Hjalager, Anne-Mette, and Grzegorz Kwiatkowski. "Entrepreneurial Implications, Prospects and Dilemmas in Rural Festivals." *Journal of Rural Studies* 63 (2018): 217–28. https://doi.org/10.1016/j.jrurstud.2017.02.019.

Horowitz, Juliana Menasce, and Kim Parker. "How Americans View Their Jobs." Pew Research Center, March 30, 2023. https://www.pewresearch.org/.

Islem, Shadman, and Angela Boatman. "Exploring Economic Returns Across Rural-serving Colleges." *Institute for Higher Education Policy* 4 (2024): ii–29. https://doi.org/10.31235/osf.io/xfw7j.

Kenner, Cari, and Jason Weinerman. "Adult Learning Theory: Applications to Non-Traditional College Students." *Journal of College Reading and Learning* 41, no. 2 (2011): 87–96. https://doi.org/10.1080/10790195.2011.10850344.

Koricich, Andrew. "Crafting Better Rural-Focused Postsecondary Policy by Identifying Rural-Serving Institutions." *The Rural Educator* 43, no. 4 (2022): 67–69. https://scholarsjunction.msstate.edu/cgi/viewcontent.cgi?article=1374&context=ruraleducator.

Koricich, Andrew, Vanessa A. Sansone, Alisa Hicklin Fryar, Cecilia Orphan, and Kevin R. McClure. *Introducing Our Nation's Rural-Serving Postsecondary Institutions: Moving Toward Greater Visibility and Appreciation.* Alliance for Research on Regional Colleges, January 31, 2022. https://www.regionalcolleges.org/project/ruralserving.

Lawrence, Elizabeth M. "Why Do College Graduates Behave More Healthfully Than Those Who Are Less Educated?" *Journal of Health and Social Behavior* 58, no. 3 (2017): 291–306.

Leist, James Ernest. "Exemplary Rural Community College Presidents: A Case Study of How Well Their Professional Qualities Mirror Job Advertisements." PhD diss., Texas Tech University, 2005.

Manly, Catherine, Ryan S. Wells, and Suzan Kommers. "Who Are Rural Students? How Definitions of Rurality Affect Research on College Completion." *Research in Higher Education* 61, no. 1 (2019): 764–79.

Martinez, Mayra Nuñez, Leandra Cate, Lia Wetzstein, and Katie Kovacich, K. "Landscape of Mentorship Programs at Rural Serving Community Colleges." Community College Research Initiatives, 2023. https://www.washington.edu/ccri/RLS_DataNote1/.

McNamee, Ty C. "Rural-Located Institutions and Rural-Serving Institutions: What We Know and Where We Go from Here." American Council on Education, 2024. https://www.acenet.edu/.

Menzies, Loic. "Continuity and Churn: Understanding and Responding to the Impact of Teacher Turnover." *London Review of Education* 20, no. 1 (2023): 1–13. https://doi.org/10.14324/lre.21.1.20.

Meyer, John P., and Natalya M. Parfyonova. "Normative Commitment in the Workplace: A Theoretical Analysis and Re-Conceptualization." *Human Resource Management Review* 20 (2010): 283–94.

Mitchell, Robert, Nicholas Fuselier, and Patty Witkowsky. "Recruiting and Retaining Higher Education Leaders for the Rural Community College 'Lifestyle.'" *Journal of Education Human Resources* 42, no. 1 (2024): 26–44.

Murray, John P. "Recruiting and Retaining Rural Community College Faculty." *New Directions for Community Colleges* 137 (2007): 57–64.

Olcoń, Katarzyna, Rugare Mugumbate, Mim Fox, et al. "No University Without Community: Engaging the Community in Social Work Simulations." *Higher Education Research & Development* 42, no. 2 (2023): 1–15. https://doi.org/10.1080/07294360.2023.2197192.

O'Meara, Kerry Ann, Lorilee R. Sandmann, Jonn Saltmarsh, and Dwighty E. Giles Jr. "Studying the Professional Lives and Work of Faculty Involved in Community Engagement." *Innovative Higher Education* 36, no. 2 (2010): 83–96. https://doi.org/10.1007/s10755-010-9159-3.

Parker, Kim. "The Growing Partisan Divide in Views of Higher Education." Pew Research Center, August 19, 2019. https://www.pewresearch.org/.

Schrank, Benjamin R., John A. Fuller, Colleen M. Gallagher, et al. "Institution-Wide Retreats Foster Organizational Learning and Action at a Comprehensive Cancer Center." *Journal of Cancer Education* 39, no. 4 (2024): 368–73. https://doi.org/10.1007/s13187-024-02418-9.

Schulte, Ann K., and Karen Schreder. "Rural Students Find Their Voice on a College Campus." *The Rural Educator* 45, no. 2 (2024): 68–73.

Scott, Alison, Ashton Anderson, Karen Harper, and Moya L. Alfonso. "Experiences of Students in Recovery on a Rural College Campus: Social Identity and Stigma." *SAGE Open* 6, no. 4 (2016): 1–8. https://doi.org/10.1177/2158244016674762.

Traba, Chris, and Moonja Yoo. "Staff Retreats: Building a Team." *Nursing Management* 26, no. 2 (1995): 54–57.

Vandenberghe, Christian, Alexandra Panaccio, and Ahmed Khalil Ben Ayed. "Continuance Commitment and Turnover: Examining the Moderating Role of Negative Affectivity and Risk Aversion." *Journal of Occupational and Organizational Psychology* 84, no. 2 (2011): 403–24.

Verma, Sahil, and Gurvinder Kaur. "Faculty Retention Dynamics: Investigating the Role of HR Climate, Trust, and Organizational Commitment in Higher Education Context." *SAGE Open* 14, no. 1 (2024): 1–17. https://doi.org/10.1177/21582440241233372.

Weissman, Sara. "The Great Resignation at Community Colleges." *Inside Higher Ed*, 2023. https://www.insidehighered.com/.

Wood, Jo Nell, Kim Finch, and Rachel M. Mirecki. "If We Get You, How Can We Keep You? Problems with Recruiting and Retaining Rural Administrators." *The Rural Educator* 34, no. 2 (2013): 1–28.

Workman, John. "Higher Ed's Reckoning with Relevance: Preview of EAB's State of the Sector." EAB, 2023. https://eab.com/.

Interview

Beyond Noir
A Writer's Interview with Lynn Kostoff
Andrew Geyer

Sometimes a writer manages to transcend genre and create lasting art. Lynn Kostoff is such a writer. Retired from his position as a professor and writer in residence at Francis Marion University, Kostoff is the author of four novels, with two more on the way. He writes the sort of dark, gritty, crime fiction known as *noir*. Like most of his characters, however, Kostoff is a transgressor. He refuses to be pinned down by the "rules" of the noir genre. In his own words: "Bottom line, you've got to tell a story; but I've always tried to do much more." He has succeeded in gorgeous fashion, and the resulting fiction is unique.

Lynn and I spoke recently about his long career as a writer, and I was most impressed with everything I heard. He has paid his dues and then some. Having grown up on a farm outside Youngstown, Ohio, he put himself through both undergraduate and graduate school with a combination of hard work, scholarships, and plain old-fashioned moxie. He built his decades-long career as a university professor using the same recipe. He began teaching developmental English to college athletes and culminated as a writer in residence at Francis Marion University. But Lynn never forgot his origins. Throughout his career, he continued to teach first-year writers, finding great reward in helping novice writers find their voices. So, it should be no surprise that, over the course of his journey as an author, Lynn has become a writer's writer—a dedicated craftsperson who has a great deal to teach those of us who aspire to write well and read with a writer's eye.

I came to our conversation having read two of Kostoff's four published books: his debut novel, *A Choice of Nightmares* (Crown Publishers, 1991), and the much more ambitious *Late Rain* (Tyrus Books, 2010). Because much of our conversation—which teased out Lynn's philosophies on writing, living, and making art—focused on those two works, a bit of background may be helpful for those who may not yet have read these remarkable novels. *A Choice of Nightmares* revolves around a self-deluded dreamer named Robert Staples, a second-rate actor who has convinced himself that he is destined to make it big. His "agent" asks him to deliver a package, which Staples promptly loses, forcing him into the heart of a bloody, high-dollar, drug-running operation and drawing him into a relationship with an alluring but pitiless femme fatale. *Late Rain* revolves around the intersecting needs and desires within a group of characters brought into contact with each other by a murder for hire. When the hit goes wrong and winds up being witnessed by a senior citizen with Alzheimer's disease, a former homicide detective named Ben Decovic—a scarred widower trying to make peace with his past—has to put together the jagged jigsaw pieces of the crime and his own life.

At the beginning of our interview, I confessed that I have never been much of a noir reader. Rather, I have always had a predilection for what

Figure 9.1. Novelist Lynn B. Kostoff on Pawley's Island, 2024. Photograph by Melanie Kostoff.

the current market would label as *literary fiction,* which is to say novels that emphasize character and theme over plot. I quickly followed up that confession with another: "But I love your books." What followed was an enlightening and delightful conversation about genre and art, language and the nature of perception, and the power of storytelling to capture the most important aspects of life.

GEYER. You said that when you set out to write *A Choice of Nightmares,* your intention was to do classic noir with all the tropes. Could you remind our readers of those tropes?

KOSTOFF. These were some of the noir tropes I was writing toward, but please remember there are many other subcategories and shadings:

- Nods toward the tenets of existentialism and the dynamics of tragedy, though, as the novelist Dennis Lehane notes, "In Greek tragedy, they fall from great heights. In noir, they fall from the curb";[1]
- Antiheroes and common/everyday men and women as protagonists who are morally ambiguous;
- A sense of fate and free will colliding, usually with fate winning;
- A woman who functions as a femme fatale, which is to say as a temptress, like an Eve or Siren character;
- A confrontation with various forms of evil, both within and without the protagonist;
- A sense of widespread social corruption;
- An ending that denies easy comfort or reassuring closure.

GEYER. Next, could you give us an example of each from *A Choice of Nightmares* and connect each with the incredibly vivid settings in which they play out in the book?

KOSTOFF. Robert Staples, the protagonist, is a definite antihero. He has deluded himself into believing he will one day catch his big break and become a well-known famous actor, but his career has gone no further than work in low-budget films like *Ninjas from Neptune, Meat Me,* and *It Won't Die.* His chasing after celebrity and fame is a mistaken and deformed version of the American Dream.

Staples is also a classic rationalizer; he is adept at blinding himself to consequences and believing his choices will lead to the fulfillment of his desires, and his blindness ultimately leads him into the starring role in a low-budget tragedy.

Staples also believes he has turned his back on "being ordinary" and is destined for fame and all that it promises. He has given up a stable marriage and life to chase his desires; but, like a line of tipped dominoes, every one of his choices leads to his tragic downfall. The femme fatale is a woman named Denice. She is stronger and smarter than all the rest of the males in the novel, but she is also missing a conscience. She is the embodiment of Robert's fantasies, but he is too blind to see how empty and dangerous they will turn out to be.

Denice is intimately involved in the South Florida drug trade, and Robert's involvement with her leads him to darker and deeper forms of corruption and evil; in particular, dealing with an "enforcer" who has renamed himself Barry From West Palm, as well as corrupt cops and DEA agents. Like the amoral greed behind the ivory trade in Conrad's *Heart of Darkness*, the presence of cocaine in the drug wars corrupts everything and everyone absolutely.

The action in the novel takes place in South Florida, particularly Miami—referred to by a character as "Maimed-ami" because of the pervasive violence and damage the drug trade has produced—and Key West. In the novel, South Florida is a fallen Eden, and Key West, the southernmost point in the United States, becomes the place where everyone's luck runs out. The settings felt like the perfect places for Robert Staples's life and dreams to crash and burn. By the novel's close, Robert has come to understand the concept of "least common denominator" and his place in the universe.

GEYER. Tell me about your choice of setting for *Late Rain*.

KOSTOFF. I had originally intended to set the novel in Myrtle Beach, since it is only a couple hours away from Florence, where I live; but I ended up creating an imaginary beach resort, Magnolia Beach, because over the course of four drafts, many of the Grand Strand and Myrtle Beach reference points kept disappearing and changing. It was more than a little frustrating. The Grand Strand, like so many coastal cities, is constantly in danger of overdevelopment, too much of its earlier beauty and charm being replaced by sprawl. I wanted a setting that was on the verge of becoming a boomtown, not one already, so I created Magnolia Beach, known in *Late Rain* as "The Other Myrtle Beach."

By doing so, I discovered that I had accidentally bumped into another piece of South Carolina history. It turned out that there also had been *another* Magnolia Beach, one between Litchfield Beach and Pawleys Island.

That beach was famous for The Magnolia Beach Club, founded in the 1930s by Lillian Pyatt. Due to segregation, the Club was for African Americans and listed in the now-famous *Green Book*. The Club booked concerts by such musical greats as Duke Ellington, Charlie Parker, and Ray Charles.[2] Magnolia Beach and the Magnolia Beach Club were wiped off the map in 1954 by Hurricane Hazel and eventually became known as McKenzie Beach. The resort, rebuilt there, went bankrupt in 1963. In many ways, the Magnolia Beach in my novels echoes the fragile dynamics of the original as well as the current state of the Grand Strand. It is a setting both inside and outside of history, existing like a promise that no one had bothered to keep or remember.

GEYER. You wrote *A Choice of Nightmares* in the third-person limited point of view. The narrator remains outside the novel's action, but unlike an omniscient narrator, cannot see everything that has taken place. Could you share why you chose to use that viewpoint and if it was part of the original design when you began the novel?

KOSTOFF. *A Choice of Nightmares* was my first novel and a big learning experience for me, particularly in choosing and using point of view. In the first draft, I let Robert Staples tell the story himself in the first person, and while that helped me learn more about his character, it ultimately worked against plotting and pacing. The draft was over five hundred pages because I was faithful to his character, especially his overriding ability to lie to himself and rationalize his choices. In the second draft, I decided to use a "close" third-person limited point of view, as if I were looking over his shoulder throughout the novel. This change immediately cut the draft in half and brought the pace and plot into sharper focus.

GEYER. Moving on to *Late Rain*, the viewpoint you used in that later novel is third-person omniscient. Why did you make that choice for this particular book? Was it your original choice?

KOSTOFF. In the early stages, I saw the characters simply as a group of people, each of whom badly wanted something, and the plot complications weren't planned out. They arose when the personalities and agendas of the characters collided. I tried to nudge and focus the characters' interactions more dramatically in each subsequent draft. The more the characters interacted and bounced off each other, the more they stayed true to who and what they were, and that's what finally opened up the complications and conflicts among them and hopefully made the characters more complex and human for readers. Since there was an ensemble set of characters as protagonists, the use of the third-person omniscient seemed to fit best.

GEYER. For me, both as a writer and a reader, the most impressive element in *Late Rain* is the way you handle that omniscient viewpoint. The way you tie it in with character development is masterful. Specifically (without giving anything away), there are two viewpoint characters with mental handicaps of very different kinds, and the way you capture their individual quirks and challenges in prose almost makes it seem like you're writing in the first person. Can you give the writers in our audience some insight into how you hit upon that strategy, and also some advice about how they might emulate it themselves?

KOSTOFF. For me, character is bedrock; the plot and conflict grow out of that. I spend a lot of prewriting time doing notes and small sketches of and for each character. I see that as an "audition" of sorts that helps me get a fuller picture of each character. A lot of what I come to discover about the characters doesn't end up in the drafts, but it does give me a larger and richer sense of who they are. For example, as a sketch exercise, I might give each character two hundred dollars and send them shopping, cataloging what they would buy at the grocery store and then where they'd spend the rest of the money and what on. Their choices suggest sides and elements of their personalities that help to round out their characters.

Another prewriting exercise I do is generating sentence patterns tied to each character. In many respects, syntax echoes consciousness, and consciousness unlocks character and how he or she perceives the world. Generating these sentences is admittedly an intuitive process; but if I stick with it long enough, I eventually find sentences that seem to fit the characters' personalities. For example, I ended up developing a character by messing around and inverting his original name: Wendall Croy became Croy Wendall. I liked the idea that something did not feel right in the latter, and that led me to developing Croy's way of perceiving the world and others. Croy is childlike and amoral and has constructed a private system of meaning based on numbers and word rhymes. Croy is a criminal and murderer, but functions in a realm beyond conventional judgments. He is the equivalent of an amphibian.

Another character, Jack Carson, is in the late stages of Alzheimer's. While I hoped a man with Alzheimer's witnessing a murder would serve as a good plot hook for readers, I did not want it to devolve into pure melodrama or a plot gimmick. I wanted to capture the feel of someone struggling to hold onto his sense of self and life since a number of sections in the novel are narrated specifically from Jack Carson's point of view. It took quite a few tries before I found the syntax that reflected the slow ghosting of Jack's former solid self.

GEYER. Speaking of characters, you said that you tend to people your books with characters who are willing to break rules. Can you expand on that idea of transgression and how you use it to define your characters?

KOSTOFF. Of all the criteria for responding to a piece of fiction, the question of a character's likeability seems to me to be the most reductive and least productive. It's the equivalent of donning a set of blinders before you go sightseeing. Crime fiction, noir even more than other genres, seems susceptible to this kind of criticism. It's hard to imagine crime writers not hearing at some point that their characters are not likeable or not likeable enough to keep readers turning pages.

That begs the question of why readers turn pages in the first place. The impulse for readers to identify with characters is perfectly understandable. It is the basis of one of the oldest bonds between storytellers and their audience. How that bond is defined, though, when it comes to noir can be problematic.

At bottom, noir is rooted in the concept of transgression. Lines are crossed. Rules are ignored. Laws are broken. Ethics and morals are tested. The fine print in the social contract is exposed. The everyday world and its foundations are put on trial. Because of that, noir does not always show the best sides of humanity. In every respect, it asks for an uncomfortable identification from the audience. Uncomfortable but necessary.

Likeable characters are a different story. They reassure us of our place in the universe and reinforce what we want to see in ourselves. In fiction, they are the mirrors that throw back flattering reflections. But, too often, likeable characters are also synonymous with the status quo. They can be the equivalent of "Do Not Disturb" signs. They may ask the right questions but duck the answers and where they lead.

Noir denies the easy dichotomy between likeable and unlikeable characters and replaces it with a different emphasis and perspective. It asks us to consider the full range of what it means to be *human*. Noir then goes on to ask the hard questions and doesn't flinch at the answers, and there's nothing comfortable in that. Because of that, the endings in noir works often are morally ambiguous or open-ended. The "mystery" is not solved, but deepened and enlarged.

GEYER. As we wind toward a close, I'd like to move to more general questions. Can you talk about your literary influences? For example, we briefly discussed echoes of *The Great Gatsby* in *A Choice of Nightmares*. Which writers have you learned the most from, and which do you recommend for our writerly audience to read and why?

KOSTOFF. Two writers have been especially important to me: Flannery O'Connor and Nathanael West. At bottom, though, I think I've learned from every writer I've ever read, both in terms of what is done well and what isn't. To read like a writer has always been important to me, and there are dozens and dozens of writers that have influenced me in large and small ways. I used to make it a practice of giving my writing students a two- or three-page, single-spaced list of recommended writers based on what they'd written for the class. The influences are everywhere once you start looking.

GEYER. Can you also talk about your love of film and whether your writing has been influenced by any films/directors in particular?

KOSTOFF. As with writing influences, it's hard to narrow down directors who have been important to me, but the primary ones that come to mind (though that could probably change tomorrow) are Terrence Malick/*Badlands*; Robert Altman/*McCabe and Mrs. Miller* and *Nashville*; Roman Polanski/*Chinatown*; David Lynch/*Mullholland Drive*; Billy Wilder/*Double Indemnity* and *Sunset Boulevard*.

GEYER. And finally, is there anything in particular that you'd like to leave our audience with? Anything at all?

KOSTOFF. Please read and read, and then read some more and support authors you love by word-of-mouth recommendations and with online reviews.

There is so much here to carry away, think over. But for me, I think the main thing that I keep coming back to from both the novels and the interview is the idea of redemption.

Raymond Chandler, another noir author whose work transcends the tropes of genre and rises to the level of literary art, once wrote that "In everything that can be called art there is a quality of redemption."[3] That is certainly the case in the work of Lynn Kostoff. The open-ended nature of the fates of Robert Staples and Ben Decovic, as each of the novels in which they figure as protagonists comes to a close, seems to imply that redemption is possible. Difficult. Costly. But possible. A different, perhaps darker, example of the hope for redemption in Kostoff's work is the reader's last glimpse into the consciousness of Jack Carson in *Late Rain,* as seawater washes around his waist. The night is falling, and the tide is rising. But the ocean is perhaps our greatest universal symbol of rebirth.

As a most important coda, in addition to *A Choice of Nightmares* and *Late Rain,* Kostoff's other published works include the novels *Broken Hymns* (Shotgun Honey, 2025), *The Length of Days* (Stark House, 2025), *Words to Die For* (New Pulp Press, 2014), and *The Long Fall: A Novel of Crime* (Carroll & Graf, 2003).

Andrew Geyer currently serves as chair of the English department at the University of South Carolina Aiken and managing editor at *The Petrigru Review.* He is a member of the Texas Institute of Letters and the South Carolina Academy of Authors Literary Hall of Fame. His latest book is *Southern Voices: Fifty Contemporary Poets* (Lamar University Press, coedited with Tom Mack). His latest individually authored book is the story cycle *Lesser Mountains* (Lamar University Press). Honors for Geyer's fiction include an IPPY, an INDIE, and two Spur Awards. He also has a long list of editorial credits, including coediting the award-winning composite anthology *A Shared Voice* (Lamar University Press, coedited with Tom Mack).

NOTES

1. This quotation is attributed to Dennis Lehane, the crime writer best known for *Gone Baby Gone* (William Morrow and Company, 1998), *Mystic River* (William Morrow and Company, 2001), and *Small Mercies* (Harper Perennial, 2023). The origins of the exact quotation have not been traced, but it appears in works with which Lehane has been involved. See, e.g., Douglas Brunt's interview with Lehane, "New England Noir." In the introduction to *Boston Noir,* Lehane makes a similar statement: "In Shakespeare, tragic heroes fall from mountaintops; in noir, they fall from curbs," 9.
2. For a brief accessible history of the Magnolia Beach Club, see "McKenzie Beach," SC Picture Project.
3. Chandler, "The Simple Art of Murder."

WORKS CITED

Chandler, Raymond. "The Simple Art of Murder." *The Atlantic,* December 1944, 53–59. https://cdn.theatlantic.com/media/archives/1944/12/174-6/132330934 .pdf.
Lehane, Dennis, ed. *Boston Noir.* Akashic Books, 1997.

Lehane, Dennis, ed. "New England Noir." Interview by Douglas Brunt, February 12, 2019. YouTube video, 44:56. https://www.youtube.com/watch?v=-MKSBn71GNw.
"McKenzie Beach." *SC Picture Project,* accessed September 10, 2025. https://www.scpictureproject.org/georgetown-county/mckenzie-beach.html.

Review Essay

Bodies and Soul

Four Books by Lowcountry Poets

Jo Angela Edwins

Marcus Amaker, *Hold What Makes You Whole* (Free Verse Press, 2023), 202 pp., paperback $19.99.

Katie Ellen Bowers, *This Earthly Body* (Main Street Rag, 2024), 94 pp., paperback $15.00.

Miho Kinnas, *Waiting for Sunset to Bury Red Camellias* (Free Verse Press, 2023), 88 pp., paperback $8.00.

Yvette R. Murray, *Hush, Puppy* (Finishing Line Press, 2023), 46 pp., paperback $15.99.

In my last review essay for this publication, I stated that so many books had been published by South Carolina poets in and around 2023 that I could not review them all in one essay. Indeed, I cannot review them all in two, but this essay will be the next in a series that will begin to try. Of course, we hope that South Carolina poets continue to publish books at such a pace that this reviewer remains in catch-up mode for a long while. This review essay focuses on books by four poets who at some point in their lives have called the South Carolina Lowcountry home and whose works explore the intersection between the physical and spiritual selves of the speakers and characters.

Marcus Amaker, inaugural poet laureate of Charleston from 2016 to 2022, published his tenth book of poetry, *Hold What Makes You Whole*, in 2023 with his publishing company Free Verse Press. Like his other collections, the book showcases Amaker's various artistic talents as a graphic designer, musician, and poet, as photographs and collages intersperse with rhythmic poems to give the book a multimodal appeal. Dedicated to his great-great-aunt Ruth Hubbard Robinson, a poet who passed away before she and Amaker could republish her 1996 collection *IMAGES: Mirrored from the Heart*, Amaker's book features poems that reflect both the musicality of poetry (for example, "Earthquake Dance," "The Acoustics Here") and the power of family (for example, "Heartline/Bloodline," "A Doctor Tells Us

It's Not a Life or Death Situation"). But the contents of the collection are as diverse as the poet's mind, reflecting especially the lived history of African Americans, most especially African Americans in Charleston. One shining example, "Black Cloth," is dedicated to the nine members of Charleston's Emanuel African Methodist Episcopal Church (also called Mother Emanuel) who were killed when Dylann Roof executed a racially motivated attack at a Bible study meeting in 2015. The poem begins with the powerful command, "Racism,/let us no longer walk in your shoes." The evils of racism are described as "cloaking yourself in a black cloth/like the grim reaper," but the poem moves on to concentrate on the men and women of Mother Emanuel who were killed in racism's name. The women are described as "speak[ing] the light that flows from love," and the men are described as "walk[ing] towards heaven with focus,/even when your shoes were stained/with the dirt of intolerance." The poem calls out to Clementa Pinckney, South Carolina state senator and senior pastor at Mother Emanuel, referencing a black cloth "at Clementa Pinckney's seat,/resting under a single rose." As the poem goes on to celebrate the unity in Charleston inspired by people of various races who were appalled by the violence, it concludes with a call to remove the Confederate flag from the statehouse grounds, a call that was thankfully eventually heard by South Carolina Governor Nikki Haley:

> And I would rather hang a black cloth
> on a flag pole
> than give the confederate flag
> another glimpse of the sun.

Other poems in *Hold What Makes You Whole* contemplate the disproportionate effect of police brutality on African Americans. "The Creepy Crawlies" is dedicated to Jamal Sutherland, a mentally ill African-American man who died in North Charleston's Sheriff Al Cannon Detention Center in 2021. The opening stanza depicts police as "cockroaches" hiding in wait on busy highways to pull over unsuspecting African-American drivers, who find themselves afraid, fearful that "[i]nstead of you/killing the bug,/the bug kills you." By the end of the poem, the "slick brown skin/that scares" the police becomes the cockroach they feel justified in killing. "Black Numerology" is dedicated to Walter Scott, the man whom police officer Michael Slager killed in North Charleston with a gunshot to the back in 2015. Slager initially lied about the circumstances surrounding Scott's death, until a video appeared showing what actually happened. In the poem, Amaker's speaker states that he watched the video of Scott's death hundreds of times and counted the thirteen steps Scott took in running away from Slager until the eighth bullet killed him. The poem imagines how many steps he took before dying and how many he might have taken had he lived, before powerfully concluding:

> My mouth
> is tired of
> sounding out the syllables
> it takes to talk
> about America's
> favorite pastime:
>
> Counting bullets
> and burying Brown bodies.

It should certainly be noted that many of the poems in *Hold What Makes You Whole* are positive in tone, poems of joy and hope and love. Some are love poems to Amaker's wife, Jordan ("Queen," "Making Love with Only Words"). Some are celebrations of the life of his daughter, Rei, and the poet's wonder at daily living ("Point of View," "Up," "South Sensory"). Others chronicle struggles ("Another Poem about Stuttering," "United States of Anxiety"). Amaker's collection is multivocal, containing both the poet's own unique voice and the imagined voices of others. In this way, it reflects both diversity and unity. As the poet declares in "Connecting the Dots,"

> I   want to hold people closer than the stars
>   hold our attention.
> I want to admire   them for
> longer than   a
> firework   spark.

Charleston native Yvette R. Murray published her chapbook *Hush, Puppy* with Finishing Line Press in 2023. A chapbook is a short collection of poems; Murray's consists of thirty-three poems spanning thirty-six pages. Divided into "Call" and "Response" sections, the collection is a hymn to the Gullah legacies that make up a central component of the rich character of the Charleston area. This slim volume resonates with celebration, frustration, triumph, anger, joy, and reverence. Murray mixes form poems with inventive free verse poems and multiple speakers to reflect the variety of voices represented in Lowcountry communities, especially African-American communities. Charleston is both celebrated and seen for all its dark history, as is illustrated in the lovely piece "Port City," in which the speaker is "[m]esmerized" by the city's mysteries:

> I am lost in the swirl
> of steel, blood and glass.
> Phalanges folded intimately.
> Your shadows leaping back into azaleas
> as if you wish not to be seen
> because you do keep secrets from me

And those secrets are the darkness that the common romantic image of Charleston belies, "Coffin-Trees on avenues/and still winds that blow." Nevertheless, the speaker declares himself a "simple man who desires/the complicated love you give." Similarly, in "Spring Street Ghazal," the poet shows the successful and the downtrodden among the crowds spotted on the busy street. The "blue suit" buying a cappuccino contrasts with the "black-hooded kid with a wood look," as the large pecan trees contrast with the nearly hidden birds' nests settled in the letters of a store sign. In the end, the poet alone notices all of it: "Yvette squints and comes the vision:/Seeing the whole if only you would look."

Some poems in *Hush, Puppy* echo each other in intriguing ways. For example, "R. K."—whose title stands for "Rice Kingdom" and echoes the rice trade in South Carolina that could not be sustained after the end of slavery—reflects on enslaved people's descendants who become property owners themselves, working for the good of their children instead of the good of enslavers. The descendants' success is symbolized by the "[s]ilverware dancing slowly/in the doors of a buffet/crammed full" with the possessions earned by a Pullman porter whose house is decorated with the "diplomas and degrees,/kin and faces,/awards and funeral programs" of a family descended from enslaved people on a rice plantation, though the descendants now live "[f]ar away from the swamp/away from the mud," so distanced from hard farm labor that "a hoe rusts on the back porch." The almost human character of household items and their ability to stand for a family's history are similarly reflected in the poem "The Lazy Susan and the China Cabinet Used to Argue," in which the speaker declares that "once a year not ever twice" these household pieces would argue about "what color

Martin's tie was/Or what type of shoes Medgar was wearing that day." Even the contents of the cabinet—teacups, seafood forks, champagne flutes—would bicker. The speaker, busy cleaning the house, concludes the poem declaring, "Long after the drying was done/I could hear them talking/loud, loud, loud to make sure I would still hear." Indeed, robust (even if ghostly) voices of ancestors resonate throughout Murray's collection in poems with evocative titles like "Carolina Blues," "Notes from Back Pew of Mother Emanuel A.M.E. Church," "Self Portrait as Sweetgrass," and "Minstrel Man," which is a finely crafted pantoum. Ultimately, the collection acknowledges the complexities of fleeing histories of racial oppression in the ancestors' homeland only to face different kinds of racial oppression elsewhere. The final poem of the collection is "Come Back; Dis Ya' Home," a titular line that acts as a refrain in this poem, which is subtitled "A Bop for 2020." The speaker quotes an elder who bemoans the fact that "[f]olk walked off plantations/into another white nightmare" and found themselves "away from rhythms, away from rhythms/that breathe underwater." The elder urges those who left to "[l]et blood memory guide you/back to Purple mindscape" where they might "[d]rink sassafras/strong horse tea,/be a midwife or potter, sew sweetgrass/and build strong mountains again." The land soaked in the ancestors' blood is also the land that nurtures their descendants in Murray's multifaceted portrayal of the South Carolina Lowcountry.

Another Charleston native, Katie Ellen Bowers now calls Heath Springs, SC, in Lancaster County home. The landscapes of both are reflected in some of the poems in her collection *This Earthly Body*. Readers might consider, for example, "A Holy City," in which the poet responds to those who ask why a Charleston native would leave the celebrated city to make a South Carolina small town her home. But, as the volume title suggests, it is the phenomenological landscape of the poet's life within her own body that becomes the central subject of most of the poems in the book. The struggles of being a woman in America, with all its gendered demands and prejudices, radiate through many of these poems, which explore mother–daughter and male–female dynamics with the brave frankness that harkens back to the Confessional poetry of the 1950s and 1960s. The speaker of Bowers's poems frequently calls out the shame visited on girls in their youth who are simultaneously sexualized by their culture and blamed for the sexuality projected upon them when their bodies begin to mature—and sometimes before they mature—as in the sadly disturbing "Rubbing Sand." In "Etymology," Bowers considers the origins of the word *love*, which comes from early terms for *desire*, and declares

> I never could quite grasp why wanting a boy,
>   the one you think you love,
> to slip his fingers between your thighs
> was invasive
>   *see also: encroaching*
>   *see also: crude*
>   *see also: slutty*

At the end of the short poem, the speaker is unashamed to be searching "for understanding/in the map of constellations/freckled onto my lover's back." Erotic poems are peppered throughout the collection, acknowledging the woman's joy in her sexuality, despite a culture that casts aspersions on it, as is illustrated in "What to Make of That," in which the speaker's male Christian friend, who was "once not a Christian," tells her that he "cannot feel the presence of Christ" around her, even though he still concludes that, despite that absence, "anyone would be a fool not to love" her. Poems like "before my new last love(r)," "The Heat of Summer," and "A Promise" show both the tender and the tentative edges of intimate relationships. In many of these poems, the speaker is struggling to love and respect herself, given the mixed messages about morality, female body image, and male expectations that shape her environment.

An additional important subject in *This Earthly Body* is the mother–daughter relationship: both the speaker's relationship with her mother and the speaker's wonder at becoming a mother herself. In the long, multipart poem "A History of Things Some Remembered and Some Not," the speaker portrays a fraught relationship with a mother who struggles with posttraumatic stress disorder, alcoholism, grief, and mental illness. She recalls a childhood when the mother, wracked with grief for her own dying mother and father, refuses to be a supportive parent to her own child, whose father is working hundreds of miles away. The mother's failures become a lesson to the speaker, who sees her mother soften toward the speaker's daughter in a way she never could toward her own. The final section of the poem, in a tone of prosaic resignation, declares, "Anyway, this is fine./We learn from the failures of our parents." By contrast, the last section of the book contains several poems in which the speaker expresses her love for and surprise at her relationship with her own growing daughter. In "Things I've Learned While Taking a Bath with My Daughter," the daughter washes her mother clean and then wants to lie back on her in a posture that reminds the mother of carrying her as a baby, "My body her home again." In "Take That, Fire

Ants," the speaker notices, in the person of her child, the contradictions in human sympathy, as the child leaves cracker crumbs to feed the black ants near the porch but gleefully rides her bike through a fire ant hill, reveling in killing them. Powerfully, the poem concludes, "We seek to provide, but we long to destroy." The same principle might apply to the complicated relationships between humans who should love each other. Indeed, the complexities of love are at the heart of the struggles expressed in Bowers's book, and the same might be said of the final collection under review in this essay.

Hilton Head resident Miho Kinnas draws on her Japanese heritage in her vividly imagistic collection *Waiting for Sunset to Bury Red Camellias*, also published by Amaker's Free Verse Press. The connection between the physical image and its spiritual resonance is especially strong in this volume, as several poems depend on a sensory experience, often of the natural world, described in such a way that illuminates the situation of the soul. This illumination is perhaps most apparent in her gathering of haiku and tanka a third of the way through the book. These small poems create tones from the humorous to the contemplative, to the sad, through their brief depictions of vivid scenes and actions. Any pet owner is likely to identify, for example, with this scene: "burnt bacon/for a few seconds/the dog forgets me." Sudden waves of grief are demonstrated concretely with "I am fine/until crisp iceberg lettuce/brings out my tears." Several individual short poems throughout the collection have similar sharply imagistic effects. "Earthquake" describes the seismic phenomenon as "shaking only the air/not the house with the door that/needs a little lift to lock or unlock." "Weather Forecast" describes the opening of hibiscus blossoms into the afternoon: "those petals will grow/too large and are/expected to disrupt the sunset." "Reading Henri Cole" has the speaker distracted from poetry by noticing a blue heron watching an osprey circling in the sky. As is evident, the natural landscape of the Lowcountry is almost palpable in Kinnas's collection, but the domestic sphere also plays a large role in the book. "Spirit" shows a widow reconnecting with her late husband by digging through a freezer "[t]o find/the lemon cake her husband loved." One of the most delightful poems in the collection, "Happiness Pancake," describes two people working together to make a pancake that represents their joyfulness in their togetherness. The poem also acts as a kind of recipe for the simple breakfast comfort food, down to the "little secret" at the end: With lid close at hand, "add a bit of water./Let the pancake steam/just a little while longer." Cooking the pancake becomes an emblem of the precise makings of a strong and loving relationship.

Indeed, as blurb writer Grace Cavalieri says on the book's back cover, "the book's subject is love," which, she notes, is "a theme that is perfect to make beauty permanent"; that love, romantic and platonic, ties body and soul together in Kinnas's poems. "The Last Swim," dedicated to Maggie Schein, unites pleasant memories of a winter hike in distant years with a more recent swim at the coast and uses the poetical description of both memories to act as a kind of love note to the speaker's friend. Several poems also touch on the complexities of familial love, especially the fraught devotions that emerge between an aging mother and an adult daughter. "The Pitch" features the speaker's mother telling her daughter of dreams set in the mother's native Manchuria, in which she and her friends "sold cigarettes to passersby" by shouting sales pitches in both Chinese and Russian. The mother interrupts her dream recollections to say ominously, "I may die soon/If you leave now I won't see you again." The speaker doesn't believe her, but the poem implies that the mother was right, as it concludes with the speaker saying, "I still hear her voice repeating the pitch/with a chuckle in between." The apparent accuracy of the mother's dark prediction is further supported by the placement of "The Pitch" immediately after "Yokohama," in which the speaker notices her mother's physical decline illustrated by her need to rest on walks and her dependence on a cane. As the poem approaches its end, the speaker explains, "The day I saw my mother for the last time/she staggered out of the house without a cane./*I am fine, I am fine, don't worry, I'm fine.*"

It should be noted that this book demonstrates well Kinnas's skill with using white space and line breaks to create poems that use the page to help construct meaning. In "Three Shrimp Boats on the Horizon" individual words are mapped in a grid of three words by three lines, making three nine-word stanzas, to build both evocative concrete imagery and a kind of concrete poem reminiscent of boats spaced along the ocean's horizon. "A Breath in the Wind" is a two-column mirror poem (or, perhaps, more precisely, two mirror poems) that may be read forward and backward with words consciously placed in reflective positions. The first poem in the collection, "The Sea Foam Arrives to Hide the Lies of a Woman Poet," is divided into eight sections stretching across eight pages. It contains physical placements of stanzas and words in ways that suggest images of staircases or stepping stones, or forms that suggest but do not quite match the structure of the haibun. Kinnas is clearly concerned with craft, and, in several cases, the appearance of the poems on the page invite as much contemplation as the words themselves.

Each of these poetry collections in one way or another contemplates the mysterious intersections between the physical and the spiritual and, likewise, encourages readers to question their assumptions about complex subjects such as love, death, history, and cultural imperatives. Although the poetic voices are diverse, the landscape that nurtures those voices is, in each case, the complicated echo of the lushness of South Carolina's Lowcountry. South Carolina has a long tradition of storytelling, song singing, and poem making. These four collections carry that tradition forward, as living readers and writers make new South Carolina history, looking with characteristically mixed emotions toward the second quarter of the twenty-first century.

Jo Angela Edwins is professor of English and Trustees' Research Scholar at Francis Marion University. A widely published poet, she currently serves as the poet laureate of the Pee Dee. Her recent collection, *A Dangerous Heaven*, was published in 2023. She is the 2025 recipient of the J. Loren Mason Distinguished Professor Award.

Reviews

Jon Tuttle (ed.), *South Carolina Onstage* (Academica Press, 2023), 298 pp., cloth $99.95.

In "About this Book," the short essay that introduces *South Carolina Onstage*, editor Jon Tuttle writes that the compilation, which features seven plays, "is not . . . a Greatest Hits anthology"; instead, as Tuttle explains, the plays were chosen to "represent different periods in the state's history as well as different geographical areas." He readily admits that the works included, which span two hundred years, are "of uneven quality." The value, then, of *South Carolina Onstage* is based on its representation of South Carolinian playwrights, tracing the history of dramatic conventions beginning in Charleston, then the Upstate, and finally the Midlands.

Tuttle, himself a playwright and professor at Francis Marion University for thirty-three years, is the just the right scholar to serve as editor of this excellent collection. Not only was he a member of the Board of Governors of the South Carolina Academy of Authors, but his interests also have always been to promote playwriting as a means of both discovering and uncovering cultural heritage. Tuttle explains that the anthology does its best to maintain "the integrity of each text while reconciling it to the expectations of a modern reader." This means amending archaisms, correcting idiosyncratic punctuation, combining stage directions, and correcting misspellings—a mammoth but necessary endeavor.

As a playwright myself and a past South Carolinian, one who has always greatly admired Tuttle's dramatic works and his myriad accomplishments at Francis Marion University, I very much appreciated the introduction, in which Tuttle traces the history of South Carolina theatre, beginning in antebellum Charleston and especially concentrating on its first theatre, Dock Street near the battery, and continuing through the Civil War. Tuttle documents theatre's relationship to industrial growth, British influences, and even the advent of the railroad. He takes into account the popularity of opera and how that ignited performative interest in the state (consider the opera houses in Abbeville, Sumter, and Chester, among others). Most intriguingly, this detailed introduction shows not only how shifts in social and economic standing contributed to the growth of theatre in South Carolina but also—and, ingeniously, I might add—how the history of theatre shaped, and continues to shape, the state's identity.

South Carolina Onstage shares seven plays, beginning with William Ioor's *The Battle of Eutaw Springs, and Evacuation of Charleston; or the Glorious 14th of December, 1782.* As Tuttle explains, Ioor "ought rightly be considered South Carolina's first dramatist.". Tuttle chose *The Battle of Eutaw Springs* rather than Ioor's first pastoral play because it "was the first to dramatize Revolutionary War combat in the southern colonies." Each play is introduced thoroughly by Tuttle both to justify and explain the rationale for the work's inclusion in this anthology and to provide strong background that informs each drama. Fictionalizing the war in five acts, Ioor describes his take on the war using historical figures, especially General Francis Marion and Colonel Henderson, and a chorus of continental soldiers. Although the play itself is heavy with lengthy speeches and Republicanisms, its prototypical Southern gentleman protagonist, Jonathan Slyboots, proves that "Whig sensibilities reap material rewards," especially because he harbors a fugitive British sailor, Queerfish, who, later in the play, willingly becomes an American citizen.

Modern Honor, the second play in the anthology, features the work of John Blake White, described as possibly the "first dramatist in the South to write a substantial body of work," which was eclipsed by his reputation as a painter. Tuttle chooses *Modern Honor* primarily because it is his first that addresses social reform—in this case, a treatise criticizing dueling—which was prevalent in South Carolina in 1812. White had lost several good friends to this (ironic) nod to chivalry and wrote passionately in favor of gun violence as a means of civilized self-protection. Written in verse and heavy with Platonic dialogue, White's dream of ending dueling would not occur in the author's lifetime, but the play advocates effectively for such reform, especially in the character of Hammer, who serves as a second in the process of dueling, primarily acting as mediator and even as an obstructionist to combat.

Tuttle also includes the first play written by a female author, Sarah Pogson, whose *The Young Carolinians, or Americans in Algiers* describes the siege of San Antonio as a southern border romance. In addition, the anthology includes *Michael Bonham, or the Fall of Bexar,* by Charleston writer William Gilmore Simms; *Sand,* a melodrama by prolific playwright Rebecca Dial; and, most intriguingly, *Wedding Band: A Love/Hate Story in Black and White,* by Alice Childress, who preceded Lorraine Hansberry as the first African-American author to be produced professionally in New York for an earlier play not included here.

Wedding Band, the best work in the anthology, is based on Childress's grandmother. It aggressively attacks antimiscegenation laws at the time by featuring a mixed-race couple forced to move from neighborhood to neighborhood to escape the persecution that arises from archaic conventions and unjust laws. Filled with fascinating minor characters, the play imaginatively pushes for Black nationalism in sometimes fantastical ways and always with an eye toward establishing more equitable racial laws.

South Carolina Onstage ends with Sarah Hammond's *Kudzu*, written in 2003 and appropriately named after the invasive vine that pervades the South. Hammond uses the vine metaphorically to uncover the darkness behind the veneer of Southern gentility. *Kudzu* openly addresses contemporary topics such as homosexuality and drug abuse and is based on Confederate reenactments.

The true worth of *South Carolina Onstage* comes from Jon Tuttle's incredible affection for and knowledge of the history of theatre in the state. A recipient of the South Carolina's Governor's Award in the Humanities and both the Founder's Award and Lifetime Service Award from the South Carolina Theater Association, Tuttle's commentary about each play justifies their inclusion while providing a very readable, intelligent history of theatre in the state where Tuttle has spent his career as an educator and a playwright. I greatly admire the anthology and believe that its greatest value lies in Tuttle's ability to relate these plays produced in South Carolina convincingly to the culture and history of the state.

Mark Charney, Texas Tech University

Millicent E. Brown, *Another Sojourner Looking for Truth: My Journey from Civil Rights to Black Power and Beyond* (University of South Carolina Press, 2024), 224 pp., cloth $26.99, paperback $18.99 (2026), ebook $18.99.

Millicent Brown's memoir, *Another Sojourner Looking for Truth*, provides a personal, emotional history that reflects on the author's lived experiences as a "first child" of South Carolina public school desegregation and as a constantly evolving activist-historian still grappling with many of the same questions about equity encountered in her youth. In the preface, Brown asks, "What does *freedom* look like in the United States for Black people like me?" Born in 1948, Brown's awareness of both Black excellence and the realities of Southern segregation emerged during the height of the civil rights movement, grew into a more global sense of Black Power through practical and academic experiences, and continues to grow in her local and regional roles as a scholar and advocate for liberation.

The memoir's accessibility and emphasis on lived experience make it appealing to a broad readership interested in civil rights history through a personal lens, and the focus on South Carolina makes it especially appealing to those looking to engage local histories. Most specifically, Brown's oscillating sense of belonging and her consistent sense of transformation may appeal to those grappling with their own sense of inclusion. Brown shares instances of leading from the front lines of progressive empowerment movements, as well as moments of exclusion and alienation. Often, these experiences occurred simultaneously, and Brown's reflection on this dissonance alongside her experiences of historic civil rights events make this text a thoughtful choice for a common read in high school or introductory university courses.

Chapters One through Seven recount Brown's family and early life in a "highbrow" Black neighborhood on Charleston's west peninsula. The first two chapters, named for the home built by her grandfather Arthur Brown at 270 Ashley Avenue and later lost to the expansion of the causeway, recount the central role of her family in her early development as an activist. Political participation permeated her home experience; her father, J. Arthur Brown, a former local chapter president of the National Association for the Advancement of Colored People, "modeled and surrounded [his children] with people who did not operate out of fear." This local commitment was supported by Brown's first integrated experiences outside of Charleston through participation with the Highlander Folk School in Monteagle, Tennessee. Here, she also encountered similar backlash to the threats to which she had become accustomed in Charleston. During one of the family's visits in 1955 or 1956, the school was raided by local law enforcement on false charges of unlicensed alcohol sales, which resulted in a number of dubious arrests as well as the addition of a new verse to the already well-known protest song, "We Shall Overcome," added by a teenage participant from Johns Island during the raid.

Brown's dual experience of being in a liberatory environment surrounded by state and social oppressors mirrored prior experiences and foreshadowed upcoming ones. This section culminates with her role in the 1963 court case *Brown et al. v. School District No. 20, Charleston, South Carolina*, known as "Little Brown," after the landmark 1954 case *Brown v. Board of Education of Topeka, Kansas*. On September 4, 1963, Brown and Jacqueline Ford, daughter of Reverend Clarence Ford, integrated Rivers High School in Charleston.

This landmark event was met with press coverage, ostracism from white students and faculty, new friendships with Jewish students, and numerous bomb threats made in the same month as the white terrorist attack on the Sixteenth Street Baptist Church in Birmingham, Alabama. Of this constant tension that persisted until her graduation in 1966, Brown writes, "The students saying all kinds of ugly sentiments or staring angrily at me were in my face and I ignored them by showing charm. The responsibility of 'representing the race' was the most important I had ever taken on. And I was not about to fail." More information about Brown's experience at Rivers High School can be found in the extensive oral history projects of the Avery Research Center for African American History and Culture, a once-independent center of Black excellence now administrated through the College of Charleston.

After her 1966 graduation, Brown's extended sojourn from Charleston began. Chapters Eight through Eleven recount Brown's first encounters with higher education in Boston and Atlanta, as well as life experiences in Mississippi and San Francisco. At Emerson College in Boston, Brown began her study at an integrated college and notes that "after three generations of college-educated family members on both maternal and paternal sides, I would be the first not attending a historically Black college in the South." It was in Boston, although not formally at Emerson, that Brown began to encounter a more "self-loving, African-rooted rejection of long held white supremacist thought and indoctrination," which caused her to question the implications of her impeccably respectable upbringing and the assumption that life in the North was less permeated by racism. Brown left Boston after three semesters to pursue an education more rooted in the Black experience at the Atlanta University Center (AUC) consortium. Of her move from Boston to Atlanta, Brown writes, "My time off the plantation severed any notion that I would seek to be a model of racial respectability as a means of being accepted by white America." The 1969 student takeover of Harkness Hall, the "lack of support from Black administrators," and the dismissal of associated Black students and faculty members contributed to Brown's decision to leave AUC and academia for the foreseeable future. Brown had again encountered the dual experience of inclusion and alienation in her search for truth, which compelled her to continue her sojourn toward more practical activist experiences.

In the wake of her growing awareness of global systems of oppression and disappointments with academia, Brown was recruited at a Student Non-violent Coordinating Committee meeting to work with Liberty House, the main economic arm of the Poor People's Corporation, at their workshop in Jackson, Mississippi. This position allowed Brown to "do the people's labor while utilizing whatever intellectual understanding of struggle that [she] had." This position expanded Brown's awareness of the experiences of Black people living in rural poverty in Mississippi—a new experience, given her relatively privileged background—and the possibility of cooperative labor provided her an opportunity to travel the country selling Liberty House products to retailers from Seattle to Chicago to Philadelphia. The horror of the Jackson State University attack in 1970, an incident in which authorities fired on unarmed students, killing two and injuring twelve, just eleven days after the Kent State massacre, and a later incident in which Liberty House volunteers registering Black voters were shot at by white Mississippians, prompted Brown to leave Jackson for San Francisco.

Brown's relatively short sojourn to San Francisco resulted in a newfound sense of self-reliance through personal economic struggle. She arrived with "just under $300 in [her] pocket" and "the very act of surviving replaced all thoughts of civil rights, Black power, fighting the system, and all other concerns [she] had carried everywhere [she'd] ever been." This experience of urban poverty allowed Brown to step "outside the intellectual platforms and just [see] what was in front of all our eyes." The knowledge she gained from her one-year California "disengagement," along with a simultaneous expansion and contraction of pride and guilt, sent her back to Charleston to "be quiet and listen a little more patiently . . . for a while."

Completing the memoir, Chapters Twelve through Fourteen narrate Brown's reintegration into academia and activism in South Carolina. Rebuilding a support system on her return was necessary, and this system helped Brown complete her bachelor of arts degree in history at the College of Charleston and a master of arts degree in counseling education at The Citadel, as well as her work in a variety of positions of direct action. A brief academic sojourn to Howard University for doctoral study, disrupted by the sudden death of her father, resulted in yet another return to and sojourn from Charleston, and Brown later completed her PhD studies at Florida State and re-entered academic life as a faculty member at multiple institutions, ultimately joining the faculty at Claflin University. Throughout this period, Brown remained engaged in activism to empower Black communities and support equity in education through work with more organizations than this review can address.

Brown closes the memoir by addressing some of the same questions she encountered as a "first child" of public school desegregation. After speaking at a Charleston County School Board meeting, Brown notes that it seemed as though she had "entered a time warp and the same resistance to racial and class parity [she] experienced as a teen persisted," and the persistent lack of acknowledgment that "Black models of education [are] worthy for all students" continued to frustrate Brown, whereas other, more positive experiences with organizations such as the nonprofit Center for Creative Partnerships continued to drive Brown's commitment to advocacy. The maturity that Brown gained through intellectual and practical experiences comes through in the final chapters, allowing her more patience and understanding as she continued the good fight. The last line of Brown's memoir encapsulates this forward drive: "While I breathe, I hope."

Delilah Clark, Francis Marion University

Richard W. Hatcher III, *Thunder in the Harbor: Fort Sumter and the Civil War* (Savas Beatie, 2024), 246 pp., cloth $32.95, ebook $32.95.

On average, over three hundred thousand people per year come to Fort Sumter in Charleston Harbor to see where the Civil War began. However, many guests are shocked, even unimpressed, by the small stature of the original fort, which is overshadowed by the large, black structure that forms Battery Huger. Many visitors assume that the battery, constructed in 1899 in response to the Spanish-American War, is part of the original fort construction and survived unscathed during the five years of the Civil War. The rest of the fort's history falls into the background, and several fascinating stories, facts, and people go unnoticed and unheard. Recovering this overlooked history, Richard W. Hatcher, a former historian of Fort Sumter–Fort Moultrie National Park, does an excellent service to everyone from the academic scholar to the layperson.

Chapter One covers the most extensive period, 1829–1860, explaining why Charleston was on the list for the nation's Third System of Seacoast Defense as a site for a principal fort; why it was named for Thomas Sumter, the Revolutionary War hero and South Carolina native; and how the artificial island was created over fifteen years using enslaved labor and northern granite. After the War of 1812, Congress knew that a better layered shoreline defense was needed. The nation could not afford to re-experience the burning of the White House or the burning and bombardment of coastal communities. Designed to hold one hundred thirty-five guns and a garrison of six hundred fifty troops, the immense, pentagon-shaped fort with five-foot-thick walls was intended to repel invading forces. The fort remained incomplete when the new harbor garrison commander Major Robert Anderson took charge in 1860.

Chapter Two provides a well-written summary and analysis of the tense period in November–December 1860 when South Carolina seceded, and local forces set out to encircle the eighty-nine federal troops stationed in Fort Moultrie on Sullivan's Island. Anderson needed to hold the garrison and the government fortifications and avoid war. Hatcher masterfully lays out these two months of complex political maneuvering, back-and-forth communications, and rising stakes. Chapter Three unpacks the period from December 1860 to early April 1861 as South Carolina and Charleston, the newly formed Confederacy, and the Buchanan and Lincoln Administrations grappled with the implications of Anderson's choice to hole up inside Fort Sumter while he continued its construction. Hatcher makes plain that the Confederacy was willing to fire the first shot if it meant capturing the fort and thereby humiliating and humbling the North.

Chapter Four, "Grand and Awful," masterfully traces the bombardment of Fort Sumter on April 12–14, 1861, the most famous moment in the fort's history. Readers who are well versed in the shots that started the Civil War will find their knowledge refreshed through Hatcher's thrilling prose. However, it is through the subsequent chapters that Hatcher graces readers, be they experts or amateurs, by filling in the fort's role during the remainder of the Civil War. Maintaining his chronological approach, Hatcher carefully lays out the major and minor bombardments of the Union Army and Navy, the stubborn Confederate defense, and Charleston's belief that the fort would prevent a Union invasion.

Chapter Twelve, "It Don't Look Much Like a Fort Inside," invites readers to witness the return of the American flag to Fort Sumter on the fourth anniversary of Anderson's evacuation, a celebratory event designed by Abraham Lincoln and Secretary of War Edwin Stanton. Robert Anderson, now retired, hauled the flag atop a new flagpole to the cheers and tears of a few thousand northerners inside the reduced structure. Civilians, soldiers, sailors, politicians, preachers, and other guests flocked to Charleston for this ceremony and toured the devastated city. The flag ceremony itself is overlooked, generally lost to the memory of people today, as Lincoln was assassinated that same night.

Chapters Thirteen and Fourteen are enlightening, as Hatcher reveals the largely unsuccessful efforts to rebuild and rearm the fort. By the end of the century, the fort became the site of a new coastal battery and a lighthouse station. After the centennial anniversary of the start of the Civil War, the fort became a national monument, a capacity it held until 2019, when it was upgraded to a National Park. Visitors rarely ask about this part of Sumter's history, and history students seem to ignore it.

Hatcher provides numerous fascinating snippets of the fort's story that are worthy of more concentrated scholarship, including the fact that the fort's first tourists were locals, who paid to visit after Anderson's evacuation. There were also mutiny and military executions, holiday balls, various celebrations, and a possible murder investigation. Perhaps most important, there were the experiences of enslaved laborers during the siege. Although it is generally a smooth read, Hatcher sometimes overwhelms the reader with too much technical detail, especially concerning artillery and munitions.

Overall, this is a much-needed addition to anyone's Civil War library and a boon to scholars hoping to understand the fort's history beyond the opening days of the Civil War.

Mike Emett, University of Alabama in Huntsville

Tim Sommer, *Only Wanna Be with You: The Inside Story of Hootie & the Blowfish* (University of South Carolina Press, 2022), 296 pp., cloth $26.99, paperback $18.99 (2024), ebook $18.99.

Anyone who has traversed the musical landscape of the early nineties remembers well the shot across the bow that was Nirvana's single "Smells Like Teen Spirit." Seemingly overnight, the makeup, leather, and teased hair that served as cultural makers for a particular time were replaced with flannel shirts, thrift shop boots, and an unwashed ponytail. Seattle was the breeding ground for this new sound and thus became the sonic hub for the entire country. Artist and repertoire representatives (A&R reps) stormed the streets of the Northwest looking to sign any band that fit the template for success. Meanwhile, down in South Carolina, a group of college buddies were playing golf, writing songs, performing in pizza joints, and getting ready to launch one of the most successful albums of all time. In *Only Wanna*

Be with You, music journalist and industry insider Tim Sommer chronicles the inception, development, success, and struggles of Hootie & the Blowfish. As a friend to the band members and Atlantic Records signing representative, Sommer presents the story as both witness and collaborator, providing detail that puts the reader both in the room and on the stage.

From the outset, Sommer provides a first-person perspective on the events that led to Hootie's development and fame. He begins by reminding the reader that "Hootie" is not a person but, rather, the common abbreviation for Hootie & the Blowfish, which always has been and always will be a band. Sommer then reflects on his first live exposure to the group at a concert in Charleston. Sommer was there as a representative for Atlantic Records, and he recalls how, the minute he saw them live, he knew he would be offering them a recording deal. Sommer offers little details like this to bring the book to life in fresh and surprising ways. In the subsequent chapters, Sommer lays out the familial groundwork that eventually leads to the Hootie & the Blowfish inception. The band includes vocalist Darius Rucker, guitarist Mark Bryan, bassist Dean Felber, and drummer Jim Sonefeld. As fellow students at the University of South Carolina, they all shared passions for sports, music, and a good party. Guitarist Mark Bryan heard Darius singing in the dorm one day and asked him to form a band. Before long (and after some shuffling), the rest of the crew lined up, and the band was complete. Sommer spends quite a bit of time addressing the development of the band name. Hootie & the Blowfish was not at all attractive to the record labels initially, and Sommer played a large role in selling the band to the record company executives. Once Hootie connected with manager Rusty Harmon and attorney Gus Gusler, the pieces were all in place, though success was far from guaranteed.

Unsurprisingly, Sommers's close personal and professional connection to the band helps bring to life the sections of the story for which he was not yet present. Sommer presents Hootie as, quite often, more of an event than just a band. Playing covers in local bars in Columbia and university frat houses, the group built an impressive following, in large part, on the fun and joy they brought to the stage. Sommer describes the members of Hootie as kind, thoughtful, and always approachable. The fact that they somehow managed to convey this on stage through their music and performance was one of their greatest strengths. As an A&R rep, Sommer's principal role for Atlantic Records was finding new talent. At the point that Hootie was brought to his attention, the American South was on nobody's radar. An Atlantic staff member discovered that Hootie was selling a very impressive amount of merchandise throughout the mid-South, and Sommer was tasked with traveling to Charleston to see what the fuss was about. Here, again, Sommer details the impact that the trip and concert would have as he approached Rusty and offers the band a recording contract.

Throughout the middle portion of the book, Sommer deftly draws the reader through the challenges and near-calamities of the album recording and release process. Sommer's background as a record label rep again proves pivotal to the sinew of the story. Although this is the story of one particular band and particular stretch of time, it could also serve as playbook for dealing with record labels and the immense challenges of operating within an opaque top-down corporate structure. Sommer recounts how the band was already quite financially successful and, as such, weren't approaching the label with dollar signs in their eyes. They wanted no major monetary advance and asked simply for their album to be recorded and released. Being huge *R.E.M.* fans, they managed to secure the seminal Athens group's producer Don Gehman to help spearhead their freshman release. Sommer details this process beautifully, as he was an integral part of the process. What resulted was the album *Cracked Rear View*, the title of which was drawn from a classic John Hiatt tune. Although Sommer describes the recording process as magical, he still presents two near-fatal collisions that could have stopped the band in their tracks. A superior at Atlantic decided to completely shelve the project, and Sommer had to go above his head to push it through. Perhaps even more dangerously, some unlicensed Bob Dylan lyrics were questioned, and the band had to reach a financial settlement to move forward. Regardless of the snags, within two years, *Cracked Rear View* became one of the highest selling albums ever in the history of Atlantic records.

Perhaps victims of overexposure or just professional burnout, Hootie was never quite able to replicate the success of *Cracked Rear View*. The band released several more albums and maintained their legendary tour schedule, but the crowds shrank, and the sales dropped. Although both Sommer and the band have always maintained that Hootie & the Blowfish never "broke up," the group's hiatus has been lasting. Darius Rucker has, of course, found another level of stardom on the country charts, but the band still maintains their position as a brotherhood and are still active through the numerous charities they continue to support.

Tim Sommer is perhaps the only person who could have written this book with such visceral clarity yet from a compellingly objective point of view. His lifelong love for the band and their music shines through on every page, but at no point does the reader sense a glossing over of the challenging bits. The reader needn't be a fan of Hootie & the Blowfish to be pulled deeply into their story. This book is about music, brotherhood, and the challenges of success and failure. It is a fantastic read for anyone.

Brandon Goff, Francis Marion University

Elizabeth Ellis Miller, *Liturgy of Change: Rhetorics of the Civil Rights Mass Meeting* (University of South Carolina Press, 2023), 204 pp., cloth $114.99, paperback $32.99, ebook $32.99.

For many people, the most important events of the civil rights movement include the Montgomery Bus Boycott, the sit-ins, the Freedom Riders, and the March on Washington. These public-facing events brought much needed attention to the injustices of Jim Crow. Elizabeth Ellis Miller focuses on lesser known events: the mass meetings that were held within Black communities, often in churches. These meetings not only encouraged Black citizens to resist oppression but also provided the tools necessary for successful nonviolent resistance. Miller's insightful study, part of the University of South Carolina Press's innovative Movement Rhetoric/Rhetoric's Movements series, takes the reader into those meetings; introduces the everyday people whose contributions to racial equality have been overlooked; and bears witness to the astonishing power of song, prayer, and personal testimony. *Liturgy of Change* is extensively researched, carefully argued, and clearly written. It will appeal to a wide range of readers, including those interested in rhetoric, the civil rights movement, and the intersections of religion and social progress.

Miller focuses on meetings that occurred between 1955 and 1965. She makes extensive use of contemporary sources; most important, the audio recordings of individual meetings. Doing so allows her to recover many lost voices and demonstrate the profound impact that the meetings had on participants. In setting up her argument, Miller uses the terms *liturgy* and *genre* in ways that may be unfamiliar to some readers. By *liturgy*, she means "an embodied spirituality," or, more specifically, a ritual made up of recognizable components. Those components, which she terms *genres*, "structure collective religious experience." When assembled into a liturgy, the genres create shared emotional responses among the congregants, which establish cohesive communities and strengthen resolve for action. In this way, the mass meetings were "transformative through the rhetorical, religious experience that collective participation created." Equally important, liturgies empowered activists to "move out into more public protest in unique and authentic ways." Using Carolyn Miller's expansive understandings of genre as "dynamic, power-laden sites" that "shape and coordinate social action," Miller argues that the particular genres of music, prayer, and testimony generated an ideology of liberation and gave shape to the most effective civil rights protests.

In her first full chapter, Miller frames her discussion of mass meetings through a discussion of "religion's rhetorical role in the civil rights movement." Here, she broadens her understanding of liturgy by introducing Thomas Merton's claim that "liturgies are recurring sites for sanctification," which "shape the ongoing transformation that characterizes Christian experience." Equally important, she demonstrates that liturgy does not necessarily provide an "otherworldly escape" from life's injustices but can also shape civic and political action. To substantiate her claim, Miller calls attention to the Black church's efforts from the time of Reconstruction to provide a "space for African Americans to speak freely, engage in rhetorical training, and perform literate action." Moving beyond academic theory, she enriches her discussion with insights from the late activist and congressional representative John Lewis and Georgia senator and minister Raphael Warnock.

Miller also explores religious feeling, a topic that has not received sufficient scholarly attention. The emotional experiences of the mass meetings "prompted participants toward action and sustained them to continue working over the long haul of the movement." Even negative emotions such as "fear, sorrow, and pain" could become useful, as the liturgical power of the meetings "transformed these feelings into . . . courage, faith, love, and defiance." Equally important, Miller notes that previous studies of mass meetings have underappreciated women's contributions, in large part because those studies have overly focused on the sermons provided by male preachers. Neglecting the "collective genres open to women," scholars have provided an incomplete understanding of mass meetings. Only by examining all the components of the liturgy can we grasp how through "one song, one prayer, one testimony . . . people tested out Christian non-violence and explored how it felt to be this kind of activist, working through faith toward an integrated world."

The second chapter focuses on music, particularly the invention of the freedom song. Bernice Johnson Reagon, an activist and musician from Georgia, receives well-deserved credit for her unacknowledged contributions to this developing genre. While singing the spiritual "Over My Head, I See Trouble in the Air," Reagon realized that the lyrics seemed inappropriate for an occasion focused on hope and action. Substituting the word *freedom* for *trouble*, she transformed a song about disempowerment into one "where freedom, glory, and justice reign." In her discussion of freedom songs, Miller recognizes the importance of white groups, such as the Highlander Folk School, but focuses on the contributions of Black musicians who, through mass meetings, developed a forward-looking genre that extended the "African American tradition of merging music and resistance." Mass meetings also included songs that crossed racial barriers, including "Onward Christian Soldiers" and "My Country 'Tis of Thee." These songs, familiar to both Black and white congregations, celebrated "spiritual and national freedom" and advanced the "Christian ideals of love and peace." More important, they celebrated "interracial unity" by showing the shared values and traditions of both oppressor and oppressed.

Song became an essential venue for women and girls to participate in mass meetings, a point Miller explores through her discussion of the white song leader Guy Carawan and Mrs. J. N. Rucker, who grew up within the Black church tradition. One gets the impression that Carawan, who mixed commentary and song, saw himself as a teacher. Rucker, in contrast, relied only on the music itself. Without offering "extensive arguments about songs," she reminded her listeners of "how powerfully singing functions to sound freedom." Those who are unfamiliar with folk song traditions may be pleased to learn that the summer-camp staple "Michael, Row the Boat Ashore" originated as a spiritual sung by enslaved people in South Carolina. Miller ends the chapter with an in-depth analysis of Matthew Jones's "The Ballad of Medgar Evers," which shows the "capacity of freedom songs" to respond to "recurrent violence."

Prayer, the subject of the third chapter, becomes a form of "reverent resistance." Miller begins her discussion by calling attention to the public prayers that followed early lunch counter protests. By praying visibly on the street, the young Greensboro Four not only displayed peace but also "unsettled" a "segregated space." Their actions demonstrated that prayer could serve as an "unruly genre," because it disrupted the norms defining the spaces that "Black bodies should inhabit" and where "prayer should occur." Miller's frame of reference is expansive, and her analysis draws upon writers and activists as diverse as Frederick Douglass, W. E. B. Du Bois, Adrienne Rich, and Andrew Young. Examining the roles of prayer in mass meetings in Greenwood, Mississippi; St. Augustine, Florida; and Americus, Georgia,

Miller extends her discussion of prayer as a "mode of peaceful resistance." She concludes the chapter with a brief discussion of Stokely Carmichael's efforts to move civil rights protests away from freedom songs and prayers and toward the more aggressive advocacy of the Black Power movement.

If prayer serves as an "unruly genre," testimony becomes a "fuzzy genre," which is to say a genre with "permeable boundaries and a range of usable social actions." Miller introduces Fannie Lou Hamer, one of "the most outstanding civil rights orators." She also takes the reader into meetings in Hattiesburg, Mississippi, and Danville, Virginia. In Mississippi, testimony helped transform the participants' "sense of themselves and who they could be." In Virginia, Miller discovers the underlying anxiety of participants who feared repercussion for their testimony. "At times," Miller notes, "people needed a break from the recorder to testify." Despite these understandable worries, people did testify and used their own words as a "mode of loving confrontation." In doing so, they demonstrated the power of testimony not only to give voice to the experiences of ordinary people but also to focus attention on social issues outside purely religious concerns. In this way, testimony becomes an essential vehicle for connecting the values of a faith tradition to the immediate concerns of those denied justice.

Miller's final chapter explores the intersections of mass meetings and racial violence. The meetings, the reader learns, were often attended by individuals and groups who were hostile to their purpose. The Citizen's Council and Ku Klux Klan were a constant presence, as were law enforcement officials, some of whom installed microphones to record the meetings. Rather than excluding these groups, activists welcomed them and used their attendance to model "radical pacificist" engagement and "Christian nonviolence." The liturgical structure of the meetings, of course, helped advance this purpose by situating the meetings within "already accepted Christian genres." In one of the chapter's best moments, Miller discusses how speakers would refer to police microphones as "doohickies" and humorously remind speakers that others were listening. Turning an instrument of surveillance into a comedic prop, they disempowered those who sought to control them.

Without question, Miller has great appreciation of the impact of mass meetings and great admiration for the courageous men and women who participated in them. Examining the records, she finds courage, selflessness, and a laudable commitment to nonviolence, even in the face of overt threats. Miller is not, however, an uncritical apologist. In her conclusion, she calls attention to several paradoxes within the mass meetings. She notes, for example, that although the meetings were "designed to invite collective participation," they never promoted an "egalitarian leadership structure." Similarly, the meetings focused on the experiences of men and, by so doing, "missed key aspects of the injustice Black people in the United States faced." The mass meetings, the reader discovers, were the products of their age, and however beneficial they may have been, they reflect the values of the mid-twentieth century, not the twenty-first. Miller brings these dynamics to light by contrasting mass meetings with the more recent activities of the Black Lives Matter movement. The latter, she shows, abandons hierarchal structures and promotes greater inclusion, not only of women but also of lesbian, gay, bisexual, transgender, queer/questioning, intersex, and asexual/aromantic/agender plus other (LGBTQIA+) communities. In this way, the Black Lives Matter movement corrects the "myopic, gendered vision of freedom and citizenship" offered by earlier activists. Miller ends her study by examining the works of two modern rhetoricians: Michael Eric Dyson and Barack Obama. Dyson's important 2017 book, *Tears We Cannot Stop*, continues the work of the mass meetings in its insistence on a nonviolent resistance that welcomes opponents in dialogue. Moreover, the book is structured like a liturgy, with a call to worship, hymn, invocation, sermon, and benediction. President Obama's powerful response to the 2015 murder of nine innocent people within Charleston's Emanuel Baptist Church similarly evokes the power of mass meetings and replicates their liturgical emphasis on song, prayer, and testimony. These examples suggest that, however imperfect and dated, mass meetings continue to shape responses to injustice and violence.

Elizabeth Ellis Miller has written an exceptional study. Students of rhetoric will find her analysis fresh and convincing. Professors preparing courses on Black and civil rights rhetoric would do well to put her book on their reading lists (the paperback edition is a veritable bargain in today's academic marketplace). Historians will relish Miller's insights, particularly as they relate to little-studied events and people. Most important, readers outside the academy will find much value within *Liturgy of Change*. Even those who do not think within academic contexts, such as genres and imaginaries, will find Miller's arguments accessible and convincing. They will be reminded that oppressors are never as powerful as they seem and that ordinary people can assemble the materials of their experiences and traditions to advance the causes of inclusion, peace, and justice.

Christopher D. Johnson, Francis Marion University

Edda L. Fields-Black, *Combee: Harriet Tubman, the Combahee River Raid, and Black Freedom During the Civil War* (Oxford University Press, 2024). 776 pp., cloth $39.99, ebook $39.99.

In this rich volume, Edda Fields-Black weaves together lesser-known parts of Harriet Tubman's life, the story of her ancestors, and the June 3, 1863, raid of seven rice plantations along the Combahee River in South Carolina that resulted in the freedom of seven hundred fifty-six enslaved people. Fields-Black explains, "This story is as local as it is national. Central as she was to the Combahee River Raid, in this book Harriet Tubman shares the spotlight with the men, women, and children who utilized the raid to seize their freedom and create a new community." Using previously neglected US Civil War Pension Files alongside compensation records from plantation owners who lost property—including the people they enslaved—during the raid, Fields-Black names numerous enslaved people in print for the first time. For generations, white plantation owners enslaved Fields-Black's ancestors along the Combahee, and her great-great-great uncle, Jonas Fields, and great-great-great grandfather, Hector Fields, served in the US Colored Troops during the Civil War. Jonas's pension file revealed ancestors' names she had not previously known. For the Combahee's freedom seekers, the Civil War catalyzed their Gullah–Geechee culture, which "ultimately crystalized in the early twentieth century." Fields-Black divides the book's nineteen chapters into four parts, moving chronologically from the late seventeenth century through early Reconstruction.

The seven chapters of the first part explore the antebellum period. In the first chapter, she emphasizes how "enslavement was not the same across the South, and the Lowcountry's was distinct." Tubman experienced enslavement in Maryland, where tobacco was the dominant crop. By the start of the nineteenth century, most of the enslaved population there was Creole, not African-born. Chapter Two shifts to South Carolina, providing significant vocabulary, details of plantation society, and the genealogy of seven Combahee plantations raided. To grow rice on their plantations, the enslavers relied on "skilled and strong field hands, known as 'Prime Hands.'" The seven plantations belonged to the Blakes, Middletons, Heywards, Lowndeses, Kirklands, Nichollses, and Pauls. She explains the complexity of the names of the enslaved, especially as it relates to understanding and identifying pension files. Some enslaved people used the surnames of enslavers, but they may have had more than one enslaver. Enslaved people referred to their surnames as a "title," and many went by a "basket name" or nickname within their own communities. Enslaved people along the Combahee had an internal hierarchy based on age, where "those considered Old Heads—born between 1780 and 1823 and married many years before the Civil War began—commanded respect from younger enslaved people."

Chapters Three, Four, and Five examine the effects of slavery on families. The third chapter moves back up the eastern coast to Tubman and Sojourner Truth to discuss the breaking apart of enslaved families. When male enslavers died, they often bequeathed enslaved people to their sons and daughters. This was the case with Tubman's grandmother, Rit Green. On the other hand, a New York enslaver sold Isabella Van Wagenen (later, Sojourner Truth) and her siblings after freeing her parents, so he did not have to care for them in old age. Seen ultimately as property, enslavers split up enslaved families to serve their own interests. This was true with marriage as well. Although enslavers did not typically support "abroad marriages" where enslaved people on differing plantations wed, when they did, the children lived separately from one parent. The fourth chapter also examines the objectification of enslaved people to secure loans. Fields-Black asserts that "planters in the Lowcountry bought, sold, and mortgaged the people they held in bondage whenever they saw fit" and "during the 1840s, fluctuating rice prices and the deaths of planters increased uncertainty for Blacks enslaved along the Combahee River." The author also further analyzes the hierarchy of the enslaved through drivers. Typically male, enslaved drivers ran most day-to-day work on plantations by means of a task system. Prime hands often held these positions of power, earning them little protection from enslavers splitting up their families and hatred from other enslaved people. The sixth chapter returns to enslaved children and enslavers' intergenerational wealth. Enslaved children died at higher rates on rice plantations—nearly two-thirds died before the age of fifteen—than on cotton or sugar plantations. The author notes, "The planters' intergenerational wealth was created by the labor of unfree Black people toiling in the pestilent rice swamps and losing their children in large numbers."

Chapters Five through Seven focus on efforts to liberate the enslaved. Fields-Black highlights the Underground Railroad in the fifth chapter. Self-liberation was extremely dangerous for the enslaved, and absconding from enslavement further divided families. Prime hands were the most likely to seek their freedom. White and Black abolitionists risked their livelihoods and relationships in helping freedom seekers as well. Fields-Black stresses how exceptional Tubman was in her willingness to risk her own hard-won freedom by returning to the South to help others gain their freedom. Despite the Fugitive Slave Act of 1850, also known as the Bloodhound Act, enslaved people still sought their freedom via the Underground Railroad, as evidenced by reporting on the Dover Eight in 1857. The final chapter in the first section shifts to Tubman's radicalization after John Brown's raid on Harpers Ferry. The two met in Canada in 1858 and had a mutual respect. After Brown's martyrdom, she engaged in violence in response to the arrest of Charles Nalle, who was to be re-enslaved in the South. Up to that point, she risked her freedom and life for people she knew, but moving forward, she "resolved to risk her life for people she did not know."

Part Two's five chapters examine Tubman and South Carolina in the American Civil War. Chapters Eight, Nine, and Eleven cover the Battle of Port Royal, the Port Royal Experiment, and the Sea Islands. Union forces won the battle, allowing the United States to implement an Atlantic blockade called the Anaconda Plan. The Gullah–Geechee refer to the battle at "Gun Shoot at Bay Point" and the resulting chaos of fleeing white South Carolinians as the "Great Skedaddle." These events further divided enslaved families, as some accompanied their enslavers "whether by force or by choice" to the interior, whereas others sought refuge in the woods until they could reach Union forces. In the early 1860s, slavery was still legal in the United States, so Union forces at Port Royal labeled the freedom seekers "contrabands" and put them to work "building fortifications, transporting goods, cooking, washing, serving, and even bearing arms against the rebellion." This action became the Port Royal Experiment. Although the workers received wages, they were too low for them to sustain their families. Despite the tribulations of the experiment, Tubman was able to embed herself among the refugees and earn their trust. In Chapter Nine, Fields-Black notes, "Though she could not understand the dialect the Lowcountry Creoles spoke nor their cultural practices, she knew that they all understood freedom and the willingness to sacrifice to attain it." Chapter Eleven examines the differences between Tubman and Charlotte Forten and their engagement with South Carolina's Black refugees. Forten was of mixed ancestry, was educated, and had never experienced slavery, yet both women "faced bigotry in the North when they stepped outside of free Black communities and abolitionist circles." Tubman cooked, did laundry, and collected intelligence, and Forten taught the formerly enslaved in makeshift schools.

Chapters Ten and Twelve focus on Black men in Union forces. In May 1862, General David Hunter issued General Order Number Eleven, freeing enslaved people in South Carolina, Georgia, and Florida and requiring the men to fight for the Union. However, when forces delivered his orders and took formerly enslaved men into custody, they gave no explanation, spreading distrust. Some deserted fearing their sale back to the Confederates. However, President Abraham Lincoln nullified Hunter's orders. Two months later, Congress passed the Second Confiscation Act and the Militia Act freed enslaved people in Confederate territories, six months before the Emancipation Proclamation, reaffirming "the president's authority to marshal the labor of formerly enslaved individuals in whatever capacities were beneficial to the war effort." The author recounts the well-known story of Robert Smalls's heroic escape and seizure of the CSS *Planter*, as well as the names of a handful of lesser known Black boatmen from the Lowcountry. After the Emancipation Proclamation, Black men helped deliver it to the enslaved people in the South. Part of the First and Second South Carolina Volunteers, they also fought alongside white soldiers in the attack on Jacksonville, but they were "sorely disappointed and dejected" when they had to evacuate without the enslaved people who sought their protection. The author's great-great-great-grandfather Hector Fields was a member of the Second South Carolina Volunteers.

Fields-Black finally gets to the Combahee River Raid in the four chapters of Part Three. Chapters Thirteen and Fourteen trace the events of the raid. Despite the Combahee being "breadbasket of the Confederacy," the Confederates prioritized protecting railroads over rice plantations. However, there had been rumors of a Northern attack, and gunboats surveyed the river for torpedoes. Tubman led at least eight men, but only two of her "ring of scouts, spies, and pilots" enlisted in the US Army. She sang an abolitionist song, "Uncle Sam's Farm" to signal that the forces were there to free the enslaved and "give them land" to sustain their families. Fields-Black analyzes Tubman's service on the Combahee despite limited sources to give her "some credit," as the author titles Chapter Fifteen. The sixteenth chapter takes up the Confederate response to the raid. There were questions of who to blame, but "the Confederate Army's military strategy . . . was never on trial." Despite Union forces coming to liberate the enslaved, some stayed on the plantations because they did not want to break up their families. For those who did flee, however, the plantation owners sought compensation from the Confederacy.

The final section of the book looks at South Carolina after the raid and the emergence of the Combee identity. At Battery Wagner, Colonel Robert Gould Shaw's Massachusetts Fifty-Fourth, the first Northern regiment of Black troops, proved that "Black men would and could fight for their freedom and the freedom of people still in bondage." Black women also served as nurses for Black soldiers. Building the Swamp Angel on Morris Island left many members of the Second South Carolina ill and even disabled. During the war, Northern volunteers in South Carolina continuously remarked on the language of Black people in the Lowcountry. In the 1930s, an educator noted the Creole language spoken by the Gullah people, as teachers like Forten recorded in the 1860s. This unique language developed because the enslaved spent most days in relative separation from white influence, and they held onto this localized identity even after freedom. Fields-Black explains, "The Combahee refugees identified themselves as 'Combee' because they 'came from the Combahee River.'" When General William Tecumseh Sherman marched from Charleston into the interior, he issued Special Field Order Number Fifteen, promising formerly enslaved people forty acres of land. However, President Andrew Johnson reversed the order when he pardoned Confederate plantation owners. Most of the free Black population did not have money to purchase land after the war. However, Hector Fields was able to do so through white intermediaries. Having survived slavery and the American Civil War, the Gullah–Geechee created a new community, and "one of the most enduring legacies of the Combahee River Raid is the window it opens into the process by which Lowcountry Creoles became those whom we today call the Gullah Geechee."

Combee: Harriet Tubman, the Combahee River Raid, and Black Freedom During the Civil War is more than just a monograph. The afterword acknowledgments section will be insightful for students pursuing a career in history as she explores the fascinating process of re-enacting and researching these stories amidst a global pandemic. Educators could easily assign most of the reasonably short nineteen chapters or four parts separately, making the size of this tome a little less intimidating for undergraduate students. With the inclusion of a detailed timeline at the beginning and primary sources in the center and appendices, this is sure to become a textbook for many classes and a reference book on countless scholars' shelves.

Erica Johnson, Francis Marion University

Carrie Tipton, *From Dixie to Rocky Top: Music and Meaning in Southeastern Conference Football* (Vanderbilt University Press, 2023), 320 pp., cloth $99.95, paperback $34.95, ebook $19.99.

In *From Dixie to Rocky Top*, Carrie Tipton argues that the college fight songs of the Southeastern Conference (SEC) reflect the cultural politics of the American South in the twentieth century and beyond. Tipton grew up near Davis Wade Stadium, home to the Mississippi State University Bulldogs. On game days, Tipton heard what she described as "the unmistakable sounds of war." Like other children growing up in the US South, these sonic memories established an indelible connection between SEC football and an epistemological cultural identity. According to Tipton, SEC fight songs are the skeleton key for understanding the sociopolitical fault lines of the white South from the perspective of race, regional identity, gender, and capitalism.

In tune with Karl Hagstrom Miller's *Segregating Sound: Inventing Folk and Pop Music in the Age of Jim Crow*, *From Dixie to Rocky Top* uncovers a hidden musical history: The expressive culture of the South was a fluid ecosystem that encompassed a much wider variety of commercial music than it is often given credit for. Like Miller, Tipton wisely argues that, to comprehend such a vast aesthetic infrastructure, one must explore how the market and pecuniary conditions influenced the rise of fight songs as a marker of cultural identity. By examining the ways in which school spirit is commoditized in the form of a tune, Tipton's study of fight song history is an important intervention into the economic history of commercial music in the American South.

Tipton organizes her study into eleven chapters devoted to revealing the numerous connections between the book's imbricated themes: how the commodification of school spirit took place, the ways in which SEC football traditions engendered the construction and expression of race, how fight songs represented regional identity, and how the contributions of women affected the SEC soundscape. Chapter One explores the aural sphere of the burgeoning praxis of white college football in the American South in the 1890s. Chapter Two sutures the residue of minstrelsy and Civil War songs in early southern football culture to plantation tropes and "Lost Cause" ideology. Chapters Three and Four document case studies of the emerging "school spirit" commercial music genre among southern universities. Chapter Five explores the ways in which women participated in the proto-SEC football soundscape in the South before World War II. Chapters Six, Seven, and Eight—case studies on the influence of jazz and popular music in the school spirit genre, the business of fight songs, and the fight song mania of the 1930s—document the heyday of the fight song, 1920–1940. Chapter Nine examines the curious marriage of music and politics through the lens of Huey P. Long's involvement with Louisiana State University football pageantry while serving as Louisiana governor, US senator, and presidential candidate. Chapter Ten, "Three Postwar Fight Songs," examines three songs adopted as the official fight songs at Auburn University, the University of South Carolina (USC), and the University of Tennessee between 1955 and 1972. Tipton is particularly insightful in her explication of how USC's "Fighting Gamecocks Lead the Way" journeyed from the Broadway theater to the football stadium. Key to the song taking a foothold in becoming the main fight song at USC was the collaboration between football coach Paul Dietzel and band director James Pritchard. Dietzel's vigorous support of the "Fighting Gamecocks Lead the Way," the USC Marching Band, and football pageantry in general represents the only case study in Tipton's book in which a coach was explicitly involved in the aesthetics of school spirit. The book concludes with Chapter Eleven's exploration of the changes that took place in SEC football pageantry during the course of the twentieth century, including a critique of "southern exceptionalism."

From Dixie to Rocky Top is an interdisciplinary work that draws on the methodologies of various fields of study, including musicology, American studies, Southern history, and sports history. Mining both physical and digital archives, Tipton utilizes a sweeping variety of sources: manuscript collections and oral histories, newspapers, magazines, trade journals, football programs, sheet music, legal records, recordings, university student and alumni publications, and US government documents. In this regard, Tipton's research into the business practices of college song publisher Thornton W. Allen is particularly impressive for its scope. Tipton's chapter on Allen is at once economic history, a musicological examination of Allen's work as a composer and lyricist, and a psychological portrait of greed. Additionally, Tipton organizes Allen's entire catalog of "College Songs Published, Written, or Copyrighted by Thornton W. Allen" in an appendix, highlighting in physical form just how important the publishing industry was in cementing college songs as a legitimate commercial musical subgenre.

From Dixie to Rocky Top is an exceptional addition to the literature of musicology, American studies, Southern history, and sports history. Tipton's insightful amalgamation of economic analysis and cultural theory provides a shrewd and unique look into the history of the musical ecosystem of the SEC. Scholars in the fields of musicology, music industry studies, American studies, women's and gender studies, sports history, and Southern history will utilize *From Dixie to Rocky Top* to seek a deeper understanding of how SEC football pageantry and the commodification of college fight songs became a marker of cultural and political identity in the American South.

Brian Edward Jones, Francis Marion University

John D. Miller (ed.), *Honorable and Brilliant Labors: Orations of William Gilmore Simms* (University of South Carolina Press, 2024), 324 pp., cloth $59.99, open access ebook $0.00.

The monumental William Gilmore Simms Initiatives series concludes with John D. Miller's consideration of William Gilmore Simms as orator and public intellectual, complementing the series' prior efforts to flesh out our understanding of Simms, best known as novelist and poet, through his personal correspondence, reviews, and editorials. Miller's treatment of Simms's orations as the subject of study (rather than as adjunct to studying something else Simms wrote) meaningfully enlarges our view of a writer whose era was a golden age of oratory, when public speaking was regarded as a high-prestige art form of social consequence, especially, Miller argues, in the Old South. Although Miller's book is billed as an edited collection of primary sources, it is, in fact, both less and more. *Honorable and Brilliant Labors* is neither a complete collection of Simms's orations—it includes nine, fewer than half of those known to exist—nor a purely representative sample. Miller's selection and arrangement are meant to illustrate the critical thesis that he advances explicitly in well-developed volume and section introductions: that Simms's oratory responds to "the contradictions of progress by synthesizing the different responses of his era to it, including seemingly incongruous perspectives"; specifically, Southern conservatism and Northern progressivism. Although Simms's conservatism and sectional partisanship are widely noted, Miller's claim of synthesis with progressive perspectives in Simms's public orations is more provocative and certainly makes a case for reassessment.

The book begins with the same excellent biographical overview included in other series volumes (and available at the Simms Initiatives online) by independent scholar David Moltke-Hansen, founding director of the William Gilmore Simms Initiatives. The overview is a model of the genre that achieves breadth of coverage with concision and economy, and it constitutes an insightful, at-a-glance reference for the Simms novice and veteran scholar alike. As for the presentation of primary texts, Miller's editorial apparatus seems purposely designed to interfere only mildly or not at all with a reader's direct experience of Simms's words as they were spoken. Aside from two of his own brief notes to "Barnwell Agricultural Society Oration," for instance, Miller eschews editor's notes altogether. Whenever possible, Miller uses manuscript sources for the orations rather than the versions Simms himself prepared for publication, aiming to come closer to Simms's actual delivery. Although many of the orations included in this volume have been otherwise broadly accessible to scholars—including through the digitization efforts of the Simms Initiatives—three ("Choice of a Profession," "The Social Moral, Lecture 1," and "Antagonisms of the Social Moral, North and South") are newly available outside of manuscript collections of the South Caroliniana Library at the University of South Carolina. *Honorable and Brilliant Labors* resides in Open Carolina, the open-access repository of the University of South Carolina Press, so the entire volume is available digitally.

After Moltke-Hansen's biographical sketch, the book includes Miller's brief general introduction to William Gilmore Simms as Orator, followed by four parts, each consisting of an extensive critical introduction followed by two or (in Part IV) three of Simms's orations. One way to get a sense of how this book stretches beyond the confines of the typical edited collection is by observing how many of its pages are Miller's and how many are Simms's: Of the two hundred eighty-two pages of the main text (excluding the appendix, bibliography, and index), for example, almost a third are Miller's. Miller's critical introduction to Part I exceeds the length of either one of the orations that succeed it and, in fact, approaches their length put together. Although some of Miller's pages are owing to the editor's comprehensive grounding of Simms's texts in their historical, biographical, and bibliographical contexts as any editor of primary texts might do, Miller also produces less expected critical analysis in service of his larger argument about Simms's synthesis of Southern and Northern responses to progress. The result is that Miller's parts are somewhat less like cohesive categories that organize primary texts and somewhat more like book chapters.

Nowhere is Miller's central argument clearer and more compelling than in Part I: Nature and Its Social Uses. Drawing on Simms's earliest major oration, "Barnwell Agricultural Society Oration" (1840), and his last oration, "The Sense of the Beautiful" (1870), delivered mere weeks before Simms succumbed to cancer, Miller argues for the essential congruity between

Simmsian and Emersonian conceptions of nature as a sign of moral and spiritual truth. Here, Miller's claims are nuanced and considered, asserting neither too much nor too little; at least, he argues, such affinities bespeak the influence of European Romanticism that Simms and Emerson held in common. Given the dim view of New England's historical and contemporary enthusiasms taken by the South of Simms's day (and in the South's intellectual history well into the twentieth century), Miller's line of reasoning will be seen as provocative, and, in some quarters, even heretical. Unlike Part I, Parts II–IV are arranged chronologically as well as thematically. Part II: Progress and Its Fragility examines Simms's account of the historical roots of American social development and liberty, and the contemporary forces of materialism and abolitionism that threaten them, through the lens of two orations of the 1840s, as Simms was becoming known as an orator: "The Social Principle" (1842) and "The Sources of American Independence" (1844). Part III: Class, Gender, and the Purpose of an Education includes two 1855 orations, "Choice of a Profession" and "Inauguration of the Spartanburg Female College," that advance obligations to family and community as necessary constraints on personal freedom in the lives of South Carolina postgraduates. In Part IV: Loud Voices, Empty Rooms, the historical context of rising sectionalism and looming war becomes central, as Miller introduces a trio of orations from Simms's failed Northern tour ("South Carolina and the Revolution" [1856]) and his follow-up "Our Social Moral" series in Charleston the following year ("The Social Moral, Lecture 1" [1857] and "The Antagonisms of the Social Moral, North and South" [1857]).

Miller's thesis, already a bit attenuated in Parts II and III, arguably disappears in Part IV. If these final orations of the volume develop or exemplify Simms's synthesis of Southern conservatism and Northern progressivism, Miller leaves unsaid how. The mere continuation of some characteristically Simmsian themes, perhaps, now marshaled to prepare Simms's audience for disunion and conflict, is the extent of what may be pointed out. What Miller leaves unsaid in Part IV might be missed less if the volume included a critical conclusion; that is, undoubtedly, an odd thing to want in an edited collection of primary sources, but Miller's unusually elevated critical ambitions seem to call for it. Nevertheless, *Honorable and Brilliant Labors* is both a welcome new collection of Simms's primary texts and an unfailingly thought-provoking critical assessment of them, as well as a worthy culmination of the Simms Initiative's publication project.

Shawn E. Miller, Francis Marion University

Claudia Smith Brinson, *Injustice in Focus: The Civil Rights Photography of Cecil Williams* (University of South Carolina Press, 2024), 256 pp., cloth $39.99, ebook $39.99.

Injustice in Focus highlights the powerful role that the people of South Carolina, particularly the people of Orangeburg, played in the civil rights movement, concentrating on one Orangeburg native, Cecil J. Williams. From an early age, Williams seemed destined to use his camera as a tool for social change. Brinson's book takes the reader from the 1940s, when a young Cecil first began photographing, through the 1950s and, ultimately, into the 1960s, presenting key events that Williams photographed that were influential in the state's struggle to attain racial equality. Beautifully printed black-and-white photographs, mainly attributed to Williams, illustrate these powerful events and leave the reader longing to see more of his work.

The book is presented chronologically in four parts, starting with Cecil Williams's early life in Orangeburg. Throughout the chapters, Brinson unfurls Williams's flourishing devotion to photography, which is intertwined with his dedication to the social change unfolding in South Carolina. The preface outlines the book's purpose and Williams's purpose as a photographer. Brinson emphasizes how the events that took place in Orangeburg, as documented by a savvy young photographer, played a fateful and consequential role in the history of the civil rights movement. Through Brinson's insightful analysis, the reader discovers that Cecil Williams was not just a passerby with a camera but was, instead, an engaged observer immersed in the science and art of photography and, equally important, an active participant in the events that unfolded in front of his camera.

After the preface, the book explores Cecil J. Williams's early days in the 1940s. Williams, like many photographers, including me, got his start with a hand-me-down camera from his brother. It struck me that one never knows what might become of the future of a child when they are introduced to different tools or experiences and are surrounded by impassioned people. Throughout the book, the reader gets a sense of what it was to be a photographer in the midtwentieth century. Photographs were not instantly available on a screen as they are today. One had to wait for the images to be processed, either in a personal darkroom or through mail service. Williams was so enthralled with photography at a young age that he set up his own darkroom in his house. I was impressed that Williams shot his first wedding at the age of twelve and very quickly learned how to make photography a vocation. He was able to serve as an apprentice to Edward C. Jones, who would introduce him to his role as a storyteller, documentarian, and historian. Although this section of the book focuses on Williams's beginnings in photography, it also details what life what like for him growing up "not white" in Orangeburg. There was a parallel in the difficulty that Cecil Williams had in carrying his heavy equipment (Crown and Speed Graphic cameras are especially cumbersome) and the struggles of steadfast parents, educators, farmers, and business owners who were working toward equality day by day.

The next chapter of the book takes the reader through the 1950s, during which time Orangeburg and Clarendon Counties showed leadership, innovation, and persistence through nonviolent resistance. The chapter also follows Williams's increasing photographic skills through to his decision to attend college at Claflin. In 1950, twelve-year-old Williams was already a photographer and, from an early age, felt as though he was on a "divine mission." He and his camera would be used by God to exchange evil for good. He photographed marches, demonstrations, and key figures, his camera always ready to tell the story of a people understandably not satisfied with separate but equal. Williams seemed to be everywhere things were happening, answering the call to photograph this event or that key figure. Ultimately, his persistence led to the fulfillment of one of his goals: his photographs being featured in *Jet* magazine. The chapter on the 1950s ends with fifteen black-and-white photographs of events, figures and the Black way of life in South Carolina, all of which would challenge the South to push past segregation.

The chapter on the 1960s reads like a bursting timeline of sit-ins, marches, lawsuits, pickets and petitions organized by the Black citizens of Orangeburg. Williams, now in his twenties, continued to be a godsend with a camera, making images that recorded pivotal turns in the pursuit of freedom and racial equality. The 1960s for Williams seemed to be a time of marked advancements. The student became the teacher, with his own line of assistants. He also opened a photography studio, focusing on all types of portraiture, photographed celebrities and civil rights dignitaries, and even made a connection with President Kennedy. Breakthroughs in social equality were happening in the 1960s, but not without heartbreak. Williams witnessed and photographed painful events—arrests, beatings, and even death. He continued to photograph for *Jet* magazine and was a valuable resource for outlets that sought to highlight events in South Carolina. The chapter ends like the previous one, with eleven momentous black-and-white photographs that record the people, places, and events that changed our nation forever.

The last chapter of the book is aptly titled, "And So Much More," which properly describes Williams's life outside of photography. Although he seemed to be everywhere, photographing everything with his camera, he did so much more. He was not just a photojournalist. He was also a businessman, entrepreneur, designer, artist, protester, self-taught architect, visionary, and inventor. The book concludes with a discussion of the awards and honors Williams received for his remarkable contributions. It is my hope that his legacy will continue to be passed on to future generations, particularly young South Carolinians, so they can get a glimpse of the grit and perseverance of a generation of Americans as they fought to gain their freedom.

This book is for everyone. Photographers, like me, will enjoy reading about the common feelings that many photographers experience, such as getting your first camera, seeing images emerge in darkroom chemicals, and the challenges of telling your story. Those who want to learn more about the people of South Carolina, with Williams as a role model, will be equally satisfied as they read about brave people who sacrificed so much to secure a better and more equal future for their children.

Before reading this book, I was appreciative of Cecil Williams's work and legacy. After reading this book, my appreciation has deepened. I have realized the importance of introducing his photographs to my photography students in the hopes that they will see opportunities to use photography as a tool for change and not forget South Carolina's path to racial equality.

Julie Mixon, Francis Marion University

Judy Goldman, *Child: A Memoir* (University of South Carolina Press, 2022), 160 pp., paperback $19.99, ebook $19.99.

Beautifully written and immensely readable, *Child* is a love story for the ages—and of its age. That age is midtwentieth century Rock Hill, SC, where Jim Crow is prevailing over its residents and everything they do. Bucking the trend, quietly and politely, are Peggy and Ben Kurtz, a Jewish couple raising their three children in comfort and privilege. They also are raising them with invaluable, immeasurable help. That's Mattie Cherry Culp, the Black housekeeper who keeps the children safe and the family fed and, shockingly, lives with them full time. That wasn't done in that place and time, particularly with only one bathroom in the house.

But such was the unconventional reality and genuine love in the Kurtz home. Despite the obvious differences between the races—Mattie was always "Mattie," Mrs. Kurtz was always "Mrs. Peggy"—an unlikely family bonded in the respectable Eden Terrace neighborhood. With *Child*, the youngest of that family, at eighty, looks back and writes about it.

"Can we ever tell the whole truth to ourselves?" Judy Goldman wonders midway through her memoir. "Insights are tenuous, imperfect. It's so hard to go beyond the familiarity we have with our own stories, interrupt what we've known forever." Goldman questions herself throughout *Child*, recognizing that memories can be faulty, different to different people. We sit with her at her mother's dressing table, which was passed, on her death, to Mattie and then, on Mattie's death, to the author. Goldman studies the photos of Mattie on the table and tries to piece together the truth about the woman who helped raise her, whom she loved devotedly since she was three. For Goldman, Mattie's mystery lies in her own child, a daughter she gave up to work for and live with the Kurtzes. That daughter, Minnie, lives with Mattie's brother and sister-in-law in Charlotte, NC. Goldman tries to understand how Mattie can be mother to them both and how Minnie thinks about her biological mother. In Goldman's mind, she, Minnie, and Mattie form a triangle.

But in the beginning—Judy Kurtz Goldman's beginning—there's no other child. It's just Judy and Mattie in their private world of love and play, with Mattie cutting colorful papier-mâché dresses for Judy to wear, sharing a bedroom and double bed "that felt as wide as the world." Mattie walked young Judy to school—picking her up and carrying her once they were out of Ben Kurtz's strict view. And she carried her most dramatically when seven-year-old Judy fell through a jungle gym, cutting her underarm to the bone. Mattie ran through the streets, Judy in her arms, until she found someone to call a cab to the hospital. Once there, waiting for the doctor, a nurse whispers to Mattie, who then loosens herself from Judy's grip. "Child, you go on now, go with the nurse," Goldman recalls Mattie telling her. "I'll be waitin' for you. You gon' be all right." Goldman recounts waiting in the whites-only room while Mattie waited in the "colored" room.

"I didn't know then that one thin wall separated us, a frightened woman on one side, a frightened child on the other, a child whose arm would need layers of stitches, who did not even think how the separate waiting rooms might be affecting Mattie, how it felt to her to be judged not good enough to sit in a room with a child she was certainly good enough to take care of every other day of the year, the child who only knew she wanted Mattie."

Mattie Culp would carry Goldman much of her life, eventually helping with her two newborns, becoming godmother to her son and like a grand-mother to all the Kurtz grandchildren. "My white children," she called the Kurtz children. "My best friend," she and Peggy Kurtz called each other. In truth, Mattie carried the whole family, cooking Thanksgiving dinners for decades, even after retirement, and helping tend Peggy Kurtz when Alzheimer's disease robbed her of her elegance and generosity. For their part, the Kurtzes kept Mattie safe and solvent, buying her a home when the children didn't need full-time care.

Still, the times were what they were, and Mattie, too, had unfathomable reasoning about race and class. Goldman questions why Mattie—as close as she was to the Kurtz family—would never eat at the table with them and bristled noticeably when Goldman's brother, Donald, then in the Army, brought home a Black friend who did. Nor would Mattie go to the Carver Movie Theater, which local Blacks patronized and Kurtz family members owned. "In that neighborhood? With that rough crowd?" she says when Goldman asks. "I wouldn't set foot in that place."

Goldman doesn't shy from describing those incongruities, always in her search to understand why and how her family and Mattie came to love each other so thoroughly in such thoroughly unfair conditions. Despite what many have told her—that her parents as members of a minority race would of course be sympathetic to Blacks—the author disagrees. Goldman con-cludes they were remarkably strong in different ways. Ben Kurtz was formi-dable in his ability to do the right, hard thing—hiring a Black woman to be a saleslady decades before that became normal and standing down a pair of New York men who came to their home one night, threatening him about his pro-union stances. For her part, Peggy Kurtz bloomed with empathy. She, too, did the unthinkable: She befriended a Catawba Indian family in a drugstore, visiting them for years at their home in the Lancaster County reservation.

Told in "micronarratives," *Child* unfolds as memories do: brief flashes from childhood alongside adult wisdom and curiosity. An important gift is its portrait of Rock Hill in that era, with Winthrop College and its stu-dent-teachers' school for local children, and its economy-driving "Bleach-ery" textile plant, which experienced a violent strike in 1956 that rocked the whole town. Goldman's descriptions of segregated Trade Street are riveting, particularly the lively Black section with its pawn shops, cafes, pool halls, and backslapping clientele. We learn that the late Chief Blue of the Catawba Indian Nation was a downtown fixture, posing for photos in his regalia. And we learn through Goldman's clear, poetic prose and sharp memory that Rock Hill was a town of dichotomy: both a gracious place where ladies put camellias in cut-glass bowls and an unfair world in which Black yardmen magically appeared with their shovels to kill the snakes that scared the white children. "This was our landscape," Goldman writes. "Camellias and snakes. The particulars of our lives. The irregular ground on which our life stories were built."

Above all, *Child*—a title with multiple meanings, the most significant of which the author doesn't reveal until the end—is a love story. That is, perhaps, best illustrated by the time Judy and Mattie were separated in the hospital, when Judy fell through the jungle gym. She wouldn't have waited for the doctor long, she writes; that wouldn't happen with a white child. But love doesn't separate. Seven-year-old Judy left the white waiting room and found Mattie in the colored one. Then she climbed into her lap, "and we were waiting there, together."

Aïda Rogers, University of South Carolina

Ruth R. Martin, with Vivian B. Martin, *Beatrice's Ledger: Coming of Age in the Jim Crow South* (University of South Carolina Press, 2022), 148 pp., cloth $29.99, ebook $29.99.

In *Beatrice's Ledger: Coming of Age in the Jim Crow South*, Ruth R. Martin, along with collaborator Vivian B. Martin, provides an essential first-person account of growing up in South Carolina during a time of intense racism. Part memoir, part researched history of the region in and around Smoaks, SC, Martin's memoir invites readers into a personal account of growing up in 1940s as a Black woman. She speaks to both the hardships and beloved memories, creating a fuller picture of the region and a deeper understanding of the time, while focusing on her own family's story.

Martin begins by setting the tone for all to come within the book: telling the story of a white woman bringing the sheriff to her house to force Martin's father to pay a debt. As her father insists that he has paid his debts, young Martin watches in fear, because "even as a young girl, I knew being in the right did not mean that a Black man would not be harmed." After her father shows a record book that proves his claim, the author notes that the woman does not apologize to her father, as "I already knew that [the need to apologize when wrong] did not apply when it came to whites." In this anecdote, readers understand both her father's pride in the work he has done as well as the fear all Blacks live under for the very fact of their race. The remainder of Martin's story is suffused with this dual pride and fear—pride for lives well lived and fear of a larger racism within which they exist.

Often, Martin tells stories of beloved memories from her personal life that have roots in chattel slavery, creating a more complex story behind many parts of her life that she holds dear. For example, she describes the Lovely Hills Missionary Baptist Church as having been founded by permission of enslavers in 1850. She then goes on to discuss how this place of worship would be an important place in her life. She describes it as where her family chooses to worship and as the place of worship for many Black leaders in the community. She writes, "It's no wonder that throughout my life it has been to Lovely Hill . . . to which I return to bury my loved ones, to attend family reunions, and to worship when I am in the area." Martin leaves readers to grapple with the beloved place created by a horrid history, a commonplace occurrence in her own life.

Her description of the education system for Black people in Smoaks is no less complex. She describes the segregation at Simmons Elementary School, which she attended as a child, stating, "South Carolina was especially aggressive passing Jim Crow laws to control Blacks and whites, and denying Blacks education was a key tactic." Still, she describes Simmons as "a monument to how, not long after slavery, Blacks set about trying to get education for themselves in their children." Repeatedly, Martin's story places racist laws in direct relationship to the people who lived under them. Again and again, she shows the tenacity of her family and her community, highlighting the people who fought for a better future under a racist system. Although we hear stories of this courage on the national stage, *Beatrice's Ledger* provides witness to the ways that this resistance happened at every level of society.

Of course, Martin provides at least as many examples of racism's effects on her life and the lives of those around her that did not have a silver lining. She describes a life with separate rules for Blacks and whites, often stating, "I never questioned it; it was just the way things were." From Black children watching the school bus full of white children pass them by as they walked to school to helping with yardwork for white families because "you couldn't have white folks thinking you were uppity," Black and white lives were governed by a different set of regulations.

Besides being unfair, those rules were often unclear and ever changing. Martin describes witnessing a fight between two white girls, not knowing whether she should try to separate them or whether she should let it take place. "Race relations in the South had not prepared me to know what my role was in this situation." She considers separating them but knows it could result in her being beaten, yet when she does nothing, she's accused of "letting them fight." Although readers may understand conundrums such as these on an intellectual level, *Beatrice's Ledger* provides firsthand accounts against the larger historical backdrop. Furthermore, although readers may have an intellectual response to these events, Martin's accounts force an emotional response.

Martin's story often meanders, moving between the subject of living in South Carolina during Jim Crow and more mundane or personal recollections of her childhood and the families who lived around her. Still, *Beatrice's Ledger* provides an essential firsthand account of what it meant to live during these times in this place. She tells the story of being Black and living alongside whites, often in an uneasy peace. Martin's book is one of many important stories that showcase how legalized racism played out on individual lives and how people managed to overcome even in the face of such adversity.

Laura Leigh Morris, Furman University

Diane Catherine Vecchio, *Peddlers, Merchants, and Manufacturers: How Jewish Entrepreneurs Built Economy and Community in Upcountry South Carolina* (University of South Carolina Press, 2023), 280 pp., cloth $34.99, ebook $34.99.

Peddlers, Merchants, and Manufacturers offers a case study of a unique geographical region to examine an overlooked question in South Carolina history: Why would Jews settle in the Upcountry (now known as the "Upstate") of South Carolina when they had no established Jewish community? Diane Catherine Vecchio's story unfolds chronologically beginning with first-generation Jewish immigrants arriving to South Carolina in the late seventeenth century as skilled traders and merchants who connected trans-Atlantic businesses with the port city of Charleston and ending with contemporary Jewish professionals in the Greenville–Spartanburg corridor who work as doctors, dentists, lawyers, accountants, realtors, educators, and managers at international corporations. Along the way, Jews filled important economic niches as peddlers who helped transition subsistence-based farm households into sites of consumption and merchants who supplied goods and services to the rapidly growing population of textile workers. However, Vecchio's main argument is that Jewish-owned manufacturing companies launched in the midtwentieth century contributed significantly to the economic and community development of Greenville and Spartanburg Counties. Sociology enthusiasts will appreciate how Vecchio grounds her argument in opportunity structures, group characteristics, and strategies.

Opportunity structures are pathways that make entrepreneurship possible. The Upstate was a hospitable business climate for textile and clothing manufacturers seeking low corporate tax rates, nonunionized workers, an abundance of cheap labor, and proximity to cotton fields that reduced transportation costs. Furthermore, the desire for a "New South" image may have compelled non-Jewish community leaders to overlook religious objections and welcome Jews who had skills to match the market needs in Greenville and Spartanburg, particularly the fast-growing consumer interest in clothing, high-end footwear, and jewelry.

Group characteristics refer to the skills and goals that people bring with them to an opportunity as well as the social networking necessary to mobilize labor and resources. Vecchio explains that many post–World War II Jews who migrated to the Upstate were well educated sons of successful Northeastern Jewish businessmen skilled in the needle trade. Jews who relocated to the Upstate applied their knowledge of the clothing industry and the cultural trait of resourcefulness to provide work clothes for laborers and business attire for executives. Their connections with European businesses also helped introduce Upstate consumers to innovative marketing ideas and products, such as one-price clothing and double-knit clothing.

Strategies are purposeful actions taken to confront the numerous problems and uncertainties of founding and operating a business. Access to capital represents a significant challenge. Jews adopted the strategy of offering credit to other Jews "rooted in the Judaic concept of tzedakah, the communal obligation to help others." Vecchio also describes chain migration. For instance, foreign-born Jews often settled in large northeastern cities to work in the garment industry before migrating to Upstate South Carolina in search of more fruitful opportunities. The wives of Upstate Jewish businessmen would board Jewish migrants temporarily in homes, and their husbands found managerial positions for them in Jewish-owned factories. Another strategy consisted of intermarriage in middle-class Jewish business communities, which consolidated the resources necessary for expanding businesses.

Vecchio not only provides a solid theoretical framework but also supports her claims with a dazzling array of sources that would humble the most rigorous methodologist. She uses transcripts of life histories based on interviews conducted between 1936 and 1943 as part of the Federal Writers project. Other evidence originates from her personal interviews with thirty-nine different people, including the well-known civil rights activist and politician Reverend Jesse Jackson, who is a Greenville native. Other relevant sources include photographs, books and peer-reviewed articles on Jewish American history, church temple records, journal and diary entries, letters, obituaries, memoirs, school yearbooks, manuscript collections from libraries and historical association, minutes from city council meetings, city directories, newspapers and periodicals, census data, Ancestry.com, master's theses, and a PhD dissertation. These myriad sources allow Vecchio to present competing views of the motives behind antisemitic threats and violence encountered by a surprisingly small number of Jewish merchants in Greenville before the Civil War. They also help explain why upstate Jewish business owners shied away from direct involvement in the 1960s civil rights movement. Additionally, Vecchio presents different arguments on whether the transition from segregation to integration occurred more peacefully in South Carolina than other deep Southern states.

It is interesting that Vecchio departs from a holistic understanding of Jewish history in the Upstate to a reductionistic approach in the final chapter of the book, where she briefly revisits the controversial South Carolina Fourth Congressional District campaign race in 1978 between Democrat Max Heller and Republican Carroll Campbell, who eventually became the one hundred twelfth governor of South Carolina from 1987 to 1995. Campbell won the election by a relatively small margin of 5,793 votes. Vecchio suggests that Campbell found his way to victory through his campaign manager and an independent party candidate who messaged voters about Heller's Jewish and foreign-born status. Some readers may wish that Vecchio had balanced this assertion with broader political and economic factors, such as South Carolina's transition from a solid blue state to a swing state, tremendously high levels of inflation, and failing textile industry, all of which Campbell emphasized aggressively during his well-funded campaign. In defense of Vecchio, she documents other antisemitic episodes directed toward Heller leading up to and during his tenure as popular mayor of Greenville from 1971 to 1979. It cannot be ruled out that religious bigotry cost Heller the election.

Vecchio asks us to recognize that the Jewish contribution to economic and community development in the Upstate has been overshadowed by non-Jewish contributors such as textile giant Roger Milliken, who relocated his company headquarters from New York to Spartanburg in 1954, and the more recent massive recruiting of hundreds of international businesses, including Michelin, BMW, and Adidas. She writes a little-known but convincing story about how Jewish immigrant families paved the way for their success in Upstate South Carolina and, at the same time, paved the way for our success.

Russell E. Ward, Francis Marion University

Daniel Wolff, *How to Become an American: A History of Immigration, Assimilation, and Loneliness* (University of South Carolina Press, 2022), 248 pp., paperback $24.99, ebook $24.99.

How to Become an American, Daniel Wolff's latest book, raises as many questions about what it means to be "American" as it answers. This makes it a compelling read. Wolff is a prolific biographer, capturing American history and culture through the lens of famous Americans. Here, he diverges from that method, instead excavating the lives of "so-called unimportant Americans" to tell a poignant story of immigration and belonging. It is interesting to consider that the result may be the same: People's lives, well-known or not, move with history and inevitably reflect some cultural themes. Average people may not have the drama of fame punctuating and elevating their lives, but Wolff shows that private, ordinary experiences reverberate with larger significance.

Beginning with a woman's diary found while cleaning out a home, Wolff pieces together a multigenerational saga of one family trying to become American, questioning at each stage whether this identity has been attained. To underscore their "un-specialness," as he puts it, Wolff chooses to keep the family anonymous. Emigrating from a Polish village in 1839, a young Bohemian Jew landed in New York and peddled his way to owning a paint shop in Charleston in the 1840s. The man was welcomed by an established Jewish community. Thanks to its religious tolerance, South Carolina has been home to Jews since 1695. At the beginning of the nineteenth century, Charleston had the largest Jewish population in the United States. The man built a family, a home, and a thriving business within the relatively prosperous stratum of merchants who existed in between opulent plantation owners and mixed-race working classes. Although life in Charleston offered Southern Jews like this family social and economic stability, even freedom, it also required setting aside the moral contradictions of slavery, which may have been particularly difficult for Jewish immigrants to reconcile. As Wolff explains, they "left the Old World because they'd been denied the right to marry or start a family, to own land, to vote.... But part of how they'd become Americans was by denying other people the right to marry or start a family, to own land, to vote." Moreover, Southern Jews in antebellum Charleston were just white enough to be left alone to pursue their livelihoods, but they always remained cultural outsiders in this fiercely hierarchical society. The immigrant couple pinned their hopes on their children, and their children's children, becoming true Americans as the tarnish of the Old World would fade and they would all eventually melt in.

The growing family lived through the Civil War relatively unscathed, but Charleston struggled to recover. It did not industrialize along with the New South. In 1873, some cousins opened new stores in St. Augustine and then Jacksonville, which were more lucrative markets. Florida needed paint stores not only to rebuild its housing stock after the war but also to transform its jungles into winter getaways for a new class of Northern tourists. Jacksonville had a small but strong Jewish community. It also offered some greater promise of American equality for Black people and immigrants alike: "Maybe it was easier to fit in, to become American, as part of a growing middle class in a growing city," Wolff muses. The paint business, like many of the trades, was democratizing too, shifting from an Old World guild of master craftsmen into an industry of factory products, distribution chains, and less specialized workers. There were rumblings of labor unrest. The merchants and shop owners were getting squeezed between the interests of new corporations and intensifying strikes for workers' rights. The next generation of the family looked north for new opportunities. They moved to Minneapolis and opened the city's first paint store in 1880.

Wolff recounts two generations of this immigrant family making Minneapolis their home. Minneapolis was a burgeoning city, thanks to the largest flour mill in the world that processed the area's wheat and shipped it across the country. It also became the financial center of the upper Midwest, overseeing one of the country's largest economic booms of the Gilded Age. In addition to their profitable store, the family invested in properties throughout the city as real estate values grew exponentially. But here, too, they were still betwixt and between: They were neither the region's "empire builders" (gentrified New Englanders and robber barons) nor the city's workers (farmers, miners, lumberjacks, railroad men, and millworkers who tended to be German, Irish, or Scandinavian). Once again, this immigrant family was part of a growing merchant class interested in assimilation but not easily finding a pot to melt into. They did have a Jewish community, but even that was fraught with tension between newly arrived Russian Jews and well-established German Jews. Notably, Minneapolis's Jewish population grew rapidly in the first half of the twentieth century, and the city became home to a range of differing but intertwined Jewish organizations that were all confronting a backlash against "foreigners" and non-Christians. Ultimately, the Minneapolis chapters of this family's history are marked most by the labor wars and the difficulty not only of religion and culture but of class wedging them out from above and below. As small business owners, they shared workers' contempt for large corporations and the mechanization of labor; name-brand companies were scooping up large shares of the paint market. Yet they bristled at some of the union demands and struggled to keep their business going amid all the strikes. As Wolff recounts, "if assimilation in the South meant accepting slavery, in Minneapolis, a small business owner was expected to be antiunion." This was a difficult line to walk. The political winds kept changing. The definition of *American* kept shifting.

With one family, Wolff conveys many parallel histories of nineteenth- and twentieth-century America: South, North, immigration, citizenship, industrialization, Jewish America, labor. Running through them all are intensely personal trials of identity and belonging. Each generation of this family secured significant levels of comfort and stability, but isolation and loneliness never left their sides. Americanness was continually elusive. If Wolff takes readers into finely textured experiences of these individuals' disillusionment with assimilation, he also probes their larger implications. As a nation of immigrants, all of us exist somewhere in the in-between, each a little too much of this and never enough of that. "American" is capacious, to be sure, but in all that space, there is a lot of distance.

Shevaun E. Watson, University of Wisconsin–Milwaukee

Daniel B. Friedman, Tracy L. Skipper, and Catherine S. Greene (eds.),
*From Educational Experiment to Standard Bearer, University 101 at the
University of South Carolina* (University of South Carolina Press, 2022),
272 pp., cloth $114.99, paperback $32.99, ebook $32.99.

The University of South Carolina (USC) is well known for having the
nation's best first-year student experience. *From Educational Experiment to
Standard Bearer* is a captivating historical view of USC's efforts to ensure
first-year student success and develop a globally replicated University 101
course.

Fifty years ago, the student experience on this beautiful campus, located
in the heart of Columbia, was quite different than it is today. As civil rights
protests broke out, USC students perceived that the administration was
tone-deaf to their needs and rights. Student activism of the 1960s and 1970s
led to much change across the campus. The administration needed to bridge
the gap between the student body and the administration, faculty, and staff.
Student life was of the utmost concern for both students and the university.
The authors describe this period of collision and how the then–university
president, Thomas Jones, assembled a group of stakeholders, including students, which became the President's Committee on Academic Atmosphere,
to address the current affairs of the university and develop plans to move
the university into the future. Perhaps the most critical and lasting initiative
derived from the committee was the development of University 101.

University 101 was designed to assist first-year students with the transition to college life and allow faculty to build relationships with students.
Before the development of this course, students were expected to succeed
without having the tools necessary to do so. The university's motto, *Emol-
lit Mores Nec Sinit Esse Feros*—learning humanizes character and does not
permit it to be cruel—would become reality as President Jones worked with
faculty and students to build the program from the ground up.

University 101 seemed to be the solution to President Jones's vision for
the continued growth of the university while addressing the unique needs
of the students. Because of the increasing size of the university, it was critical for this course to allow faculty to build strong, impactful connections
with students. Participating faculty were tasked with building relationships,
teaching the history of the university, and creating a sense of pride and love
among students for their university. The goals of the course included orient-
ing students to the purpose of higher education, improving retention rates,

and building communication between students and faculty. University 101's success drew national attention. Universities across the nation started adopting the USC model in hopes of seeing similar impacts. By the 1980s, international interest was also evident, and an international advisory board was established.

President Jones wanted the course not only to benefit students but also to transform faculty. Faculty teaching University 101 are trained to be open-minded in connecting with the students as they help them become acclimated to the university. The authors highlight research that faculty became more student centered and focused on student success after training for and teaching University 101.

Today's model of University 101 stays true to its initial efforts while also reflecting years of development and refinement. Three broad goals with ten learning outcomes define the course. These goals are to foster academic success; discover and connect with USC; and promote personal development, well-being, and social responsibility. Building community is widely considered the most essential part of the course. Peer involvement has also led to the use of student leaders in the course and the strengthening of the relationship between students and the university. Research across the University has narrowed down six areas that students feel are most influential and impactful in the course. These six areas include connection to the USC, connection with faculty and staff, connection with peers, campus involvement and engagement, awareness and use of campus resources, and academic success.

From Educational Experiment to Standard Bearer provides an in-depth historical background of how the university built a successful University 101 program from the ground up. As a former student at USC, I enrolled in a section of University 101 as an education major during the Fall 2006 semester. This book gives me great insight into the work it took to offer such a course. However, in my experience, I felt that my particular class focused more on producing teachers than on student success in higher education. As a first-generation student, I desperately needed the transitional piece of the course more than the teacher preparation that I already received in other courses. Still, I have fond memories of the course, and, as a current professor in higher education, I appreciate the preparation that went into the development of University 101. Without reading this book, I would have never considered the years of work it took to develop such a strong program. This book is an excellent read for any future or current student, faculty member, or anyone interested in the growth and history of the University of South Carolina.

It also gives great insight to all stakeholders of higher education in turning challenges into triumphs in the continued growth of their university.

Krystin McCormick Williams, Francis Marion University